The *ART* of Cultivating
Preferred Customer
Status

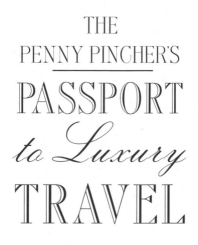

THE
PENNY PINCHER'S
PASSPORT
to Luxury
TRAVEL

3RD EDITION

D0369624

CRITICAL ACCLAIM FOR
*THE PENNY PINCHER'S PASSPORT
TO LUXURY TRAVEL*

"This book delivers on its promise—indispensable, hard-earned knowledge on how to get more luxury and value in your travels."
—Joseph DiGiovanna, American Airlines

"In snappy, first-person narrative, Widzer helps us travel beyond our means. Fly first-class at coach fares. Sleep in suites at rack rate costs. Drive luxury cars at economy prices. It's no wonder the *National Geographic Traveler* calls this the 'definitive guide to living large on the road.'"
—*ForeWord Magazine*

"The tips Widzer has can pay for the book at the first check-in counter you come to."
—Drew Griffin, CNN News

"It's the only book I turn to when I want to travel in style without breaking the bank. It's that good!"
—Christopher Elliot, contributing editor,
National Geographic Traveler

"Joel Widzer, the ultimate insider, bares his all in this third edition, updating readers with the latest and greatest ways to travel like the rich and famous."
—Marcus Tilley, host of "Tilley Talks Travel"

"Joel Widzer's *Penny Pincher's Passport to Luxury Travel* is a real upgrade from the usual travel-on-the-cheap line of advice."
—Randy Curwen, travel editor, *Chicago Tribune*

"Read this book once purely for inspiration. Then read it again as a step-by-step guide to planning a truly deluxe trip, without busting the budget."
—Tim Winship, FrequentFlier.com

"Top-of-the-line travel at bottom-dollar prices is an unbeatable combination—and this book tells you how to do it."
—Ed Perkins, travel columnist

"It's rare we feel compelled to recommend a travel book, but we can't resist telling you about *The Penny Pincher's Passport to Luxury Travel*."
—*The Washington Post*

The *ART* of Cultivating
Preferred Customer
Status

THE
PENNY PINCHER'S
PASSPORT
to Luxury
TRAVEL

3RD EDITION

JOEL L. WIDZER

TRAVELERS' TALES
AN IMPRINT OF SOLAS HOUSE, INC.
PALO ALTO

Travelers' Tales and Travelers' Tales Guides are trademarks of
Travelers' Tales/Solas House, Inc. 853 Alma Street, Palo Alto,
California 94301. www.travelerstales.com

"The Extra Mile" by Tim Winship © 2007 first appeared on
FrequentFlier.com, reprinted with permission from the author.

Art Direction: Stefan Gutermuth
Interior Design: Kathryn Heflin and Susan Bailey
Page Layout: Cynthia Lamb

Library of Congress Cataloging-in-Publication Data

Widzer, Joel L.
  The penny pincher's passport to luxury travel : the art of culti-
vating preferred customer status / Joel L. Widzer. — 3rd ed.
       p. cm. — (Travelers' tales)
  Includes bibliographical references and index.
  ISBN 1-932361-57-X (pbk. : alk. paper)
  1. Travel—Guidebooks. I. Title.
G153.4.W5 2008
910.2'02—dc22
                        2008003474

Third Edition
Printed in the United States
10 9 8 7 6 5 4 3 2 1

It is funny about life: If you refuse to accept anything but the very best you will often get it.

—W. SOMERSET MAUGHAM

Table of Contents

A JOURNEY INTO THE GREAT UNKNOWN
Traveling Like the Rich and Famous

Ten years ago I embarked on the rewarding journey of writing a book on strategies for travelers with the sole purpose of enriching their travel experiences. I knew it was a good idea, but I had no idea what the road ahead would bring. Throughout the process I found the mystery of writing a book equivalent to the thrill of discovering the great unknown through travel. While I did not initially know how my book would unfold, I had a plan, which is the same approach I take with all of my travels. To reach my goal of writing a book that would serve to optimize a person's overall travel experience with methods of traveling in luxury at a fraction of the price, I strategized, researched, and immersed myself in books on the topic. My research ultimately led me to securing an agent, a publisher, and, finally, promoting my finished book, the first edition of *The Penny Pincher's Passport to Luxury Travel*.

The first two editions of this book have helped readers enhance their traveling with first-class air upgrades, hotel suites, and luxury car rentals, while still saving copious amounts of their hard-earned money. I was able to provide less experienced travelers with essential keys to better planning and research that ultimately allowed them to fulfill their quest for top-notch travel without breaking their budgets.

Like its predecessors, this edition of *The Penny Pincher's Passport to Luxury Travel* is all about creating and owning a strategy. Simply put, that strategy is maintaining astute loyalty to a select few travel providers, traveling where and while others are not, and treating all with whom you come into contact with respect and dignity. Over the years, my travel writing has transformed me from one person with an idea to a journalist who has participated in hundreds of television interviews, countless radio interviews, contributed to a regular column with MSNBC, and been asked to speak at many a conference, often to top-level travel executives. In the end, this cumulative experience, along with my trips exceeding 200,000 air miles annually (to date collectively 3 million miles), has given me the ability to go straight to the heart of the essential strategies that work for everyday travelers, strategies that lead to luxury travel at a fraction of the cost.

THINKING OUTSIDE THE BOX

Packing my bags for over twenty years, I have become nothing if not passionate about travel. I feel I am at my best when on a plane, in a foreign city, or dashing down the autobahn in a sporty car clocking 200+ kilometers per hour. Like with any passion, I have engrossed myself in the ways and means of travel. I have made it a habit to understand what makes travel providers tick. This understanding has become a specialty. Rather than writing about where to go and what to see, I write about how to go. The sheer excitement of planning a trip wherein you receive far more value than the price of admission thrills me, as it does many of those with whom I've been privileged to work over the years.

Throughout my travel experiences I have learned that getting to know a destination is the easy part of your trip, especially with increased access to myriad guidebooks and online reviews and postings. Not so easy to understand are the nuances of working with a travel provider, how to leverage your travels into something great, and, ultimately, how to read the travel tea leaves to understand the best places to go at the right times. These essential travel skills indeed take time to develop, but once firmly in place they allow you to explore the world while simultaneously staying in the best hotels throughout the world.

Prior to the release of the first edition of *The Penny Pincher's Passport to Luxury Travel* in 1999, much of the travel talk focused on low-budget travel. Thankfully, many of today's travelers have evolved beyond the mindset of staying in a hostel for $10 a night with such amenities as a community bathroom down the hall. Many of today's travelers, young and old, are interested in a memorable experience, something that brings added value to their journey. However, those same travelers, myself included, can't afford to pay movie-star prices to secure such an experience. This premise was the genesis of the time-proven tools outlined and discussed in detail within *The Penny Pincher's Passport to Luxury Travel*. Since its release, many have joyfully jumped on the "get more for your money" bandwagon. While it's flattering that numerous writers, bloggers, and pundits have caught on to a theory I first espoused, I believe that many copycat guides lack the solid foundation of a few simple key principles that have proven successful for almost two decades. These simple principles remain the difference between luxury at coach prices and the noisy, crowded back of the plane.

In the upcoming pages you will read entertaining anecdotes with important messages, and learn timeless travel strategies including how to maintain flexibility in changing flight and departure times, and how to plan, research, and position yourself as a prized and courteous traveler to whom travel companies will always want to provide their best service. When all is said and done, I believe the one skill that has allowed me to consistently upgrade on every flight I take, stay at wonderful five-star hotels, and drive exciting cars every trip I take, remains my ability to understand change.

The travel industry is in a constant state of flux. In 1999, the travel industry was doing quite well, and technology's effect on the traveler was still in its infancy. When the second edition of my book hit bookshelves in 2004 the industry was still suffering the aftereffects of September 11th, but technology continued gaining ground. Today, travelers are hitting the road in record numbers, filling planes, hotels, and many a rental car. In addition, companies have increased their respective investments in technology that eases the process of booking travel, while simultaneously tracking consumers and their needs better than ever, thus hampering what customers' agents can and cannot do. One example of recent changes is the computerization of airline upgrades. This means it is much harder to receive an airline upgrade with a sincere smile. Not impossible, of course, but more difficult. These new industry changes require fresh strategies that work in today's ever-malleable environment.

Make no mistake: getting the best value in travel requires work, deliberate planning, and patience, but it will lead to travel success.

As previously noted, the success of *The Penny Pincher's Passport to Luxury Travel* has prompted a new track in travel-guide writing. Others have added their voices to the ongoing discussion about how they have procured their flashy, advertised "luxury" with far-flung schemes, elaborate point-earning methods and, sometimes, even a bit of trickery. Over the years I have remained steadfast in my conviction that acquiring superb service must center upon building relationships with travel providers. As such, I have been careful to avoid penny-saving methods which take advantage of travel providers; even if you get away with it once or twice, rest assured that eventually your travel provider will catch on, and the doors leading to a good and amicable business relationship will be shut for good.

I remain loyal to the fundamental principles I first espoused in 1999, however, I realize that changes in the travel industry affect how you utilize your travel services. While much of the game remains the same, mid-course adjustments are necessary, much as a pilot reroutes through a storm or a football coach adjusts the offense after halftime. In today's playbook, travelers are faced with more upgrades being doled out by an automated computer system, so I now have a strategy for beating the computer in Chapter 6. Likewise, your choice of hotels is more than ever the key to a memorable trip and I explain why in Chapter 7. These, among many other new theories and strategies, are what you'll find in this newly revised book.

I hope you enjoy your journey into this third edition of *The Penny Pincher's Passport to Luxury Travel.* It's the work I am most proud of, another crucial and memorable step on a journey that has been long in the making, and more rewarding than I could ever have anticipated.

A LIFETIME OF LOYALTY

Reaping the Rewards of Leverage

At a time when every major travel provider offers a loyalty program with homogenous services and perks, one has to wonder if consolidating your loyalty is still a worthwhile proposition. I found myself pondering this fifty-four days into the new year, when I had skyrocketed to 80,000 qualifying miles on Delta Air Lines, extending my top-tier elite status for the next two years. I found that reaching Platinum Medallion level in such a short a time was easy, given my travel patterns. I flew three international flights and three transcontinental flights paying about $5,000 total for coach-class tickets, which were upgraded to first or business class on every flight. After those flights came the hard part—should I continue to remain loyal or spread my airline wealth with another airline?

Of course, no airline is perfect, so it was certainly tempting to give another carrier a go. But instinctively, I also recognized that giving in to temptation can be dangerous. So I mapped out the pros and cons of each route. Here are the results:

Upgrades. By far the best reason for being loyal is for the upgrades. My current loyalty has placed me at the front of the line for a shot at the good seats. In reality, any airline would favor my business and offer me elite status with noteworthy upgrading opportunities. But I would be establishing an entirely new profile with that airline, forgoing my long history of previous seat time.

Service. Second to being upgraded is the preferred service a loyal customer receives, and I can't fault Delta Air Lines for its service. However, temptation does set in when I read about the exceptional service offered by other airlines, including such amenities as flat-bed sleeper seats. (At the time this book went to press, Delta was expected to introduce lie-flat seats in 2008.) As tempting as a quiet bed on a long flight sounds, I doubt that my initial entry into their loyalty program would yield me such benefits at the discounted prices I currently enjoy. While many foreign carriers are renowned for their unsurpassed service, service on most domestic carriers doesn't reach the heights of Singapore Airlines, where virtually every whim is looked after. As a tradeoff, I wouldn't fly a foreign carrier as much and would not reach very high in their loyalty programs— meaning I would not enjoy all the benefits I can with a domestic airline.

Relationships. Loyalty programs are all about building mutually beneficial relationships. Sometimes it can be a really small thing that supports the relationship. For example, when a ticket agent puts my tickets into a ticket jacket I always give it back to her and joke that this might save the airline a penny and keep it flying. Think about this, if a million people did this, it could save the airline real money. I also enjoy familiarity with gate personnel at the airport I most frequently fly from, giving me a leg up when it comes to upgrades and seating assignments. Another key to relationship building is how airline employees go out of their way for you. Whenever I fly internationally, flight attendants routinely approach me to offer a choice of meals before all other business/first class passengers. They'll say, "Mr. Widzer I see you're Platinum Medallion so I would like to make sure you get your first choice of meals. What would you like?" It's nice to know that you'll get pasta, not a steak, when you don't eat red meat.

The key to a good relationship is continuity. In real life, being seduced by every temptation that comes along would result in utter chaos. In my opinion, this is the same thing as chasing the newest or latest loyalty program. Whether you reach first-tier elite status or ultra status, continued loyalty is the consumer's half of the equation, rewarded with upgrades, preferential service, and the occasional special reward.

Although I remain a passionate supporter of consolidating your travel business to build loyalty with a few quality travel providers, there is a catch to be aware of. Mere elite status in a travel loyalty program does not have the same cachet it did a few years ago. Remember the day when a Gold American Express or a Platinum Visa Card made an impression? Nowadays, offers for these cards are sent to millions of homes every day. The real distinction comes from invitation-only programs such as the American Express Black Card.

This is true with travel providers as elite membership becomes diluted with ease of entry. Even if you're not invited into one of these skull-and-bones programs (which I have yet to be), your cumulative long-term history with a select group of travel providers will position you as someone who earns rewards worthy of devoted loyalists. These invitation-only programs may well be the future direction of all loyalty programs, which is moving away from offering generic awards to all customers and toward tailoring exclusive rewards that will create purposeful incentives for each unique customer. For example, during a recent "Hyatt Free Night Promotion" I earned three free nights that, due to the restrictions and other requirements, had virtually little value to me. Instead, Hyatt offered me an equivalent but customized award more suited to my needs.

This all has a trickle-down effect on occasional or infrequent customers. As travel companies grow in their understanding of consumers' behavior, they are able to spot those consumers who have a long-term history with their company but who might not otherwise count as their top spenders. I will discuss this topic in detail later in the chapter.

MISSING THE VALUE OF LOYALTY

Tom, an early adopter of frequency programs, never moved away from the mindset of signing up for every available program—a strategy that just doesn't work anymore. A frequent traveler for more than twenty-three years, Tom collected loyalty points like someone would collect coins or cars—in various denominations, shapes, and models. But I have come to recognize that when it comes to travel loyalty programs, variety does not work.

Tom had collected an assortment of over 1 million miles and points through a total of twenty-eight different frequent-user programs: five airline accounts, fifteen hotel programs, four car rental agencies, three credit card programs, and the refinancing of his home. I asked Tom what he planned to do with all of his miles. He said, "I never really thought about it. I was just having fun collecting them."

If Tom had realized that travel providers bestow the most rewards on those customers who provide them with a consistent and predictable stream of revenue, that is, their loyal or "right" customers, he could have gotten a lot more out of his miles than simply the pleasure of collecting them. To get the most value out of those miles and points, you need to be loyal to the few, not the many.

CONSOLIDATING YOUR LOYALTY

Let's take a closer look at how Tom could have invested his twenty-three years of point collecting. Tom did one thing right: he was absolutely diligent about earning his points and miles. He always made sure that the points for whatever flights he took or hotels he stayed in were credited to his frequent-user accounts. However, he accumulated points in so many accounts that he only averaged about 35,000 miles or points in each, not nearly enough to get the rewards he should have been able to reap after so many years of frequent traveling. Thirty-five thousand miles might translate to one round-trip coach ticket for each of his five frequent-flyer accounts (a free coach ticket ranges from 25,000 to 50,000 miles). However, if Tom had a million miles in one frequent flyer account he could have traveled around the world in first class—with enough points leftover to stay in the world's most luxurious hotels —free!

Tom should have chosen to remain loyal to one airline that had reciprocal agreements or alliances with other airlines. This way Tom would have been able to travel to most destinations throughout the world with his airline's alliance partners and still earn points in his one account.

Accumulating all those points in one account would have qualified Tom for the highest level of elite status with his one airline's frequent-flyer program. That high-level elite frequent-flyer status would have opened the door to a number of benefits, only one of which is free upgrades. (I will explore airline elite status in more detail in Chapter 5). By the way, in most frequent-flyer programs, 25,000 miles is all Tom would need to qualify for the minimum elite level. But at 175,000 miles (35,000 miles x 5 frequent-flyer accounts consolidated into one account), he would have been 75,000 miles above what he needed for the highest elite status and the highest level of preferred service.

With respect to hotels, it is likely that twenty-three years ago Tom would have had to belong to the frequent-user programs of a few different hotel chains to obtain adequate coverage for the places he traveled—but certainly not fifteen programs. Tom would have been well served if he had limited his travels to the four major hotel chains during that time: Hilton, Hyatt, Marriott, and Sheraton. During the past few years, however, many of these chains have expanded their offerings with hotels that range from super-deluxe to conservative, by buying other brand hotels. Thus, travelers can limit their travels to only one or two chains and consolidate points.

GETTING THE MOST MILEAGE
WITH THE RIGHT PROGRAMS

In addition, Tom could have taken advantage of the expansion that occurred in airline mileage programs over the past ten years and chosen a select few travel providers that had reciprocal points programs. For example, he could have traveled with an airline that offered bonus miles for nights spent at a certain hotel, and he could have rented cars from a company that offered points redeemable with his airline. He could have earned even more miles by paying for his travels with a credit card that also partnered with his particular grouping of travel providers.

If Tom had managed his mile-collecting efforts wisely through reciprocal points programs, he could have parlayed the 1 million points he had accumulated throughout his twenty-eight different and unrelated accounts into approximately 3 million useable miles in one account. He would have also spent time developing mutually beneficial relationships with the right travel partners that would have been more valuable to him in terms of preferential treatment than any number of miles acquired.

To SWITCH OR NOT TO SWITCH

Tom's story is not uncommon. If you are as budget-conscious as most of my readers, then you know it is all too tempting to switch airlines and hotels every time you travel. After all, the travel provider that gave you the best deal for your last trip may not have the lowest fare for this trip. However, if your goal is to become a first-class traveler on a coach-class budget, you need to take the long-term view and realize that your steadfast loyalty will reap luxurious travel benefits far beyond the few dollars you might save on today's transaction.

Is It Time to Jettison Your Preferred Airline?

If you're getting bad service, you've moved, you can't get an upgrade anymore, or your carrier is in financial trouble, the answer might be "yes." You need to spend your loyalty dollars wisely. I review my travel partnerships once a year to make sure I'm not throwing away my money. If I need a loyalty tune-up, I switch programs.

Why switch? Here are four good reasons:

1. Poor service. If you're consistently irked during your travels, chances are your vacations and business meetings will not be very pleasant. When you're experiencing poor service with no hope of change—enough said—change programs! If poor service is the root of all evil, good service is heartwarming. First-class service paves the way for an enjoyable and productive trip. Whether it is a first-class seat, hotel suite with a Central Park view, or a sporty rental car, getting upgraded enhances your travels.

2. You're relocating. If you anticipate a change in your travel destinations due to territory realignment or your prime customer moves, you might consider if your current travel partners will still best meet your needs. If not, determine who will. If you have been flying United Airlines because 90% of your flights went through Chicago, but now you'll be flying through Atlanta, you might consider switching loyalties to Delta. The same goes for hotels. If the Hyatt does not have suitable properties in your new destinations, check with another hotelier.

3. Getting rewards is impossible. Competition for upgrades is progressively higher the lower you are on the loyalty chain. For example, my top-tier elite status with Delta Air Lines provides me a 95% probability of being upgraded. While someone with Delta's minimum elite membership is upgraded only 25% of the time. If you're finding too much competition for upgrades you might consider a program that is more suited to your travel frequency.

4. Your airline is about to go belly-up. If your travel partner is on the verge of non-existence it could be a good time to jump ship. Currently many air travelers are struggling with their loyalties to U.S. Airways. While many travelers have given up hope for the airline, you might reconsider. If they do manage to emerge from these difficult times, those loyal customers who "stuck it out" with them will greatly benefit. Your trust and dedication in the airline will position you to better negotiate your way into first class, receive waivers on ticket change fees, and any other special request you might need. As a caveat, be careful with your air miles. Either use the miles quickly or transfer them into one of U.S. Airways' partner's account.

If you find yourself in any of these situations, and it's time to change loyalties, follow three steps:

1. Contact your current travel provider and inform them why you're switching loyalties. Give them a chance to make amends. If you're still unsatisfied, then contact the loyalty program of your new travel provider and tell them that you are switching to their program. Ask them to match your previous elite status, or to grant you their minimum status.

2. If you're a beginning or low-frequency traveler consider a second-tier program. By this, I do not mean second tier

in service. Rather, forgo American Airlines, United Airlines, or Delta Air Lines, the top three programs respectively, and consider Continental Airlines or Alaska Airlines—both of which offer excellent service. These airlines have fewer members and even fewer high-elites. So your chances for getting an upgrade are dramatically increased. This same theory holds true with hotels and car rental companies.

3. Decide how to use your old miles, redeem them, donate them, or transfer them. Build the highest level of elite membership you can with your new partner.

As a loyal customer you have power, and that power gives you leverage. Just be sure it's with the right company.

LOYALTY IS THE MOST ESSENTIAL STRATEGY

Since I began flying, 97% of my flights have been flown on one particular airline. Consequently, I have become a Three-Million Miler, which means I have accrued over 3 million miles in my frequent-flyer account with that airline. Because of my steadfast loyalty, I am privy to many special concessions and benefits. And although I always pay the most discounted fares, I am automatically upgraded to first class—every time. When I fly overseas, I usually receive a two-class upgrade, from coach to first class, and I am provided entrée to luxurious first-class lounges. Whenever I need an exception to a rule or restriction, my loyalty has given me the leverage to supersede this airline's strictest rules.

WHY LOYALTY PAYS

In the travel industry, most consumers perceive very little, if any, difference between competing companies. As a result, travel providers must work hard to create and maintain loyal and satisfied customers, which are crucial to their economic vitality. Here's why:

➤ Approximately 15% of travel providers' customers provide 90% of the companies' profits. During economic down cycles the percentage of profitable customers is even slimmer.

➤ Travel industry experts estimate it costs about six times as much to attract a new customer as it does to retain an existing one.

➤ Industry analysts estimate that only 4% of disgruntled travelers complain to their travel providers. Those who do complain are more likely to return because the provider gets a chance to make amends. The other 96% of unhappy customers do not make the effort to complain; they simply do not use that travel provider's services again.

➤ It is also estimated that each disappointed customer tells between eight to ten other people about his or her dissatisfaction, while only 5% of satisfied customers express their satisfaction to friends and family members. Nevertheless, a satisfied customer is not necessarily a loyal customer, making customer retention even more important. I will discuss this phenomenon later in the book.

Travel providers also know that loyal customers provide many more economic benefits than merely spending the same amount of money every time. They know that over time, loyal customers become less price sensitive and are less likely to switch to a competitor. Loyal customers become more receptive to purchasing ancillary services such as credit cards that earn points on their favorite airline, spa services from their favorite hotels, club memberships in private airport lounges, or cellular phone or GPS system usage with their rental cars. And as we will see later in this book, generating ancillary revenue has become a key source of profitability to travel providers. This again is a reason that an infrequent traveler can take advantage of the golden egg of loyalty.

Loyal customers also cost less to maintain. They get to know the drill—in essence, they become experts at being the companies' customers. This "expertise" decreases costs because such customers demand less attention, make fewer mistakes, and allow faster execution of transactions. For example, repeat airline passengers typically know an airline's specific rules and procedures. As a result, they know exactly what questions to ask and what to expect from the airline. This ease of doing business places fewer demands on the staff, providing the airline with the ability to serve more customers in less time, which increases their productivity, lowers labor costs, and ultimately increases profits.

Take, for example, my travel habits: I intimately know how my travel providers' web sites work, hence I book my tickets, rooms, and cars online, check in and out online, leaving me with very little if any interaction with human personnel, which frees up my providers' human resources for more pressing issues, as well as helping to reduce their labor costs. When I do need an additional layer of service I usually know the programs so well that I can get right to the point, minimizing the length of the interaction and this saves money. When I really need a favor, I stress my behavior, reminding the provider, "Hey, I'm very good at saving you money (explaining how). Can't you make an exception for me here?"

For these reasons, loyal customers add value to travel providers. Consequently, it is to their advantage to give you the kind of preferential treatment that keeps you coming back and maybe even spreading the word to your friends and colleagues.

Bear in mind that this preferential treatment usually does not add to your travel provider's cost of doing business. For example, Sheraton Hotels began offering their loyal guests the opportunity to check out of their rooms as late as 4 P.M. This seemingly small incentive, which cost Sheraton slight inconvenience with their housekeeping and front-desk staff, increased their guest loyalty by about 10%.

Even what appears to be a bigger-ticket customer incentive can actually reduce your travel provider's red ink. Think about it: an empty hotel suite, oceanfront room, or first-class airline seat is revenue irrevocably lost after that night passes or that flight departs. If, however, a hotel perceives you as a loyal customer, the front-desk representative might offer to upgrade you to one of their empty suites for as little as an extra $15 a night. You win by getting a suite and attendant amenities for a little more than what it would have cost to stay in an ordinary room. The hotel wins by getting the extra revenue and increasing its chances that you'll be back.

Understanding the importance that travel companies place on customer loyalty is your opportunity to profit as a consumer. It is essential that you establish a history of loyalty with select travel companies in order to consistently obtain preferential treatment and services that are normally reserved for those who pay first-class prices. Therefore, begin to build partnerships with high-quality travel companies. This will be the cornerstone of your strategy of traveling first class at coach prices.

Yet all the perks and lavishness that come with loyalty are not limited to the über-traveler. My friend Tina flies about five times a year, however, following a bit of advice from my book, Tina got to know the local gate agents at her airport. On a recent trip, Tina was greeted warmly by the airline's gate agent and the airline's airport manager even came out to introduce himself to her and thanked her for all of her business. She asked why she was receiving all the special treatment, to which the manager replied, "You've reached elite membership for the year and we wanted to let you know how much we appreciate your business." Tina didn't even realize that she had reached 25,000 qualifying miles for the year, but she sure did appreciate the personalized treatment.

BE ASSIDUOUSLY LOYAL TO YOUR TRAVEL PARTNERS

I cannot emphasize enough the importance of adhering to this principle. By maintaining loyalty to one travel partner, you are more likely to achieve the most elite levels as a customer, giving you access to the greatest number of benefits. To maintain your loyalty, you will need to remain flexible. This principle is discussed in full detail later in the book. For now, keep in mind that your chosen travel partner might not always be the most convenient. This means that you might have to take a connecting flight rather than a non-stop flight or stay at a hotel that is five minutes away from your intended destination. Yet, you will find that your flexibility is well worth the effort when you are luxuriating in the finest travel experience imaginable.

SECRET PROGRAMS

Many readers write telling me that they spend their travel dollars on a potpourri of travel companies, thinking that this is the best way to save money. As already discussed, many approached their frequent-flyer or loyalty programs much as they would a coin collection. The reality is that your loyalty and role in loyalty programs is a valuable tool, and that currency is just as valuable as your credit card, computer, or cell phone. When I tell travelers that I routinely earn more than 250,000 annual qualifying miles with just one airline they ask why, often telling me that they would leverage their points with multiple providers. In one sense they make a good argument, however, unless you plan on making a drastic change in lifestyle, you are better served by funneling all you can into the one program that best meets your needs. I say exceed their stated guidelines. The reason for this is what one airline executive described to me as "under the radar programs."

Most organized loyalty programs have a formal structure of benefits and perks achievable at certain levels. For example, most airlines award their minimum level of elite membership with an annual earning of 25,000 qualifying miles. However, as mentioned earlier, sustained loyalty can enter you into an entire world unknown to most. Often qualifying for these programs is by invitation only and is based on your annual earning as well as your total lifetime earnings. Once you enter these doors, airline seats, unavailable hotel rooms, and sporty luxury cars are yours for the taking. The most significant benefit of these programs is that these loyal customers hardly if ever hear the word "no." They want to change their flight without paying a fee—no problem. Want to upgrade to an oceanfront suite—it's available. Although, at the time of writing, I personally have not been invited into one of these programs, those I know who have enjoy their added perks very much.

These programs are only a cornerstone toward what is an all out initiative for the truly loyal. As stated, I am not a member of any skull-and-bones club, but because of my long-term loyalty to a select group of providers I pretty much get most of the same benefits. What this means to you, the average traveler, is that any level of sustained loyalty will go a long way toward enhancing your travel experience. The simple key is that even if you are not a frequent traveler this technique will work for you. All you have to do is invest a little time to research your travel partners and call them to express your intended loyalty—and then follow through.

THE CONTINUING CUSTOMER RELATIONSHIP

Since 1999, the technology used to track and monitor consumer behavior has become sophisticated and fairly inexpensive. This allows the travel industry to monitor who brings them value and who does not. This is also how they can drill down into sub-categories of their data and tailor programs that benefit all levels of travelers.

One way in which travel providers keep you coming back is by giving you personalized attention much in the way that they offer under-the-radar programs to their most loyal customers. As noted in the above paragraph, advances in technology have given travel providers the ability to tailor their marketing programs toward individual needs rather than take a one-size-fits-all approach. This personalized approach has become a cornerstone of a travel provider's competitive advantage and leads to stronger individual relationships between the company and its customers.

To provide personalized service, travel providers track all aspects of their customers' habits, creating a profile that includes purchasing history, ease of individual transactions, any complaints filed or complimentary letters sent, and traveler preferences such as seats they like on the plane or type of room or car they like to rent. The extent of technology available to track customers is nothing short of amazing. At a recent conference I attended for loyalty program managers, I was astonished with the varying technologies I saw. The industry has become such a large part of corporate business that companies literally spend millions of dollars on software and tools to serve their customers. If I wasn't a believer in consumer loyalty before that—seeing what I did sure turned the tide in their favor.

IF YOU BUILD A LOYAL PARTNERSHIP, REWARDS WILL COME

If your aim is to develop mutually beneficial relationships with your travel providers, you want to put the same effort into building and maintaining your travel profile as you would your personal credit profile. The more your travel profile makes you look like a loyal customer, the more likely you are to receive the preferential treatment that constitutes a first-class travel experience.

When you establish a loyal customer relationship with a business, you are in essence building a mutually beneficial partnership with that business. Building a partnership is what allows you, the consumer, to use your loyalty as a valuable investment. This investment pays huge dividends and greatly enhances the way these companies treat you. Remember, your repeat business has value to even the biggest companies, no matter how little or how much you spend. After all, the long-term promise of even the modest amount of income your business brings to a company is worth a great deal, especially when multiplied by the hundreds of thousands of other loyal customers who are just like you. Expanding on the credit analogy, if you had a credit score of 750 you would be considered a prime candidate to offer credit. Now even if you did not spend tens of thousands of dollars a year on your credit cards, because of your diligent efforts in building a prime credit profile you would be sought after by any creditor. The same goes with your travel history. Think about it: If you were the CEO of a major airline, wouldn't you feel secure knowing that hundreds of thousands of people will continue to spend even a few hundred dollars flying your airline every year?

These days, almost all types of businesses promote and track the loyalty of their customers through incentive programs that offer preferential services, prices, and rewards to their most loyal customers. A major force in retailing, Neiman Marcus, offers the InCircle Rewards program in which shoppers can earn rewards ranging from lavish trips to New York City or Hawai'i, to a private performance by well-known musicians, or traveling throughout Europe with fifteen of your friends with exclusive use of a private luxury jet—just by being a loyal customer. Even small businesses compete for loyal customers by offering incentives. After ten purchases, your neighborhood car wash might offer you a free car wash, and your corner yogurt store might give you a free yogurt.

Even if a particular company doesn't have an organized incentive program, you can find ways to profit from your loyalty. I have used Verizon as my wireless carrier for years. When I went to upgrade my phone I was given the customary two-year retention discount. But I also wanted a few accessories and a better deal. So I called their corporate office asking if they could offer any special incentives. They ended up giving me roughly a 50% discount on my accessories and discounted my regular rate for the next year by $10 a month. Now, as stated, they don't have any formal program that I know of, but even my limited spending and loyalty made Verizon consider me a customer they wanted to keep.

In today's global economy, competition is fierce, and any smart business recognizes the value of a loyal customer. Savvy consumers are aware of the benefits of building loyal relationships with astute companies. As a result, both the consumer and the companies profit in a win-win situation.

Quick Review

- Approximately 15% of travel providers' customers provide 90% of the companies' profits.
- Successful businesses seek out and reward loyal customers.
- Build a partnership with a company by being a loyal customer, and become eligible for valuable amenities.
- Customer loyalty is a win-win situation for you and the company with which you do business.

THE RIGHT CUSTOMER

As mentioned previously, travel providers keep a detailed, computerized personal travel profile on each of their customers. This personal travel profile is how travel providers track the value that you bring to them—not just today, but over time. The right travel provider knows that the relationship being built is greater than any individual transaction.

Today's travel providers are not willing to dole out preferred services and upgrades to just any frequent customer; you have to be the right customer. One day while making an airline reservation, I learned firsthand how sophisticated travel providers' customer tracking systems are. During my conversation with this representative she told me that I needed 17,537 miles to re-qualify for platinum elite status (the airline's highest elite level). I then asked her if she thought that the airline would automatically give me this level of elite status even if I did not fly the required number of miles. She clicked away at her keyboard and then said, "Well, I can see that you spent X dollars this year, X dollars last year, and have spent X dollars over your lifetime." I quizzed her further about my record and she continued to tell me that overall my profitability ratio was 83%, and that I was considered generally pleasant to work with. Stunned by all this information, I sheepishly asked how she knew all this. She replied, "It is all here on my computer screen." Whenever you have contact with a travel provider, your record is readily accessible via a computer screen displaying comprehensive data such as the total amount you have paid in fares or rates over your lifetime with the provider, the amount of time it takes for you to make reservations, check-in, the number of questions you ask, and even the number of complaints or how you treat employees.

Frequency is Only Part of the Equation

In the past, it was possible to reap the rewards of loyalty without adding much to a company's bottom line. For example, I, along with numerous other travelers, made a habit of purchasing the lowest possible airfare or paying the lowest room rate to obtain preferred services such as first-class seat upgrades, oceanfront suites, fast check-ins, bonus miles, and an array of other benefits—just by flying the same airline or going to the same hotel chains, no matter how little we spent on the trip or how high maintenance a customer we were. However, during the past few years, travel providers who have lost billions of dollars have taken a down-to-business approach towards unprofitable customers.

Today, it's no longer just about frequency. If you want your travel provider to give you preferential treatment, you have to demonstrate your value as a customer in other ways. Knowing how to do this will set you apart from all other travelers and position you as a five-star customer sought after by travel providers.

A Three-Step Approach to Becoming "The Right Customer"

Your travel provider should see you as:

1. Profitable to the company,

2. Willing to spend a little more than rock-bottom prices, and

3. A pleasure to do business with.

You give a little, but you gain a lot in the form of preferential treatment.

1. Does your travel provider see you as profitable to the company?

While your current spending on travel services is part of the equation that determines your profitability quotient, penny pinching luxury travelers know how to make their past and future spending count today. These savvy travelers know that travel providers look at their customers' past and current histories as well as their projected profitability. For example, suppose an airline has two customers, Larry and James. Larry spent only $5,000 this year but is expected to remain a customer for ten years. James spent $7,000 this year but is not expected to return as a customer. Although spending less up front, Larry brings greater value to the airline because of the promise of return business.

2. Does your travel provider see you as value-conscious but willing to pay a little more in exchange for preferential treatment?

When the first edition of *The Penny Pincher's Passport to Luxury Travel* came out, the rule was that even the most discounted fares were upgradeable. Today, that is no longer the case. If you want to have a chance at those upgrades, you must be willing to pay a slight premium. If you do, you will be amply repaid with first-class treatment.

The reason for this change is that today's travel providers are forced to sell their services at a huge discount in order to remain competitive. Therefore, getting you to book the next, upgradeable fare level rather than the cheapest, non-upgradeable ticket makes a huge difference to them (as it does to you, if an upgrade is what you're looking for.) So does encouraging you to book directly with the airline or hotel rather than through travel discount web sites such as Expedia or Orbitz. Travel providers don't make nearly as much money on those web site transactions, and most airlines, hotels, and car rental companies will not upgrade you or offer other preferential services unless you book your travel through them. Most travel providers offer a money-back guarantee if you book your travel on their web site and later find a lower rate. And as we'll see in Chapter 13, buying direct most often gives you the lowest overall price.

3. Does your travel provider see you as a pleasure to do business with?

My friend, Jack, is by all outward signs an ideal customer. He flies over 100,000 miles each year with one airline, often paying full fare, stays with the same hotels, and rents cars from the same rental company. However, he often does not receive the preferential services he deserves. Last summer while taking a trip with him I learned why. The reason: he is very obstinate and demanding with anyone who has the power to upgrade him and offer him preferred services. After seeing how Jack treated the employees at the airport and on the plane, I suggested that, when the plane landed, we rent separate cars and meet up at our hotel. Not wanting to be at the hotel when Jack checked in, I took a detour and arrived at the hotel an hour later. When I approached the front desk I saw Jack sitting on a chair facing the front desk, pouting. I ignored him and proceeded to check-in. While the front desk agent processed my arrival, I causally ask him if he knew why "that gentleman" was sitting over there on the chair. He told me that he was waiting for a room upgrade. When I replied, asking if upgrades were available and if I could have one, he provided me with an executive suite. I then asked if he was going to upgrade the man waiting. Without hesitation he said no. He continued to say that every time this guest visits the hotel he always has something to complain about, and even though he is a frequent guest, the manager decided that he was too abusive to the staff and that having him as a guest actually cost the hotel more in terms of his bad behavior and the time he consumes with his complaints. Obviously, this type of approach only works against you.

Likewise, once before boarding a flight home from Atlanta, I noticed a man with a Delta Air Lines Three Million Miler tag, meaning that this man has flown over three million miles with the airline. Curious how his loyalty has paid off in preferred services, I inquired as to what his experiences were with the airline. Rather abruptly, he said, "Aw, an airline is an airline—I don't expect much from them." Then I found out why. He approached the gate agent and in a disrespectful manner demanded that the gate agent tell him when his upgrade was going to clear. When the agent told him he wasn't sure, he huffed off with an angry look on his face. Seeing this I went up to my traveling companion who has achieved Delta's lowest elite level—Silver Medallion. I told my friend how to approach the gate agent and ask for an upgrade. Following my guidance, she pleasantly walked up to the gate agent and politely inquired about being upgraded, and following the simple principle of showing respect she was eventually upgraded while the heavy-duty Three Million Miler was not.

To gain preferential treatment, politeness and courtesy go a long way. As another example, say you fly a number of flights on the same carrier every year but typically exhaust the reservation agents and other staff by changing your itineraries multiple times and insisting on all sorts of special concessions. Remember, all of your transactions are tracked and accessible to the contact employees so, even with all your miles, you are actually less likely to get a free or low-cost upgrade than the traveler who has fewer miles but is a pleasure to deal with.

AN AIRLINE EXECUTIVE'S IDEA OF RIGHT AND WRONG

During lunch with a high-level airline executive, I asked him how he would define the right customer. He said the right customer is someone who consistently flies on his airline, is mostly satisfied, and provides positive word-of-mouth advertising. When dissatisfied, the right customer doesn't just complain, but offers constructive feedback. This customer perceives the airline as superior to the competition and becomes emotionally attached to the company over time. In addition, the right customer plays by the rules to get the benefits of preferred services.

When I asked this executive to describe the wrong kind of customer, he named a well-known consumer travel advocate who flies 400,000 miles per year but is also known for beleaguering the travel industry and is markedly tough on the airline industry. This particular individual advocates circumventing airline rules to get lower fares and other concessions. (By the way, the airline executive wasn't the first person to tell me about this individual. One airport gate agent told me that when he serves this person he is always on his guard, because he knows that he could end up seeing a negative account of even a minor slip-up in a future article.) The airline executive said that, even though this customer is a frequent traveler who spends a lot of money every year flying this particular airline, the company would not consider it a huge loss if that customer never came back. "Nor do we go out of our way to give that customer preferential treatment," he said.

"The hassles associated with this traveler are just not worth it."

Make it a habit to show your travel providers respect by using good manners. When you demonstrate your willingness to understand your travel provider's point of view, you validate your intent to build a lasting, mutually beneficial relationship. As a result, you'll find that the professionals who work for your travel provider will be more likely to extend preferred service to you.

A Few Last Words about Loyalty and Being the Right Customer

Combining loyalty and the concept of being the right customer is an essential element of smart consumerism. When you establish a loyal history with a business, and demonstrate your willingness to work with your partners, you will gain access to a cornucopia of benefits. As a loyal or right customer, you have power, and that power gives you leverage. Companies that understand the future of marketing will strive to cultivate your business. These days, the products and services within most industries are very similar in nature. Therefore, competitive markets provide a broad range of options and choices for smart consumers. This is markedly true with travel providers. Maintain your loyalty, be the right customer with quality travel companies, and reap the rewards of luxury.

And remember, in addition to building a loyal history with travel partners, you can establish a history with virtually anyone with whom you do business. Almost all types of industries will reward loyalty.

Key Points

➤ *Choose your travel partners wisely. It's in your best interest to create a long-term relationship and build a high level of loyalty.*

➤ *Reap the rewards of your loyalty. Your loyal patronage will pay off with tremendous benefits and allow you to consistently travel first class while paying coach prices.*

➤ *Maintain the loyalty you have carefully built with your travel partners, even if it requires flexibility.*

➤ *Seek out all opportunities to build customer relationships. A wealth of benefits and amenities await those consumers who have the wisdom and patience to seek them out.*

Your Travel Partners: Creating a Match Made in Heaven

The Secret of My Success (and Yours): Mutually Beneficial Relationships

My approach to getting travel upgrades is similar to Warren Buffet's approach to the stock market: simple and boring, but effective. I have flown over 3 million miles on more than 2,500 flights, and since 1994 I have been upgraded on every flight I have taken while only paying coach prices. The secret of my success is that I used no hyped-up gimmicks, tricks, or loopholes. Instead, I opted for a fundamentally sound approach that has proven successful over a long period of time and in all market conditions. *My technique, not tricks, is to build ongoing, mutually beneficial relationships with high-quality travel partners.*

This idea of getting the best value for your travel dollars is the core of an important concept that I have been discussing and will continue to speak about throughout this book—that is, making sure you build your mutually beneficial relationships with the right travel providers. Like the concept of the right customer, the right travel provider is all about perception, but this time from the traveler's point of view.

There are several more considerations for choosing the right travel provider. These include your individual perception of the provider's quality, service, price, and the degree of importance you attach to each one of these factors. Nevertheless, while every traveler has his or her individual preferences and needs, it is fair to say that all travelers want good quality and service, a fair price, convenience, and comfort.

Depending upon your needs, some of the questions you might ask yourself when deciding if a company is the right travel provider are: Was I able to check in for my flight from an electronic kiosk or even from my home computer? Was the fare reasonable—upgradeable? Did I have a pleasant flight? Was my room clean and quiet? Was the service friendly and accommodating? Does this provider offer enough services to meet my needs today and tomorrow?

The right travel providers are concerned with more than just profit; they care about all facets of their business operations, including their customers, employees, and investors. I have always sensed that there was a correlation between happy employees, happy customers, and the cultures of the companies that create them. I have spoken with many employees in the travel industry over the years, at all levels of service, and the ones who provided me the best service had always felt a strong sense of pride and joy in their job. Finally, in my work as an industrial organizational psychologist, I was able to conduct an in-depth study that confirmed my suspicions.

In addition to my formal studies, I had the opportunity to experience firsthand the interaction between keen customer service and well-treated employees. While visiting the Park Hyatt Hotel in Mendoza, Argentina, not only did I receive heartwarming service, but I also had the fortunate experience of speaking with the hotel's general manager. When I inquired how he was able to coordinate all his staff members to offer such exceptional service, he replied simply, "I treat everyone with respect and dignity." And it showed. As I was sitting with him, a number of employees came into contact with us; the GM knew everyone by name and could tell me about each person's background. The key to his good management was caring about his employees.

The Four Seasons group of hotels is what I would call the right travel provider. In my personal experience, they have consistently provided high-quality service at every single property where I have been a guest over the years. Recently, while enjoying a cappuccino overlooking the beautiful Las Colinas TPC Golf Course in Dallas, Texas, I had a conversation with a long-term Four Seasons executive on why their philosophy is so successful at keeping them ahead of the crowd in the ultra-competitive hotel industry.

The manager told me it all begins with their highly selective process of hiring employees, who go through a series of five interviews—that is, if they make it past the first interview, which is only thirty seconds long. The prospective candidate literally has half a minute to make an impression—or that's it.

Another aspect of the Four Seasons philosophy is that employees from each department have a mutual respect for employees from other departments and understand how each person's work contributes to the overall customer experience. In fact, managers are required to spend a period of time in each department to get firsthand knowledge of how that department contributes to the overall success of the hotel, which ultimately results in happy and loyal guests.

And what is the Four Seasons' idea of the right customer? Similar to what the airline executive said earlier, my managerial contact told me the right customer is not only a repeat guest, the right customer is also someone who tells friends how great it is to stay at the Four Seasons. That is because positive word-of-mouth is the form of advertising that marketing experts consider to be the strongest and most lasting.

No matter what your travel provider's internal policies are, you as a consumer will know the value they bring to you. If your travel provider is not doing its part to provide good value, then it is time to make some changes.

QUICK TIPS FOR CHOOSING THE RIGHT TRAVEL PROVIDER

- Consider travel providers who have the geographical availability you require.

- Ask yourself what airports and cities you most often visit.

- Talk with your well-traveled colleagues about their preferences.

- Read travel publications for consistently high-ranking travel providers.

- Call the travel provider directly and inquire about what they will offer you in return for your loyal business (elite status, bonus miles, free upgrades).

- Call the company's headquarters to see how they respond to your questions. Are they friendly? Quick to dismiss? Willing to assist?

Time for a Checkup

I sometimes think New Year's resolutions are too focused on the *new* when what is really needed is a hard look at the *old*. This is certainly true of travel loyalty programs. Since most programs reset the counter on your eligibility points in January, October is the time to do a checkup, to make sure your programs are still meeting your needs. Pull out your program descriptions, your calendar, your travel schedule and some reading glasses (for the fine print). Just five check points and you're done.

1. Know your programs. Loyalty programs are in constant flux, and the ones that worked for you last year might not do the job this year. Check to see if your programs have changed since you joined them, then consider whether your travel patterns will change this year. Will you be traveling the same routes and times? Will you need different accommodations when you get where you're going (better conferencing facilities, perhaps, or a suite instead of a single room)? Will you be traveling with companions who are using other travel programs? Whatever the reason, if you are better served by another program, now is the time to change.

2. Schedule your trips for the year. Remember November and December, when you were frantically trying to squeeze in enough year-end points to qualify for the perks and awards you want? Do you want to do that again this year? I didn't think so. Remember, all loyalty programs operate on the same principle, i.e., "What have you done for me lately?" You have to keep coming back to your travel partner, and you have to build points before you can cash in for perks. Since it's a new year, your ticket for elite privileges has been renewed. So schedule your trips now, at least on paper, to make sure you can maintain the loyalty level you want. Added bonus: You'll save yourself from a mileage run next New Year's Eve.

3. **Swing your partners.** One benefit of the network airlines is that their loyalty programs often include allegiance partnerships; when you do business with one of these partners, you can earn extra privileges. But you need to keep up with the partnerships so you can get the most bang for your buck. Once you've chosen your travel programs and have scheduled your trips, determine which partnership offers will benefit you. Pay special attention to point bonuses that can put you on the fast-track to elite status. Two caveats. First, partnership opportunities come and go, so stay current with the available program options. Second, know that some of the best bonus offers require you to sign up in advance.

4. **Check online opportunities.** Most airlines and some hotels charge extra when you book by phone but reward you when you make reservations on the Web. When you need personal assistance, discuss your itinerary with an agent, book the reservation online, then have the agent make any necessary changes. This will save you money *and* get you the bonus.

5. **Think about sleeping and driving.** In the past, travelers have focused their earning efforts on airline loyalty programs. But with ever-dropping airfares and rising hotel and car-rental rates, secondary programs deserve special attention these days. Getting elite status with a

hotel or car rental company can mean cost-saving free nights and miles of free driving. I predict that 2008 will be a banner year for secondary programs, so plan your elite qualifying activities across the board to score the goods.

O.K., your checkup is done and you're good to go. Travel safe, and enjoy your well-earned elite status.

THE RIGHT CUSTOMER + THE RIGHT TRAVEL PROVIDER = BENEFITS FOR ALL

If you see a company as the right travel provider, you are more likely to give them your repeat business. If that travel provider sees you as the right customer, you are more likely to receive preferential treatment in return for giving that travel provider an economic advantage over its competitors. This is the essence of a mutually beneficial relationship.

Now that we've discussed the basic philosophy of traveling luxuriously for less, it's time for some practical tips. The first of these tips, which is the subject of the next chapter, concerns frequent-user programs and how to get the most out of them.

DON'T JUST SAVE MONEY, SPEND IT WISELY

When you are in need of medical care, you are most likely to seek out the highest level of care possible. After all, would you want an unskilled surgeon performing a triple bypass surgery on you or a loved one? Likewise, when you wish to purchase the highest quality product or service, you are not likely to shop at a five-and-dime store. The same principle holds true for travel. We learned in the last chapter the importance of doing business with quality companies. As previously stated, if you seek the utmost in luxury travel, you will find that occasionally you will need to pay a modest premium. However, when you use the strategies discussed in this book you will not pay an excessive sum of money, and you will find that the added benefits of ultra-luxurious travels will far exceed any additional amount of money you might pay. Most importantly, you will need to deal exclusively with companies that consistently offer superior service.

If you are, on occasion, faced with the prospect of paying a slight premium for the opportunity to travel in luxury, is it worth it? Absolutely. The philosophy of those who travel first class and pay coach prices is not only to save money, but also to spend it wisely in order to reap first-class rewards. To understand this, you will need to consider the overall cost of travel and the impact your travels will have on your peace of mind. This means you should consider the actual costs of a trip from both a monetary as well as an emotional perspective. The monetary side is easy to understand: you want to get the most luxurious travel experience for the least amount of money. However, as you become a more experienced traveler you will find that the lowest price is not always the best deal. The emotional aspect of your trip affects your overall level of satisfaction and the comfort in which you experience your travels. This brings us back to the important concept of limiting your business to quality companies in order to receive high-quality service. Remember that every aspect of your trip can affect your overall experience.

Without a doubt, you will be able to find airfares that might save you $100 or a hotel room for 5% to 10% less; however, consider what other costs are associated with this savings. Will you have to arrive at the airport three hours early and fight a crowd of people vying for unreserved seats or at the very least wait in a long line to get a seat? Will the quality of service you receive be poor? Will you question the safety record of the air carrier? Will you be able to cash in your miles for only limited travel destinations? Will you be able to sleep in your hotel room at night when the bed is uncomfortable and the neighbors are noisy? Will you feel comfortable with the level of cleanliness in your room? Will you feel safe in the rental car you're driving? What happens if that car breaks down en route to an important meeting or family outing?

While searching for a fare from Frankfurt, Germany to London—a route not served by my chosen airline—I was faced with the choice of going for an ultra-low fare with an unknown airline or spending a few more dollars for a more reliable experience. My internet search yielded the following results: one flight for 1 euro and another for 55 euros. Naturally the lower fare was most attractive at face value. However, when I checked the details I found that I would have to fly from a less convenient airport, pay for any luggage, and check in at least two hours before the flight. On the other hand, the 55-euro flight offered me assigned seating, departed from the main airport with convenient online check-in and the ability to check baggage without an additional fee. In short, selecting the more convenient, less restrictive flight was a no-brainer.

On another occasion, I return my Hertz rental car back to the Phoenix airport with a broken back wing window. Although Hertz could have followed the rules of their contract and charged me for the damage, they chose to take me at my word when I told them that I did not know how the damage had occurred and they did not penalize me. Now I might have saved a few dollars with another company, but in this instance my loyalty and reputation with Hertz was rewarded with compassionate and understanding customer service.

During my travels I often come across travelers who blindly follow hyperbole rather than thinking for themselves. The legendary example is the difference between flying Southwest and a full-service airline such as American Airlines. The most frequent reason I hear for flying Southwest is that they are cheaper. They are on occasion, but more often than not they offer the same price, and sometimes a higher fare than mainstream airlines. Price aside, the differences become glaring. On Southwest you wait in a bothersome line taking your chances at winning the lottery of seats. Conversely, on an American flight, you can arrive at the airport an hour before your flight, with boarding pass in hand and breeze through the security lines. Another distinct advantage is the depth of an airline's frequent-flyer program and how you can use those points. Southwest frequent flyers are restricted to the limited routes flown by that airline. In contrast, American Airlines provides worldwide coverage and the ability to fly on code-share routes. And the most important consideration of all to the readers of this book is that Southwest will not upgrade you to first class. Unlike American, Southwest does not have first-class cabins.

Another example of how consumers can become misled by hype was the mainstream media portrayal of Virgin America Airlines' entry into the U.S. marketplace. The first day of Virgin America's operations I heard almost all the local Los Angeles news stations and cable news channels talk about how great the airline was because they offered seat-back entertainment system with movies, television, games, and music. All I could think was "where have these guys been?" Delta Air Lines has been offering this for over a year in both coach and first-class cabins on similar routes. The key is to be an active and astute consumer and, as I stated in the last chapter, it is not necessary to fall for the latest tricks, hype, or promotions. Stick to your well-thought-out game plan and, like I do, you'll enjoy first-class travel at a discount.

LUXURY OFTEN COSTS THE SAME OR EVEN LESS

While it is certainly worth it to pay a little more to have a pleasant and comfortable experience, the idea of this book is to travel luxuriously and to save money. Therefore, by doing a little research and by keeping your standards of quality high, you will find that you do not always have to pay more for luxury. In fact, occasionally a luxury rental car, a more upscale hotel room, and even a first-class airline seat can actually cost you less than what you might pay for a low-frills experience. (In Chapter 7 you'll read how I avoided the world's only self-proclaimed 7-star hotel, saved $1,775 a night and had what I found to be a more luxurious experience.)

Until lately I would have never thought about purchasing a first-class ticket. However, in an attempt to generate additional revenue many airlines have dramatically lowered their first-class fares. For example, *The Wall Street Journal* once reported that airlines had lowered their first-class fares by 220%. The article stated that 94% of first class seats are given away as upgrades so if an airline could generate only a few extra dollars from these seats it would dramatically improve their bottom line. Recently, I was traveling from Orange County, California to Atlanta, Georgia. Booking my ticket the day before my departure yielded me the following choices: a restricted coach ticket costing $431 or a fully refundable/changeable first-class ticket for $491. As previously stated, my norm is to purchase discounted coach tickets and upgrade to first class. In this situation, I opted to spend the extra $60 because by doing so I had confirmed access to a first-class seat—no wait-lists or using upgrade coupons, and I earned 7,776 miles that counted toward elite qualification, whereas with the other fare I would only earn 2,230 miles toward elite qualification. I will explain this difference later in Chapter 5. Incidentally the year before this same fare would have cost $1,250.

The same also goes for redeeming frequent-flyer miles. In an interesting quirk of the system, travelers can often redeem a first-class award seat for fewer miles than a coach ticket. After encountering this a few times, I figured that I was really lucky. But then I spoke with the program director of a major airline's frequent-flyer program who confirmed this anomaly. It seems that more airlines often have higher inventory with first-class seats because most people don't even consider a first-class award.

On a trip to the Big Island of Hawai'i, I booked a first-class flight on Delta. Because Delta does not fly all the way to the Big Island, I flew on Delta to Oahu, and the Delta reservation agent arranged a connecting flight for me from Oahu to the Big Island on Hawai'ian Airlines. On my Delta ticket, the cost was split between the Delta portion and the Hawai'ian Airlines' portion. When I made my reservations, it didn't even occur to me that my Hawai'ian Airlines flight might not have the same quality of service as Delta. However, my failure to make inquiries led to an unpleasant surprise. I found out, too late, that Hawai'ian Airlines does not offer pre-assigned seating or first class on their inter-island flights. I found myself waiting in a long line at the Oahu Airport to board the Hawai'ian Airlines plane in a cattle-like manner. Once I made my way on board the plane, I was constrained by the smallest airline seat I have ever sat in. And after the plane landed, it took me over twenty minutes to deplane. Determined not to repeat this experience on my return flight, I did my homework and called another inter-island airline, Aloha Airlines, which did offer pre-assigned seating and a first-class section. What a difference this made. I purchased my ticket in a separate line, without waiting. I boarded the plane first and stretched out in a nice big seat. Adding to my contentment was the knowledge that this Aloha Airlines flight cost me less than what I had paid for the other unpleasant experience.

On another occasion, my associate Tom and I needed to travel to Denver for a business presentation. Tom booked a room in a Courtyard by Marriott, while I did a little extra planning on my own and found out that a nicer, full-service Hilton Hotel was less money than Tom was paying for his hotel. My hotel had a plush lobby, valet parking, 24-hour room service, and most important, a clean room where I experienced a restful night, awaking alert and ready for the day. Tom, on the other hand, experienced no such amenities, and the entire next day he complained about his inability to sleep the previous night due to the discomfort he had experienced at his hotel. I didn't have the heart to tell him that my room cost two dollars less per night than his!

This story brings up another important point, about which I will go into greater detail later in this book: If you are seeking luxury travel at a discount, doing your own research and bookings rather than using a travel agent is often your best bet.

BUSINESS TRAVEL

When traveling for business or at the last moment, you will find that you will usually pay higher rates than if you had more advance time to arrange your travel plans. However, there is a positive aspect to this. Hopefully, if you are traveling for business you will be reimbursed for your expenses, which should soften the blow a little. In any case, when you do have to pay higher rates, you will also have the opportunity to reap the same rewards as you would if you were that company's most loyal patron. Simply by paying a higher rate, you will be considered the crème de la crème of travelers. The reason for this is that travel companies are forced to discount most of their rates to remain competitive. Therefore, when they do have the opportunity to charge higher rates, they treat those customers royally.

Whenever you are faced with paying a higher rate, be sure to always receive additional benefits. Many airlines will automatically upgrade any passengers who pay a full coach fare. This is called a Y-up fare. "Y" is the code for full fare and "up" is for upgrade. Additionally, some airlines will offer bonus miles based on your higher fare, as you will learn in Chapter 5. Another key benefit you can often get with a premium fare is access to the preferred security lines at the airport which can literally save you an hour or more.

Likewise, many hotels will upgrade you to their best suite
and provide you with their club-floor amenities. Make sure
that whenever you pay higher rates, you inquire into what
extra amenities and services you will get in return.

When I traveled to Lake Tahoe for a conference, I
booked my hotel late. By the time I made my reservations,
all of the special discounted rooms set aside for the conference were sold out. Therefore, I ended up having to pay a
little more than $100 extra for my room. When I asked the
reservation agent if paying the higher rate meant that I
would get a nice suite, she said, "I'll see what I can do." I
ended up with a beautiful suite overlooking one of the
world's most gorgeous lakes. Moreover, when I checked in
and asked the front-desk representative if this high rate
afforded me any special amenities, she arranged for a complimentary one-hour massage.

Be sure to make it known to whomever you're dealing
with that you are paying a higher-priced business rate and
you would like to receive added services and benefits in
return. Be polite and diplomatic, but assume that extra
amenities are customary in such a situation. They are. This
holds true whether you are speaking with a gate agent or
checking into a hotel. Let them know that you are traveling
for business and would appreciate any special perks they
might extend. Travel companies will cater to business travelers as they do to loyal customers because of their tenden-
cy to pay premium prices and because of the high frequency of their travels.

KEEP YOUR STANDARDS HIGH

Later in this book I will reveal the secrets to achieving
luxury while paying the same as or slightly above what you

would pay for low-frills travel companies. In the meantime, bear in mind that as a cost-conscious traveler in quest of luxury, it is imperative that you seek out high-quality, service-oriented travel companies instead of choosing a low-frills airline or a hotel chain whose priority is volume rather than service. This point is so important it is worth repeating. Although occasionally you will pay a modest premium for luxury, do yourself a favor and plan your travels exclusively with a high-quality travel partner. In return for being selective, you will not only enjoy more pleasurable travels, but you will also have the opportunity to build loyal partnerships that will earn you even higher levels of luxury. This also really pays off in the type of service you receive and what recourse is offered when things go wrong. As the highlighted story demonstrates, high-quality travel providers strive to maintain their reputation and when things go wrong they will take personal responsibility to correct their mistakes. This will be fully explained in Chapter 12.

How to Get the Service You Deserve

We all mess up sometimes. The world traveler may forget his ticket, and even a five-star hotel can lose your reservation. When mishaps happen, the best travel providers will often go out of their way to make amends. After all, their reputations are at stake. The circumstances of the mishap and the way you present your case will determine what happens next. With patience and courtesy, a knowledgeable traveler can sometimes turn misfortune to advantage.

High-quality travel companies strive to maintain a credible reputation for providing exceptional service. An unhappy customer is the last thing they want at their door. Every mistake and mix-up, then, gives rise to two opportunities: one for the company, to uphold its reputation, the other for the customer, to achieve a fair resolution. Here is some advice for striking a balance—and getting a good deal.

TAKE RESPONSIBILITY

First things first: Responsibility for the quality of your travels starts with you. Know what to expect from your airline, hotel, cruise line, tour operator, or rental car company, and you won't be caught in a lot of misunderstandings. You'll also learn where the benefits and perks lie.

Over the years, I have gotten to know my preferred travel providers quite well. For example, I have studied the routes that Delta Air Lines flies out of my home airport, Orange County, California; I've learned what planes are used on each route; I know which flights arrive and depart on time; and I know which flights offer the best opportunities for an upgrade. Yes, I've had to read a lot of fine print. But taking responsibility means I get to fly in first class for free.

Taking responsibility also means not taking advantage of your travel providers. Fox News Channel recently ran a story about a man who suffered a heart attack while reviewing his bill in a restaurant. The problem is that this was the *eighteenth time* this man happened to have a heart attack after a meal at this same restaurant. The restaurant decided not to take it anymore, and the man got free meals for the next 90 days in jail.

ATTITUDE COUNTS

In a recent article titled "Good Views=Lousy Service?" I wrote about poor service at two hotels in coastal Orange County. Their respective responses speak volumes about their dedication to quality service.

When the owner of the Montage Resort & Spa read my article, he immediately dispatched an e-mail to his general manager to find out what went wrong. The general manager contacted me and expressed sincere concern, asking me how the hotel could improve and prevent future lapses of quality service. Prompt action, solicitude, and a willingness to change are sure signs that goodwill really matters to a travel provider. You just have to follow their lead.

Conversely, when my friend Claudia gave my article to the manager of the Ritz-Carlton, Laguna Niguel, he retorted that he knows the hotel has good service because guests tell him so. When she told him I'd received a number of e-mails from readers concurring with my assessment, he demanded that I send him some proof. Arrogance is a sure sign that a travel provider lacks consistent quality. The best providers offer top quality to every customer, whether it's a mega-superstar or an average traveler like you and me. There is little you can do with a provider like this, except take your business elsewhere.

ASK AND YOU MIGHT RECEIVE

Recently, my teenage daughter was traveling from school in upstate New York to see her mom in Dallas. I had mistakenly booked her on an itinerary with a three-and-a-half-hour layover in Atlanta. Concerned that she would be alone on a Friday night in a busy airport, I called the Delta

Crown Room in Atlanta two hours before her flight to ask if I could purchase a one-day pass so she would have a safe place to wait for her next flight. It was probably too late to contact her, so I had little hope of success. But I thought I'd ask.

Luckily, I spoke with a Delta employee who was willing to make a champion effort. She made the arrangements in Atlanta, relayed the information to Syracuse, made sure my daughter got the message—she even waived the $50 fee for the one-day pass. All the while, she was extremely sympathetic and helpful.

My friend Lance got in a similar jam. After bragging about the low fare he had gotten just one day before a trip to Washington, D.C., he took a second look at his ticket and discovered that he had actually booked a flight three weeks hence. (I have done the same thing with hotel reservations.) Lance called the airline, explained his mistake, and got a full refund. It turns out most quality airlines and travel providers will refund your purchase if your plans change within 24 hours of booking.

Extra effort and consideration are signs of real quality, and customers should reward such companies with their continued patronage.

SEEK FAIR COMPENSATION

When you have a legitimate complaint, state your dissatisfaction clearly and succinctly to the appropriate person. If your room service is a half-hour late, call the manager of room service, not the hotel's general manager. If your first effort fails, take it to the next level. But before you lodge any grievance, think about what would be fair compensation. If your soup is cold, it would be silly to expect a free week in the hotel's presidential suite.

It often pays to let the travel provider suggest appropriate amends. My friend Carol and her two young daughters sat sweltering on a hot runway for two hours when their plane experienced mechanical difficulties. When they finally returned to the gate, Carol voiced her disappointment, noting that the flight attendants had not even offered the girls water in the heat of the plane. The agent promptly provided her with vouchers for dinner and placed her on a competitor's flight in first class—much more than Carol had expected.

Finally, here are four quick pointers for getting the service you deserve:

Be polite. Very often, the customer-contact people are doing their best, and some things are simply beyond their control. Try to work with them patiently and politely to resolve your difficulty.

Don't take no for an answer. My friend Susan was stranded in the blackout on the East Coast in August 2003. She stood in line for three hours before getting to a gate agent, who then said, "Sorry, all flights are full." Undeterred, Susan (politely) asked to be put on a waiting list. The ticket agent said it would not make a difference, but she agreed to do it anyway. And Susan did get on a flight.

Use your leverage. If you are a frequent flyer or a privileged customer of a travel provider, use your status to your advantage when asking for a favor or amends. I'm sure my 3 million frequent-flyer miles with Delta helped get my daughter that pass for the Crown Room in Atlanta.

Don't waste your time with someone who won't help or doesn't care. Complacency, like arrogance, is almost impossible to deal with. I'd rather spend my money with a company that values its customers.

As a consumer on a quest for first-class travel, you have the right to expect and receive nothing less than the best. If a travel company fails to meet high standards, inform the appropriate official in a professional and caring manner. This may not always get you what you want, but it ensures that you keep up your *own* high standards, which is half the battle.

By building loyal partnerships with your travel partners you will become ever more knowledgeable about how to most advantageously cash in on your loyalty with each company. Learning the particular idiosyncrasies of your chosen travel partners will involve trial and error and a little patience, as well as the know-how you acquire from this book. Nonetheless, because your goal is to build a long-term, loyal partnership, rest assured that you will eventually understand the ins and outs of your travel partners better than some of their own employees. And by keeping your standards of quality high in selecting the companies with which you do business, you will be rewarded for your continued patronage with upgraded airline seats, luxurious accommodations, and a wealth of money-saving amenities for a reasonable and fair price.

Key Points

➤ *Pay now or pay later. Chasing big discounts can lead to disappointments. Make sure you know what standard of quality a particular company offers in return for their low price.*

➤ *Consider the value of your time and peace of mind. When choosing the travel companies with which you do business, keep your standards of quality high. An inadequate travel partner can rob you of valuable time, and poor service can make traveling more stressful than it needs to be.*

➤ *Pay a slight premium for luxury and you can reap priceless benefits. In some cases, luxury might even cost you less. In any case, whether you have to pay a modest premium, the same price, or even less than the ordinary traveler for an extraordinary travel experience, you're worth it.*

➤ *Become a straight-A student of first-class travel at discount prices. Understand the intricacies of your travel partners' programs and leverage that knowledge to enhance your travel experience. With the knowledge you gain from doing repeat business with your travel partners, you will be able to ensure that all your travels are first class.*

4

A Contrarian Strategy

Traveling Against the Grain

As you build the blocks toward your overall strategy of traveling in luxury at a discount you'll find the next principle to be one of your best allies. Contrarian travel is an approach to luxury travel that means that you travel when particular destinations and travel companies need your business the most.

Looking for great travel deals has become a pastime and to some it has become a game that can consume all sorts of time. It seems everyone has a different strategy for reaching the holy grail of travel—a great experience at a reasonable price. A few short years ago value-conscious travelers just booked a trip during the off-season. But now that everyone is traveling during the off-season, the off-season has become the on-season. Therefore, real insiders have shifted from a seasonal strategy to a contrarian strategy.

Finding the best contrarian travel opportunities requires a lot of footwork—or in my case, seat time. This is because contrarian destinations are constantly changing, as once-unheard-of destinations offering travel value become voguish and expensive (as is the case with Prague) and new, off-the-radar destinations come to the fore. In this chapter, you will see how to take advantage of current as well as future opportunities, whatever the economic state of the travel industry.

For me, a true contrarian destination must meet three criteria: (1) it must offer a good exchange rate; (2) it must offer great travel value; and (3) it must offer an appealing environment. Having a broad perspective and looking at regional opportunities is a key to successfully traveling in luxury at a discount.

One example I found in early 2007 was South Africa. While this is not a new place for travel, it is fast becoming a vibrant travel region, as Johannesburg and surrounding cities prepare to host the 2010 FIFA World Cup. This event is the Super Bowl and Olympics of soccer rolled into one, with ticket sales expected to top 3 million. As the city and region is preparing for the upcoming FIFA Cup, restaurants, hotels, and sites are getting a nice spruce up, but the prices have yet to climb, as they will when droves of fans head to the games. So in my opinion, the time to visit is not three years from now, but right now.

In essence, a contrarian traveler looks for circumstances or events that have lower demand for a particular travel service or destination. In a time of higher demand (and prices) it may be the only way to get a luxury trip at a low price. Here are five ways to go contrarian:

1. **Buy directly**. Direct contact with a travel provider is important for building a lasting relationship with an airline, hotel, or car rental company. Once you're in the door you can ask for a better rate or an upgrade.

2. **Profit when they're not**. Opportunities are created by what I call "situational uncertainty." This occurs when a

country or region experiences a natural disaster, terrorist activity, political upheaval, or economic depression. Often, the unexpected situation can make the location more desirable. After an attack on German buses in Luxor, Egypt, for example, security forces were on high alert with few tourists vying for highly discounted $50 rooms in five-star luxury hotels overlooking the Nile. When a rare tsunami hit the Asia Pacific region, thousands of hotel rooms went empty, depressing prices and the local workforce. Supportive travelers got both a great deal and helped locals keep their jobs and feed their families by pumping money into the local economy.

3. **Follow the dollar**. What a difference an exchange rate can make. In the early 2000s a European trip came with an automatic 30% discount because of a strong dollar. Years later, the same trip cost me 30% more because of a drop in the dollar's value. During a jaunt to Buenos Aires, a favorable dollar help me enjoyed a latte-and-croissant breakfast on a tree-lined street café similar to Paris, all for only $4. I also stayed on the club-level floor at the Four Seasons for $225 a night with full concierge service and meal presentations, and enjoyed a signature massage for a mere $65.

4. **Be flexible**. The travel market is in constant flux and liable to change at any moment. Developing flexibility with respect to your travel dates, destinations, and accommodations will yield excellent luxury travel bargains. I experienced this when I was asked by CBS to do a Sunday morning interview in New York. My choice of last-minute flights offered me coach on Saturday or a $304 first-class late night Friday flight, arriving Saturday morning. Adding to my value, the Grand Hyatt allowed a 7 A.M. check-in. So

basically, I got two hotel days for one, and enjoyed a wonderful Saturday afternoon in the city.

5. **Avoid trends**. The worst time or place to travel is anywhere everyone else is going. Think about it: If a travel destination is full to the brim with travelers, there is less incentive for hotels to give you a discount or a free upgrade. Also, it's more likely that your experience will not be as good since the employees will be busy accommodating a full house, leaving less time for personal attentive service.

With airlines flying at capacity levels and luxury hotels experiencing higher occupancies, getting a luxury bargain at a discount is becoming increasingly difficult. The best solution is to have a contrarian mindset.

While contrarian travel is seeking areas of opportunities it doesn't mean that you need to forgo the cultural experience you seek. During most of 2006 and 2007 I avoided Europe due to the weak value of the dollar. However, yearning for Europe's beautiful cathedrals, quaint towns, charming cafés and culinary delights, I figured out a plan to travel like a contrarian while enjoying the beauty of Europe.

Using six strategies I was able to put my five contrarian tools to the test and I saved money on a European vacation at a time when the weak U.S. dollar was making most European travel prohibitive.

Contrarian Strategy #1: Look for out-of-the-way destinations that are not overrun with seasonal tourists. Often these are the very places offering low airfares. This was the case for my first stop: Barcelona. I chose Barcelona because the flights from Orange County were reasonably priced, and I had plenty of upgrades. (**Contrarian Strategy #2**: Use your frequent-flyer miles and loyalty points.)

Upon arriving in Spain, I rented a BMW 3 series for 92 euros—not the cheapest rate, but it was a new car and Hertz has a reputation for quality. Moreover, the car came equipped with Hertz's "NeverLost" GPS system, which would allow me to travel to many out-of-the-way places in confidence. I headed out immediately, intending to enjoy Barcelona on the return trip. A six-hour drive took me to Geneva and my wonderful hotel, the Four Seasons Hotel des Bergues Geneva. The hotel, which sits on the southwestern shore of Lake Geneva, has views of Mont Blanc and offers special bed-and-breakfast packages along with a fourth-night-free promotion. (**Contrarian Strategy #3**: By combining frequent-guest points with a special promotion, you can get a better deal. I enjoyed a luxurious room overlooking the lake.)

Geneva has the flair of Paris without the expense. The city played a pivotal role in shaping Europe for centuries, especially during the Reformation; it was Rousseau's birthplace and Voltaire's refuge. Today Geneva is an important banking and watchmaking center and serves as the European headquarters of the United Nations. It is also a pretty city, with enchanting quays, lakeside promenades, leafy parks and a lively Old Town. There are many fashionable stores and art galleries, more than thirty museums, several theaters and an opera house, gourmet restaurants and a dynamic nightlife. My favorite museum in Geneva was the Patek Philippe Museum. I collect Patek Philippe watches, and it was a thrill for me to see the history of this brand unfold before my eyes. (**Contrarian Strategy #4**: Skip the "must-see" sights that you couldn't care less about, and do something you really like.)

From Geneva, I took a marathon drive to Bilbao, Spain: 1,100 kilometers in roughly nine hours. I drove nonstop because I was short on time, but if you are traveling at a more leisurely pace, I recommend spending a day or two in either Toulouse or Bordeaux, both beautiful regions in the interior of France offering charming settings, wine, and good dining.

I went to Bilbao to experience the ultramodern Guggenheim Museum. (Architect Frank O. Gehry's design for the Guggenheim Museum Bilbao is sheer genius. As I wandered through the museum enjoying the artwork, I was amazed by the curvy sometimes-passive, sometimes-interactive nature of the building's architectural design.) Happily, the prices on this stop weren't bad. I stayed at the five-star Gran Hotel Domine Bilbao, a Silken hotel. My room overlooking the museum included breakfast for only 110 euros a night. The service was superb, and the hotel's teakwood-paved terrace offered outstanding views of the museum and surrounding hills. It was also the "in" place to have breakfast. I happened to be in Bilbao during its inaugural Bilbao Music Festival, so I ate breakfast with band members from Cheap Trick and Guns N' Roses, who were also staying at the hotel.

From Bilbao I headed back to Barcelona by way of Pamplona, the Spanish city notorious for its annual "Running of the Bulls." I arrived two days after the official event but found the city to be a worthwhile stop nonetheless. Meandering among the small streets *without* the threat of a bull and his horns bearing down on me is more to my tastes anyway (see Contrarian Strategy #4). The half-mile route winding through town from a corral on Santo Domingo Street to the city's bullring is filled with charming restaurants, cafés and residences above the ground-level businesses.

The drive from Pamplona to Barcelona took me through northern Spain along an excellent *autopista*, or highway, traversing a landscape that ranges from highlands to desert to mountains. The BMW was a dream machine, and I was in heaven the whole way. (**Contrarian Strategy #5**: Spend your money on experiences that matter to you.) In four hours I was back in Barcelona, the third city on my must-see list. If you have not already visited this young, lively, multicultural European city with a Catalan flair, you're missing a true delight. If you have been there before, as I have, there are many new adventures, restaurants, cafés, shops, and beaches to explore. I stayed at the Hotel Palace, Barcelona, an early twentieth-century building with the grace and charm of that era. It's ideally located along a tree-lined street close to the popular Ramblas area of the city, which is full of restaurants, shops, and cafés. The hotel was undergoing renovations, so the rates were below market for a property of this quality. (**Contrarian Strategy #6**: Look for luxury hotel properties under new ownership or renovation, but avoid booking during reopening festivities, when prices go up.)

UNDERSTAND BUSINESS CYCLES

Throughout the publication and consequent revisions of this book, the travel economy has gone through many cycles which is why the contrarian strategy is so important.

In the first edition I wrote that the travel market experiences ups and downs. When the book hit the stores, the dollar was relatively strong against the euro and I wrote about my experience of spending a month in Vienna at a discount. At the time I stated that business cycles eventually change course and starting in 2000, declining stocks and income produced weak demand for travel services, with the airlines and other travel providers losing billions of dollars per quarter. At the time I wrote that the positive in these dark clouds was bargain travel opportunities, such as low fares to Europe while the dollar was trading at an all-time high to the euro. (At the time of this writing, the dollar is trading at an all-time low to the euro.) Readers of the early editions of this book learned about travel to Europe, paying less than $300 in airfare and then getting good value at hotels, restaurants, and when buying clothes or making other purchases. Likewise, it was possible to fly coast-to-coast for $99 one-way, and stay at a luxury hotel in New York City, including the trendy W Hotel, for under $95.

Today the travel cycle is in a different phase and currently travelers need to exert much more effort to get a good bargain. In fact one of the most significant changes is that at the time of this writing the American dollar was worth less than the Canadian dollar. Since the early 1970s, when the Canadian currency was no longer pegged to the dollar, most Americans enjoyed a price advantage with quick trips to Canada. Many travelers can recall getting $1.40 Canadian per U.S. dollar, but that has changed, and as of this printing the Canadian is now worth a record $1.05 U.S. This shifting dynamic has now made the States a contrarian choice for Canadian travelers. Likewise,

Europeans can enjoy fantastic bargains in the U.S. on the strength of the euro.

The important message here is understanding that business cycles change and adapting your planning in accordance with these changes will enable you to maintain luxurious travels while saving money. Eventually the dollar will strengthen, airlines will weaken, and hotels will lower prices. It's all part of market dynamics. The important thing is to remember this and to use it to your advantage to maximize your travel value.

Perhaps more than any other industry, the travel industry radically changes its approach to customer service according to supply and demand. When times are good for travel providers, they restrict giveaways and preferential services. When economic conditions are difficult, they offer all sorts of enticements to generate business, including unprofitably low fares, bonus miles, and other such special amenities.

The contrarian traveler knows that although there will be times when the travel industry is strong, that strength will inevitably cycle into weakness, which ultimately creates a wealth of benefits. And even when the travel industry shows overall strength, there are always areas of opportunity in which supply exceeds demand.

WHERE TO LOOK FOR VALUE AND HOW TO ASK FOR IT

Increased advertising of special prices and media reports of industry hardships will inform you that a certain sector of the travel industry is not performing well. For example, a recent issue of a travel magazine highlighted thirty prime vacation destinations that are currently going through a tourism dry spell, which in turn provides excellent opportunities for bargain travel. Hawai'i, which is usually a prized destination for many vacation travelers, was one of the areas covered in that article. Likewise most travel TV shows love to detail the hottest travel destinations, which may be enticing, but in reality are the places to avoid.

The beauty of travel is that there will always be somewhere to go that is offering good value for your dollar. As you will see in the following section, even during a hot economy one can find many luxurious opportunities for the budget-conscious contrarian traveler.

MIDEAST REGION AND OTHER DESTINATIONS AGAINST THE GRAIN

As I stated, "Contrarian Travel" is to travel against the grain: Go off-peak, follow the dollar, look for distressed properties, eschew all trends—in general, look for the destinations and travel providers that need your business the most.

Right now, the dollar is at an all-time low to most world currencies, especially to the euro and British pound. This makes hotels and meals unusually expensive in most European cities. So the contrarian traveler looks elsewhere: to Asia, South America and, yes, the Middle East.

I recently visited Jordan, Israel, and the Sinai Peninsula, and the trip was an excellent test of the contrarian strategy. Of course, the Middle East is a region steeped in history and rich in tradition; any good guidebook can give you the rundown on this most remarkable cradle of civilization. But the imperative questions for me—and all contrarian travelers—are these: How safe is the region and how affordable is it? I found the region rated high on both issues. As an added bonus, I found the people to be welcoming, sincere, and charming.

My first stop was Amman, the capital of Jordan, where I stayed at the Grand Hyatt Hotel. The hotel was the site of a suicide bombing in November 2005, along with two other hotels in Amman, yet I felt completely safe and would have no hesitation recommending the hotel to close family or friends. Security is now very tight, but it is neither intrusive nor overbearing. Upon arrival, I was greeted warmly then swiftly whisked through the security screening (the process and equipment are similar to an airport screening). All hotel guests pass though the screening every time they enter the hotel, as do all visitors. An alternative to the Hyatt is the luxurious Four Seasons Amman, which was not involved in the bomb attack; its bed-and-breakfast rates range upward from $195.

Check-in at the Grand Hyatt was pleasant. The desk clerk spoke perfect English, and he escorted me to my upgraded room, explaining everything in a congenial manner. After showing me my room, he escorted me to the club lounge. When we crossed paths with a member of the housekeeping staff, he asked that my room receive turn-down service right away, a very considerate gesture, I thought. Later that evening I had an authentic Jordanian meal of chopped salad and sea bass—with a drink, dessert, and coffee—all for a pittance. When I misread my bill and overpaid by 30 Jordanian dinars (JOD), the waiter immediately noticed and corrected my mistake: "Oh no, sir, you're paying too much. It is only 17 dinars" (about $25). My taxi driver was also helpful and honest. After dropping me off at the restaurant, he told me I could pay him later, trusting that I would call him after my dinner. When I did, he took me on a tour of the city, pointing out prominent landmarks for just 10 JOD, or about $14.

Jordan has plenty of modern shopping malls, a buzzing nightlife, and five-star cuisine, but the great draw is its many interesting archaeological sites. A few of these sites include Petra, Jerash, the Desert Castles, Um Qais and, of course, the Dead Sea.

My second stop took me to the famed King David Hotel in Jerusalem, the flagship hotel of the Dan Hotel Group and a member of the Leading Hotels of the World. The King David Hotel has been host to world leaders, including Bill Clinton, as well as to many celebrities. Despite its notable guest list, I was upgraded to a room with a wonderful view of the Old City. The hotel has remarkable restaurants, a pool and gardens, and it is within walking distance of the major historic sites. I spent an entire day exploring Jerusalem and still could not cover all the history of this extraordinary city. On my second day, I hired a driver to take me to Bethlehem and the Church of the Nativity, where believers say Jesus was born. I expected crowds but found none. In fact, the guide who escorted me through the church, describing everything in perfect English, told me that he used to take fifteen to twenty groups through the church a day, but now he counts himself lucky if he has ten groups a week. Such are the benefits of contrarian travel: You get personal attention from a seasoned guide unhurried by pressing crowds.

How does Jerusalem measure up on security and afford-ability? Very well. Security was top-notch everywhere I went, and not once did I fear for my life. The prices at the restaurants and shops were much lower than I would expect in Europe. I was able to hire a driver and a new, air-conditioned Mercedes-Benz for only $100 a day, and the driver knew exactly where to go and how to avoid precarious areas. Of course, most drivers will take you to a friend's souvenir shop, where you'll be treated to fresh tea or another drink (the driver earns a commission on the goods sold). These shops usually offer fair value, but if you don't want to be pressured to purchase anything, be sure to say that you're not interested in shopping.

I did not have a chance to venture much outside Jerusalem and Bethlehem, but Israel offers several other good tourist venues, including Tel Aviv, with its lively Dizengoff Street; Jaffa, an ancient port city now filled with artists' studios and galleries; Haifa, with its beautiful coastal and mountain views; and the sunny southern Red Sea resort area of Eilat. The Dan Hotels have properties in all these destinations, and they offer a frequent-guest program in which members get reduced rates, earn bonus points and receive up to a 12.5% discount on food and beverage purchases, among other benefits.

Across the border from Eilat is the Sinai Peninsula of Egypt, and on its northeast point, right on the Red Sea, is the Hyatt Regency Taba Heights. The resort is surrounded by mountains and has direct access to the sea. This part of the Middle East offers some of the best snorkeling and diving in the world. Points of interest in the Sinai Peninsula include the Monastery of St. Catherine and Mount Sinai, which overlooks it. The monastery is built on the site traditionally regarded as the place where Moses encountered God in the form of a burning bush. Visitors can climb the mountain by camel or by foot. I didn't do it, but I've heard it's an amazing experience, especially if you can be on the summit (7,500 feet) at sunrise.

The Middle East is not a popular travel destination for American tourists, which makes it an excellent destination for travelers with a contrarian attitude. Is it safe? Reasonably, yes. In my view, the danger is overrated, and both the governments and tourism providers are paying very close attention to security. To my mind, the historical attractions, warm welcome, and dollar value in the region all make the Middle East a great alternative to high-priced destinations. It's a contrarian pick, with contrarian benefits.

THE TEN PRINCIPLES OF CONTRARIAN TRAVEL

The strategies I followed for my Mideast trip illustrate the ten basic principles of contrarian travel:

1. Buy directly.
2. Profit when they are not.
3. Follow the dollar.
4. Stress your loyalty and build mutually beneficial relationships.
5. Be flexible.
6. Be willing to pay a slight premium.
7. Avoid trends.
8. Watch for fare wars and be ready to act quickly.
9. Have the ability and patience to take advantage of bargains.
10. Look at the big picture.

Let's explore each one of these ten principles.

1. *Buy directly*. For all their usefulness, third-party travel web sites can be as much a burden as a boon. The conventional wisdom is to check three or four of these sites before

purchasing travel services. I say: Hold on a minute. The guy who spoke to me after one of my presentations in San Francisco would agree. He had spent six hours searching Web sites for bargain airfares and found he could save only $25. "It's not worth it," he said. In the end, he purchased the ticket directly from the airline's web site. In my opinion, that's what he should have done in the first place.

2. *Profit when they are not.* Read or watch business news to stay on top of economic conditions in the travel industry. When an industry or company experiences financially challenging times, it offers incentives to increase revenues. That is how I routinely travel to five-star resorts paying the same rate I would at a lesser property.

Another basic way to "profit when they are not" is to follow the principle laid out earlier in this chapter of looking for areas of opportunity. What I mean by "areas of opportunity" is that sometimes it is a destination, rather than an industry or company or time of year, that experiences financially challenging times and therefore offers the contrarian luxurious travel opportunities.

3. *Follow the dollar.* The value of worldwide currencies can greatly influence the value you receive for your travel dollars. As we saw earlier in this chapter the value of the dollar can dramatically change from year to year. Currently, and most likely for the next few years, the U.S. dollar will remain weak in comparison to other major worldwide currencies. What this means is that you will need to wait to go to a county or region where the dollar is weak. Keep in mind that Paris, Rome, and London will always be there and most likely won't undergo any major cultural and historical changes. But what's likely to change is the value

of the dollar. Over time the U.S. dollar will gain strength and those destinations currently overpriced by the euro or pound will look more attractive. As already stated, there are bountiful alternatives. We saw early in this chapter how I took a European trip during the height of the weak dollar and still found good value by avoiding the more expensive well-beaten tracks. Later in this book I'll discuss a few other culture-rich trips that did not break the bank.

4. *Stress your loyalty and build mutually beneficial relationships.* During a typical year I'll stay at a number of hotels within the same brand. For example, I enjoy the service and value I receive at The Four Seasons group of hotels. Whenever, I visit a Four Seasons, I make an effort to meet the manager and collect their card. Then while planning my next trip to a Four Seasons property I'll pull out the card and contact that manager and ask if he can introduce me to the manager at the property I intend to visit. This works wonders as the managers' introductions show that I am a loyal repeat customer and typically get me a nice room upgrade.

5. *Be flexible.* This is the mantra for contrarian travel. More than ever, the travel market is in flux and liable to change at any moment. Developing flexibility with respect to your travel dates, destinations, and accommodations will yield excellent luxury travel at bargain prices.

The beauty of this principle is that it can lead you to some very interesting and unique places. During the fall of 2007 I had another yearning for a European experience but did not want to pay the current rate of $300 per night for an average European hotel. So instead of opting for the traditional European cities, I headed to Lithuania. And what a joy it was. I stayed at the finest hotel in Vilnius for $195 a night and ate at the best restaurants where a meal for two with a bottle of wine, dessert, and coffee could be had for only $40. To top things off, I found a new country that was rich in cultural and natural beauty.

Flexibility could mean going somewhere new but as my experience in Lithuania demonstrates, that new adventure can provide more than just cost savings—it can be an experience you really remember.

6. *Be willing to pay a slight premium*. Wherever I do a television interview I often quip to the anchor that "travelers do not need to shop around for the lowest fares and rates." They often look at me in bewilderment and say, "What?" Yes, it's true. I tell them that by booking direct with providers, as already discussed, travelers will most often get the best rates and fares. But by shopping around they often miss out on extra perks such as a first-class airline seat, upgraded hotel room, or even getting through the security line at the airport much quicker.

I've already discussed how the lowest price might not always represent the best value. I believe that it's such an important concept that it bears repeating. The fact is that the lowest fares and rates often have numerous restrictions and are not eligible for upgrades. By paying the next price level, which usually costs $5 to $25 more, you can bypass many of the restrictions and become eligible for upgrades and preferred services.

Consider what happened when I traveled to Venice, Italy. I had already reserved a rental car for $95 a week. However, when I saw the small size of the car I asked the clerk if they had any upgrades available. He offered me a new BMW 5-Series for only $30 more for the week. In this case, the premium did exceed 15%, but I would have been out of my mind to pass up the difference between a luxury ride and a cramped one for a mere $30, which amounted to just over $4 per day, less than most people pay for a single visit to Starbucks.

7. *Avoid trends.* The best time to travel anywhere is when everyone else is going to another destination. One prime example is the Olympic Games. I have a number of friends who are fans of the Olympics but tell me how they get more enjoyment by watching the games on TV and then head to the country after the games are done, when the prices drop dramatically. This year the Olympic Summer Games are expected to be a big boon to China tourism. Already hoteliers are racing to build new properties to meet the high need of Olympic travelers. But what happens when the games are over and all the tourists leave? All the nice brand new hotel rooms will still be there but with less demand. This means that rates will settle down to more manageable levels, priced in accordance with normal supply-and-demands factors. Given the large number of rooms being built in China to accommodate Olympic fans, there is bound to be a glut after the last athlete leaves, meaning a bargain for the contrarian traveler.

Another issue regarding traveling during peak times is that when a hotel is full to the brim with guests, there is less incentive for the hotel's employees to give you a luxurious room, let alone at a low price. In fact, it is more likely than not that you will be treated like a commodity, because hotel employees will probably be too busy to offer you the kind of attentive service you should learn to expect. However, when a hotel is only at 40% booking, as I found one summer at the Hôtel de Paris in Monte Carlo, you will have the pool to yourself with an attentive staff pampering you. The employees will have more time to devote to your needs, and they will increase their level of service to make up for the fact that there are fewer guests tipping them.

8. *Watch for fare wars and be ready to act quickly.* At the time of this writing, many travel providers have been testing the marketplace by offering short-term bargain rates and fares. In many cases these fares or rates need to be booked within a few days. So when you see something you like, be ready to grab it immediately. This is how I was able to get such a fabulous fare for my trip to Europe.

A recent *Wall Street Journal* article stated that the big airline carriers (American, United, Delta) are broadly matching fares of low-cost carriers by offering aggressive pricing, including deeply discounted first-class seats in order to maintain their market share. The paper stated "airlines adjust prices several times a day to make sure rivals don't have a price advantage. Tickets are priced not on what it costs to provide the service, but rather on how much money the carrier thinks it can get." The trick to finding these discounted first-class seats is to go online and do two fare searches, one for coach and the other for first class. For example, when I searched for a fare from Orange County to Atlanta, I found out that I could purchase a round-trip coach ticket for $1499, or fly first class for $599 round-trip.

9. *Have the ability and patience to take advantage of bargains.* In the second edition of *The Penny Pincher's Passport to Luxury Travel* I wrote about my friend Lance, a California real estate investor. Lance makes a living by investing in real estate by only purchasing properties in Southern California (something he sticks to because it's what he

knows), and does so only when the California economy is
weak. I wrote how Lance had built an inventory of over 100
homes, which he rented. Starting in 2005 near the top of
California's last real estate boom he sold half of his properties for a substantial gain. Currently with the market at an
all-time low he is re-investing his money in higher-end premium properties that should gain him better rental income
and higher appreciations. Remember that the travel industry is cyclical as well, and when the travel economy is weak
you will be privy to the best deals and superior service. So
if possible, stash money away in a travel fund so that when
the right travel opportunities present themselves you will
be able to jump on them.

10. *Look at the big picture.* Economic inconsistencies of traveling illustrate the importance of considering all factors and
expenditures that contribute to your desired travel experience. This is what I mean by the big picture of contrarian
travel. By considering the big picture, you can find opportunities that exist during any phase of an economic cycle.
Viewing the big picture is what allowed me to venture to the
wonderful land of Lithuania. Looking at the big picture is
the essence of what I call a "value contrarian traveler."

VALUE CONTRARIAN TRAVELER

A value contrarian traveler is a traveler who considers the
multiple variables likely to be encountered on his or her
trip and plans accordingly. For example, if you were to travel to Europe, you would need to ask yourself: Do the relatively low airfares make up for the weakness of the dollar?
Has the weakness of the dollar decreased travel demand to
the point that hotels experiencing low occupancy rates are

ready to give you a good deal? Are you able to book a flight that is less full than others so that you have a better chance for an upgrade? Did you make direct contact with the hotel manager by email or phone to inform him or her that you would be arriving (this also provides an opportunity to ask for an upgrade, a technique that I will discuss more fully in Chapter 7)? Are you willing to fly into or out of a less convenient airport to secure the best deals and the best seats? Are you flexible enough to change the dates of your travel to a period of lower demand in order to secure a more luxurious trip? Are you leveraging your loyalty with your travel providers?

Expenditures and upgrades are certainly high on the list of the contrarian traveler's big-picture perspective. In today's world, however, safety is the number-one item on many travelers' minds, and it should always be part of the big picture of your travel planning. You will sometimes find that certain destinations are experiencing downturns in business due to security issues. For example, at the time of this writing, a traveler could get great deals to parts of South Asia or East Africa but you have to ask yourself whether the cost savings overrides the potential for harm.

THE RISK OF CONTRARIAN TRAVEL

Although a contrarian travel strategy can add value to your trips, one should understand that certain risks exist. These risks include concerns about terrorism, health, and travel providers going bankrupt. Nevertheless, travelers armed with knowledge and a good, flexible strategy can overcome these issues and enjoy the best that travel has to offer. The first thing to assess is your own personal travel threshold or tolerance level. Where and how do you feel safe traveling? Where and how do you not feel safe?

Then, make sure you understand the real facts of the current travel environment. Separate the facts from rumors and conjecture. Try to read from different media sources, talk to other travelers, and check U.S. State Department travel warnings at www.travel.state.gov.

When Traveling, It Pays to Be Active

You've gone thousands of miles, so why not leave the beaten path? Increasingly, travel is woven into our daily lives. Whether for business, pleasure, or holiday merry-making, travel is as much a part of our lives as MP3 players and cable TV. With so many people traveling (42 million Americans will travel over the holidays alone), I'd like to make the case for treating travel as a hands-on adventure, rather then a passive sightseeing opportunity. It can make a big difference in the rewards you reap. Here's an example: Earlier this year I had the opportunity to visit Panama. Naturally, I ventured down to the famous canal. While dining on the top level of the canal restaurant, I watched a cruise boat navigate the lock, transiting from west to east. Passengers lined the decks, waving gaily to those along the shore. "How boring," I thought, and sad, too. Here are all these people who've traveled so far and they're stuck on a bacteria-ridden boat, waving as opportunity passes them by.

Determined not to be a passive traveler, I ventured off in my four-wheel-drive truck to see the real sights. I found a local crossing point and stopped in the middle of the canal for a close-up view of the lock mechanisms—truly a marvel of engineering. I continued along a dirt road until I literally could drive no more. I had arrived at an idyllic, tranquil cove offering a billion-dollar view. A couple of fishing boats were returning to shore—just dinghies really, with small outboard motors. I offered the guys a few cold waters I had in the truck, and we chatted about this and that. One offered to take me out for a short ride, and I accepted. It was a priceless experience—totally unique and personal, and nothing like the touristy shore excursions the cruise passengers were in for.

Another such blessing occurred when I was in Ethiopia, where I was traveling with a group to the countryside, the rock-hewn churches of Lalibela, and the giant ancient monoliths in Aksum. I was there for the nature and the history, but I found a spiritual renewal sitting among a crowd of local men drinking beer and talking about sports, music, and even a little politics. Most of the conversation was happy and trifling, but I also learned that one of the group, a youngster of about thirteen, had lost all his family and was living on the streets. Despite his sad story, you could not have found a better-adjusted kid, who joked with me when I called him Snoop Dogg for his love of rap.

Now, I am no stranger to poverty, but something about the people of Ethiopia genuinely touched me, and I was glad to have stopped by the side of that dusty road. While my travel companions were stuck watching a rehearsed, and not quite realistic, coffee ceremony, I was sitting on a tree stump talking and laughing and drinking with some wonderful people. Of course, as word got out that an American was handing out beers, more and more townspeople came out to greet me, but no one was begging for anything or taking advantage of the situation. With each beer, I received a heartfelt "Thank you."

All in all, I spent about $12 to buy 25 beers, and I got another priceless moment.

When it comes to travel I truly have been blessed. This past year I traveled to more than twenty countries. I saw the ancient pyramids in Egypt, the wonders of the Roman Empire, and the beauty of Budapest. I visited Vietnam and found it easy to understand why Senator John McCain has become so devoted to this country. I travel first class and I stay at five-star hotels, but what really hits home are the everyday people I meet along the way. The boy doing perfect back flips in the field beyond the Queen of Sheba's throne, and his luminous smile when I gave him 50 birr (about $5). The Ethiopian farmers cultivating the land as their ancestors have done for thousands of years. These are people and blessings I'll hold dear this year.

My advice is to embrace the wonderful world of travel. If you can get off that cruise ship or tour bus and rub shoulders with the locals—do it. Of course, be careful, but experience tells me that there is much in this world to discover if you let down your guard just a little. Put aside your first-class airs and humble yourself to the world around you. Open your eyes, open your mind, open your heart—open your wallet if you have to. The blessings will all be yours.

WHAT WILL HAPPEN IF YOUR TRAVEL PROVIDER SEEKS BANKRUPTCY PROTECTION?

Economic safety is another factor to consider during these uncertain times. It is difficult to predict the exact outcome of any bankruptcy filing; however, based on past events, customers of larger, well-established companies should not suffer severe consequences. In fact, between the writing of this book's second edition and this current writing we saw some of the nation's top airlines enter and exit bankruptcy with little or no disruption to the traveling public. If anything, the airlines improved their services and offerings. In essence, bankruptcy provides travel providers an opportunity to refocus their services without the burden of servicing their heavy debt load. Customers of Delta Air Lines found better customer service with new and exciting routes including Africa and Eastern Europe. Since emerging from bankruptcy Delta Air Lines has been considered a good investment as their stock price has increased since their post-bankruptcy IPO.

Customers of smaller start-up carriers may not do as well. For example, travelers holding tickets on the former Vanguard and National Airlines did experience difficulty using their previously purchased tickets. In both these instances, the airlines ceased operations altogether.

Therefore, in this time of economic uncertainty, it is usually a good strategy to stick with larger, well-established travel providers.

OFF-SEASON TRAVEL

As stated at the onset of this chapter, off-season travel was once a pretty straightforward concept. For example, off-season travel would be going to Phoenix or Vail in the summer, and flying to Cancun during hurricane season. However, the demarcations between the so-called off-season or low season, the high season, and the shoulder season (the time between high and low seasons) are becoming more and more blurred as travelers are discovering the benefits of traveling at different times of the year.

Five years ago, I wrote about how I liked going to Europe during the Thanksgiving break because it was a contrarian's paradise. Last November I read a newspaper article describing how a lot of families are not doing the traditional Thanksgiving get-together, but rather using the time to travel.

Part of this change in the way people travel may be due to the lightning-fast way in which information travels around our internet-connected world. Just e-mail a few of your friends about the luxurious travel bargains you found on a little-known island paradise in winter, and the next thing you know it's common knowledge around the globe.

This doesn't mean that basic off-season principles no longer apply. Nor does it mean that as an off-season traveler you must settle for a vacation to Buffalo in the dead of winter or Miami in the heat of July. You can travel to beach resort locations during their shoulder seasons. You can travel to Disney World while children are still in school. Your children might miss a few days of school, but with fewer crowds and lower rates, you will find that it is certainly worth the trouble. You can ask your child's teacher for a homework packet so he or she can keep up with school work while you're saving money and having a fun time.

As a contrarian traveler, it is wise to check destination-specific travel guides and/or internet travel information web sites to obtain basic information about when the high season, low season, and shoulder season generally start.

There still is plenty of good off-season traveling to be done, but I believe that the real secret of contrarian success today is more destination-oriented than time-specific. In review, expand your possibilities to "profit when they are not," broadening your travel horizons to what I have called "areas of opportunity."

LAS VEGAS: A CASE STUDY OF CHANGE

The once dusty gambling town turned ultra-deluxe center of the world typifies the radical changes a travel destination can go through. Fewer than twenty years ago travelers could get away to Las Vegas and stay at a full service hotel for less than $85 during the week and not more than $125 on weekends. Indeed many travelers also received incentives such as free gambling chips, meal vouchers, and free transport from the airport. In the old days, value-seeking travelers could head to the warmth of Vegas, enjoy drinks by the pool, a show at night, and some gambling and have a nice time without spending a fortune (unless you lost too much at the tables or slots). All that has changed. In today's world of mega-hotels and ever-flowing crowds of young hipsters heading to the city of lights in the desert, the deals are as dry as the wasteland surrounding the city. A typical hotel on a summer day during the week goes for $225, not the once herald $35 a night. Come on the weekend and you're facing at least $425. What's more, drinks, restaurants, and basically anything you do in Vegas comes with a price. The reason: Vegas is immensely popular and people are paying the prices...and as long as they do, the deals will be gone.

The story of Vegas typifies the world of travel: if demand remains high with high prices, that trend will continue. For me the good old days of the true Vegas are gone, as it has become one of the most expensive travel destinations.

By now it should be clear that these days, smart travelers are going off-peak and off the beaten path. As I repeated throughout this chapter the pillars of contrarian strategy have changed—the tactic of traveling off-season has lost some of its punch. As more people are traveling smarter, the lines between on-season, "shoulder season," and off-season have blurred, and the returns for traveling off-peak have gotten smaller. The following is a refresher list of how to get the best contrarian deals:

Think like a celebrity. Paparazzi-shy stars are often seeking out-of–the-way places to relax in comfort. Think Namibia. It was good enough for Angelina Jolie and Brad Pitt.

Consider trendy passé. The real finds are the up-and-comers, those places that have yet to catch on with the mainstream (like Prague in the early '90s, which is now overrun with tourists). Two good bets for today's traveler: the coastal towns of Dubrovnik and Zadar in the western Balkans on the Adriatic Sea.

Act like a humanitarian Natural disasters and other calamities that wreck havoc on a destination also leave the local tourism community in turmoil. Not only can you score luxury at a fraction of the usual cost, but you can also help the local economy with your tourist dollars. A friend of mine traveled to Indonesia after the 2004 earthquake and tsunami and found great hotel bargains. He also spent a few days of his vacation helping with local relief efforts. In his words: "I had a great vacation and helped people at the same time."

Play the loyalty card. If you must travel to busy tourist places, parlay your past loyalty into upgrades. The cheapest hotel rooms, rental cars, cruise cabins, and airline seats generally go first, so travel providers end up upgrading guests to higher levels of service. Get ahead of the game by notifying your travel provider of your travel plans and requesting an upgrade based on your past loyalty.

Catch the opening. Whenever a hotel, cruise line, or airline offers a new property, route, or service, try to get in the door before the crowds. The best strategy is to travel a week or two after the opening. The first weeks will be full of VIPs, but between the opening and the crush of the later-coming general public, you can scoop up some good bargains.

Skip school. This bit of advice will be appreciated by your kids. A few days of missed school can mean a truly memorable vacation and valuable family time—at preseason prices. Just make sure to get your kids' homework so they can keep up with their classmates in between swimming, rafting, and horseback riding.

Save a day. Go for quality not quantity. My recent trip to the Grand Hyatt Kauai lasted only four days. But those four days in the 2,700-square-foot Presidential Suite overlooking the blue Pacific were certainly more memorable than six days spent overlooking the parking lot.

Consider luxury. In their quest to save money, most travelers consider only budget travel choices. Ironically, luxury can be cheaper. The Four Seasons, a name synonymous with luxury, routinely offers a fourth night free with three paid nights. When you add up all those numbers, luxury can actually save you money. Other luxury hotels are well-priced to begin with. As already discussed, the Silken Gran Hotel Domine in Bilbao, Spain, offers five-star luxury with rates reasonably priced at 110 euros. And from its teak-wood terrace, you get views of the city's extraordinary

Guggenheim Museum, one of the must-see sights of Europe.

As an added bonus here's my current list of areas of opportunity for traveling off the beaten path. All it takes is a willingness to go a little farther afield. Keep in mind that these destinations can change but the theory behind how I select each destination should provide good fodder for your travel planning.

Egypt's Sinai Peninsula, not the Italian or French Riviera. Both the Hyatt and the Four Seasons have wonderful hotels in Sharm el Sheikh, a seaside resort with some of the finest beaches and diving in the world. At press time, the Four Seasons was offering a bed-and-breakfast package starting at $195 per night.

Vienna, not Paris. With a famed opera house, world-class museums, hotels, restaurants and cafes, Vienna offers a nice alternative to pricey Paris.

Panama, not Cancun. While lacking the festive reputation of Mexico's beaches, Panama offers a delightful retreat at a fraction of the cost. The Bristol Hotel, a member of The Leading Hotels of the World, offers luxurious accommodations in the center of vibrant Panama City. At press time, rooms with daily breakfast were available from $125 nightly.

Budapest, not Prague. While both cities have stunning baroque architecture, Budapest has the mighty Danube, fewer crowds, and generally lower prices. The Four Seasons Hotel Gresham Palace Budapest, a former palace, has been transformed into an Art Nouveau-and-Renaissance landmark. Many of the rooms have views of the Danube, the Chain Bridge, or Buda Hills. Delta Air Lines recently initiated direct service to Budapest from JFK.

The world of travel offers boundless opportunities, and you can find truly memorable travel at a bargain. If you're not sure how to do it, keep reading.

And remember, there's nothing better than a first-class flight to a five-star hotel.

Here's Your Money-Saving Roadmap

I was a wide-eyed schoolboy when my grandfather, an active man of 77, told me with a beaming smile, "Travel stimulates a full life." At the time, he was off with my equally spirited grandmother on yet another trip, this time a cruise along the Turkish coast and Greek islands. He continued, "Travel is an extraordinary experience, but you have to have a good *plan*." My grandfather was right. Sure, there are times when you want to just strike out on impulse without plans, reservations, or schedules. Such trips can be highly adventurous and gratifying, but most travelers are more comfortable with some kind of agenda, and a good plan can help you get the best bang for your buck (or for your euro and peso). With a well thought-out trip, your travels will be more enjoyable and less costly, *and* you can take advantage of preferential services and amenities. So let's look at some tips for making a good travel plan.

Remember supply and demand: The first economic principle I learned in college was the law of supply and demand. In travel, it means that travel suppliers will offer incentives to offset lower demand for a season or destination. Knowing how to travel around peak demand can bring you significant rewards, including low rates, pleasant weather, uncrowded museums, and preferential service. Travelers who aren't constrained by school holidays or company-imposed vacation dates can pick the best times to pack their bags. A little research on the Internet or a quick chat with a travel agent will tell you which off-peak dates savvy travelers recommend for your destination. By traveling off-peak, you can satisfy champagne tastes on a penny-pinching budget and you can do it year-round.

Fall into luxury: Traveling in autumn isn't only cheaper, it's often more pleasant (think smaller crowds, a less blistering sun, fewer squealing kids, and big shopping discounts). One traveler summed it up to me as a time when airfares and hotel prices are at their lowest, and the best rooms are just waiting for you to turn the key. Low-rate destinations such as Bermuda, Bali and the Mediterranean all offer good weather for sightseeing and swimming in the fall. Rates at some hotels fall as much as 50%, and flights can be 30% cheaper. Many seasoned travelers wouldn't dream of traveling to these places at any other time.

Win in winter: Many temperate destinations offer excellent winter deals. For example, many hotels in California's Monterey County offer a free night for every paid night from November through January. For snow enthusiasts, Quebec City is a great choice—and winter is the *only* time you can catch the city's famed Winter Carnival. Even with

Carnival, hotel rates can be low: The posh Fairmont Le Chateau Frontenac, for example, offers a 50% discount from January through March.

Spot spring deals: Discounts abound in the spring. Just avoid any destination catering to students on spring break. Before and after spring break, hotels and resorts in Hawai'i slash rates, and European holidays are almost always less costly in April and May.

Four Seasons in summer: Even summer offers deals—particularly if you head for the Sun Belt. For example, the Four Seasons hotels in both Scottsdale, Arizona, and Dallas offer rooms for less than $150 a day, and both have highly acclaimed spas and golf courses.

Think upside down: The time to go Down Under is in our late spring and summer, when it's fall and winter in Australia. That's when you can get real savings on airfares. The exchange rate is favorable, too. Smart travelers enjoy the best hotels and dine in the finest restaurants at this time of year, saving up to 40%.

Follow the dollar: It's no secret that a strong U.S. dollar can deliver a better travel experience for less money. Currently, the dollar goes a lot farther in many Central and South American countries, while the current strength of the euro will increase the cost of your European trip by about 20%.

Book wisely: Arriving at a ticket counter, hotel desk, car rental counter, or cruise line and plunking down your credit card in front of the attendant is not the best way to get good value. It's actually the worst. On ordinary itineraries, you'll save time and money if you call your travel providers direct or book your reservations on the internet. Recently, some airlines have instituted a surcharge on tickets purchased through the airlines' toll-free 800 numbers. If you do not have access to the internet personally (or through family, friends, or a local library), call the airline and explain your situation. Most likely, they will waive this fee for you. When planning an exotic trip or traveling to a new destination, don't do it yourself. Seek the assistance of a good travel agent. They can help you plan a smart itinerary that is flexible enough to allow for changes in plans and unexpected events, but still save you money.

Ask questions: By all means, ask questions—even if you think you already know the answer. While planning a trip from Orange County to Atlanta this past summer, I was told that a coach ticket would cost me $1,024; when I asked about the cost of a first-class ticket, I found it was less than half that price: $496!

Make memberships pay: If you can show evidence of membership in organizations such as the American Automobile Association (AAA) or the American Association of Retired Persons (AARP), you'll save an additional 20% to 25%.

Leverage loyalty: Now that you've got the best basic price and a well-planned journey, it's time to get a little more luxury than you paid for. Remember that loyalty pays— even if you travel only once or twice a year. Travel providers want to keep you as a customer, so they will reward repeat business with preferential services, prime upgrades, and special discounts. All you have to do is establish a history of loyalty and mention it when you travel. To maximize your advantage and bargaining power, limit your purchases to a select group of high-quality travel providers, and be sure to join their frequent user programs.

Make friends: My favorite strategy for getting a great travel experience requires no planning at all: Just be pleasant! When you show appreciation for the hard work of travel providers, you become a pleasure to do business with. Relax, smile, commiserate, spread some human kindness, and often as not, rewards will follow. This was true for my friend Laurie, who got stranded at the Miami airport after an equipment failure on her plane. While waiting to rebook her ticket, Laurie saw the customer in front of her berate the ticket agent, blaming her for the delay. When it was Laurie's turn, she kindly told the agent to take a minute to recover from that passenger's rudeness. The agent was so touched by this gesture that she booked Laurie on another airline's flight—in first class.

"Nothing ventured, nothing gained"—that's something else my grandfather taught me. So, do your research, learn these tips, plan well, and go have fun.

Key Points

➤ Follow the Ten Principles of Contrarian Travel to achieve luxury travel at a discount.

➤ Watch business cycles and the cyclical nature of the travel industry to open the door to traveling like the rich and famous.

➤ *Remember that the difference between price and value is part of the contrarian strategy that will yield you luxury travel.*

➤ *Bear in mind that off-season and areas of opportunity are important elements of luxury travel for less.*

➤ *Be aware that contrarian travel can present some dangers, so be sure to research your travels before committing to your itinerary.*

5

FLYING RIGHT

First Class at Coach Prices

During my first year as a loyal customer to Delta Air Lines, I flew only three times. The second time I flew, I simply asked the gate agent if he would upgrade me, and he did! For the next few years with Delta, I never flew more than 20,000 miles a year, yet I flew first class at least 50% of the time. In 1991, my fourth year with the same airline, I stopped flying coach. I flew first class every time except when I flew overseas. On overseas flights, I obtained a one-class upgrade to business class. Since 1994, I even fly first class overseas—every time.

The information in this book should considerably shorten the time it takes for you to reach the first-class cabin. You may get your first upgrade on your fifth flight, your third flight, or even your first! And once you've built up those qualifying miles, first class will always be yours for the asking.

FIRST, A STRONG WORD OF CAUTION

Security is an ever-present concern for airline employees, for not only gate agents and flight attendants, but also those who check your bags, work at the ticket counter, and staff the club lounges. Therefore, bear in mind when you practice the following tips in this book that you must NEVER push too hard for an upgrade. If you are seen as interfering with an airline employee or flight crew, you will end up in deep trouble. Even if you do not think that you caused trouble, a concerned airline employee can mark your record, and this can make things difficult for you the next time you fly. Whenever I see frazzled gate agents or airline employees, I first greet them by asking how they are today and if they have a minute to help me. If appropriate I try to make a light-hearted joke about how busy the airport is or about the weather or something to break the tension. Also, if I sense that I am pushing too hard (the agent's body language changes, voice gets stern), I immediately apologize and start over in a less direct manner. My major objective is to be sensitive to those with whom I am working.

With the above in mind it is fair to say that air travel poses certain challenges. Whether it's due to heightened security concerns or the bad press airlines receive, the traveling public has come to view air travel as being as much fun as having a root canal. Indeed some of these challenges are real and range from airport logjams and full planes to severe weather, long delays, and cancellations. But the incessant complaining about air travel that seems to be as popular as discussing the hottest video on YouTube or the latest celebrity scuffle with the law is unwarranted. The reality is that most air travelers fly from Point A to Point B with very little nuisance. Based on numerous conversations with travelers and personally accumulating 3 million miles of air travel as a result, I've formulated what I call the three P's of air travel: plan ahead, be proactive, and have patience. This approach simplifies the process of travel and sets the stage for the remainder of the chapter.

Plan ahead. I was sitting on a rain-pelted runway in New Bern, N.C., and the pilot kept delaying our takeoff. As time wore on, I knew I might miss my connection in Atlanta to Memphis, so I called the Westin Memphis, which was holding my reservation, and told them that I might be delayed or even stuck in Atlanta overnight. The clerk said that since I'd called, the hotel would hold my room but not charge me a no-show fee if I didn't make it. One base covered. I then called a favorite hotel in Atlanta, the Grand Hyatt, and explained the situation. Same deal: The hotel agreed to hold a room in case I needed one but would not charge me if I made it to Memphis. I was covered either way, with no cost to me but a couple of phone calls. When I arrived in Atlanta, my flight was indeed canceled, but I knew exactly what to do and where to go.

Be proactive. During a weather delay in New York's La Guardia Airport, I came across a friend who wearily told me he had been waiting in line for two hours trying to rebook his canceled flight. At the same time, he was on his cell phone trying to reach a phone representative. My friend was doing everything right, but he could have cut his wait time with two easy steps—if only he took advantage of the airline's special programs.

1. With even the lowest frequent-flyer status, my friend would have been given a special toll-free number that would allow him to bypass the public reservations line. When I gave him my own Delta SkyMiles number, he instantly reached an agent, who rebooked him on a flight for the next day.

2. A membership in an airport lounge can also get you out of a jam. While trying to get to Memphis on another

occasion, my first flight from Atlanta to Memphis was canceled. I immediately went to Delta's Crown Room, where
the agent rebooked me on a flight two hours later, and I
snagged the last first-class seat.

Reaching elite status on most airlines is not very difficult.
A co-branded credit card can usually give you a head start.
For example, with Delta's Platinum SkyMiles credit card you
can earn up to 20,000 of the required 25,000 "Medallion
Qualification Miles" with credit card charges instead of air
travel. Similarly, you can usually purchase a day pass to an
airline's private lounge for a nominal fee of $25.

Be patient. If you are patient and can remain calm and collected—that's half the battle. Review the terms and benefits of
your frequent-flyer program carefully before you travel, then
calmly ask for assistance from the airline agents whenever
you need it. When it comes down to it, there is usually not
much you can do when delayed. Therefore my best advice is
to get your MP3 player going and listen to your favorite tunes
or pull out your current book. As discussed, a $25 invest-
ment for a one-day pass to your airport lounge can be well
worth it. I experienced a four-hour delay on one trip to
Europe and since the airport was small with not much to do,
my airport lounge was a godsend. I was able to watch TV,
access the internet, and relax in a comfortable chair. While a
delay is never fun at least I did it in style. The key here is not
to beat yourself or others up, and as the adage goes, stuff happens and sometimes it's just a matter of going with the flow.

Here are a few more tricks I've learned:

➤ **Have a car ready to go.** If your destination is within a
   day's drive, and you're faced with another day at the

airport or missing your meeting or a vacation day, look into a one-way rental. Often the cost is more reasonable than the cost of a night at a hotel.

➤ **Buy a one-day lounge membership.** Not only can you get rebooked more quickly in the lounge, it is also a nice place to wait out a flight delay. In fact, if your flight is delayed three hours or more, $25 for a one-day pass might be money well spent; in Delta's Crown Room, for example, you'll get free drinks, and those add up. You can usually get a guest admitted on the same pass, as well. Another nice benefit is that most lounge memberships allow you to go through the preferred security line, making your airport transition much less stressful. Many airlines now allow you to purchase a one-day pass online or at the ticket counter. I know a guy who has one for each of the three airlines he flies, each set aside for an emergency or when he needs to get through security in a hurry.

➤ **Be in the know.** On a recent Friday night, while trying to get home to Orange County, California, my flight was delayed due to a delayed incoming flight. When I asked the agent when the flight was going to arrive, she told me, "Five minutes." I walked to the gate, only to find out that the flight hadn't even left the departure city! This time, I fired up my computer and tracked the flight on the airline's web site, knowing precisely when it departed and when it would arrive at the gate.

➤ **Book directly with your airline.** When you book through a third-party web site, or even through a travel agent, you may find that the airline cannot directly access your ticketing record, thus impairing their ability to rebook a flight for you.

If you plan well, act proactively, and keep your patience, the road bumps of travel won't take such a toll.

SOME IMPORTANT TIPS FOR GETTING UPGRADED TO FIRST CLASS

Now that you know how to navigate the rigors of air travel, the fun part begins—getting upgrades. The first key as expressed throughout this book is to communicate your present and future loyalty to airline employees at all times—present yourself as the right customer. Always remember that preferred service will be based on the value that you bring to the airline. This includes your prospective future value as well as the value your business represents right now. But what if you are just starting out? Although obtaining first-class seats every time you fly may take some time, depending on how frequently or infrequently you travel, there are many ways the inexperienced traveler can obtain first-class seats while building a solid, loyal relationship with one airline.

When I started to fly, I flew fewer than five trips a year, yet I maintained loyalty to one airline. Before I had accumulated many qualifying miles, I would do the following whenever I needed a special request honored, such as waiving restrictions or opening up a seat for me to use a free first-class upgrade certificate.

I would be talking to the reservation agent, ticket agent, or gate agent, and say, "Perhaps I am not your most frequent flyer, but since 1987 your airline is the only airline I have flown. In the past I have always received excellent service from your airline, and I am sure that this will not be an exception."

By making such a statement, you are stressing your willingness to build a mutually beneficial relationship and your commitment to future loyalty to that airline—as long as you are satisfied. The possibility of your future business is the key for infrequent travelers, because it gives you leverage. In my case, the agents viewed my expression of good faith as an opportunity to keep me as a customer. This successfully provided me access to the prized enhanced benefits I was seeking, even with a brief history of loyalty.

Keep in mind that this technique will only work if you are sincere about building a history with an airline. The worst thing you can do is be dishonest about your intentions. I recall one day at the airport when I heard a woman ask for an upgrade telling the gate agent that her mother had just been admitted to the hospital, and that she was very stressed. The agent replied by asking her how many mothers she has, because according to her record her mother had died last June and again in December. Due to the airlines' ability (and practice) to document conversations with customers on the computer, if you habitually use the same excuses—such as illness or other personal hardship—the airline will spot the pattern in your customer history and deny your requests. Honesty is key. Do say that you have flown their airline in the past, are flying on it now, and intend to continue flying on it in the future—as long as you continue to receive the good service you have come to know.

Along with communicating your honest intent to be a loyal customer, you must also realistically consider the relative strength of your bargaining position if you are just starting a history with your chosen airline. If you're a new customer, do not march up to an airline representative, claim to be the airline's best customer, and demand a first-class seat. Do be vocal about your past, present, and intended future loyalty—but do it respectfully.

Fly first class as much as possible. This may sound like a Catch-22, but it's not. When you are first starting a flight history with your chosen airline, it's important that you fly first class as much as you can. This will familiarize you with the ways of first-class travel, and you will get a feel for how your airline deals with handing out first-class seats. This will also help you when you're vying for a first-class seat on a crowded flight, because then you can say to the gate agent, "Look at my flight history. I never fly coach—it's just too uncomfortable. Could you help me out by getting me a first-class seat on this flight?" This really works to your advantage.

Believe it or not, very few first-class seats are sold at a first-class rate, although sometimes you might be surprised and find a special that you would never have known about unless you asked. To illustrate, Delta has recently been offering low-priced first-class fares, such as the one I flew between Orange County and Atlanta for only $491—so it pays to stay informed.

In most cases, however, buying a first-class ticket is expensive. Therefore, obtain and use first-class upgrade certificates to fly first class at coach prices.

If your past flight history spans multiple carriers, you'll need to decide to fly with only one airline. The only possible exception to exclusively using one airline is if you fly every week and can establish an elite frequent-flyer level with multiple airlines within a year. If you do not fit this description, you will be better served by exclusively flying one airline. Keep in mind the higher you build the miles in your chosen frequent-flyer program, the greater psychological factor you create. I recall watching football one Sunday during the 2007 season, and hearing a commentator talk about the then 8-0 New England Patriots and how even after achieving a sizable lead in a game, Quarterback Tom Brady and Coach Bill Belichick continue scoring, because it sends a message to next week's opponents. In the same manner when I ask a ticket or gate agent how many YTD miles I have in February and they see 125,000 they immediately perk-up and serve me well.

FLYING EXCLUSIVELY WITH ONE AIR CARRIER IS EASIER THAN YOU MIGHT THINK

Your only requirements are flexibility and the knowledge that you are building value with your chosen carrier. Most major carriers have very similar routes and fares, and when one airline offers a fare sale, all the competing airlines usually match the new fare. Therefore, there is no advantage to changing airlines. When flying with your chosen airline, there will undoubtedly be times when you will have to change planes while another airline offers a direct flight for fifty dollars less. If you're tempted to go with the other airline for just that one trip, remind yourself how satisfying it will be to sit in first class and receive preferential service.

HOW TO CHOOSE THE ONE AIRLINE WITH WHICH YOU WILL BUILD YOUR LOYALTY

Choose a major carrier rather than a less-established, low-cost carrier. The chief advantages that the major carriers have are their code-share alliances with other airlines, better frequent-flyer programs, and enhanced ground services such as advance check-in, plush airport lounges, and, when available, first-class seat upgrades. In addition, I have found that more often than not, airfares of the major carriers match those of the low-cost carriers.

For example, at the time of this writing, Jet Blue offers a rate between Long Beach, California and New York's JFK Airport that does not exceed $299. American Airlines, which flies the same route, has matched Jet Blue's fare, whereas previously the fare on American Airlines was as high as $1,350.

Find an airline that provides convenient scheduling from your home airport and best serves the routes you fly the most. Then consider with whom the airline has code-share or partner agreements, also sometimes referred to as alliances. These are reciprocal agreements in which two air carriers agree to accommodate each other's passengers. Code-share agreements benefit consumers because customers can continue to purchase and book tickets with their chosen airline while flying on a code-share airline, and thus still earn qualifying miles towards elite status on their chosen airline. This type of arrangement helps customers continue to build mutually beneficial relationships with one carrier.

Find out everything you can about the airline's frequent-flyer program and its financial solidity. If you are tempted to choose a discount airline that offers generous frequent-flyer rewards, be sure to find out if this carrier is financially sound. If your chosen airline goes belly up, you'll end up starting over with a new airline. When making a decision to build a relationship with a financially vulnerable airline, keep in mind the contrarian tip I offered in Chapter 4: Historically customers of larger, more established air-carriers such as Continental, Delta, and Northwest seem to have weathered bankruptcy or financial turmoil better, retaining their miles, elite status, the value of advance-purchased tickets, and in some occasions being able to transfer their miles and elite status to another airline. Conversely, customers of low-fare airlines lost all of their miles and even the value of advance-purchased tickets. Do your research into an airline's financial solidity by reading such financial publications as *The Wall Street Journal*, and contact the U.S. Department of Transportation (www.dot.gov).

Investigate the relative benefits of various frequent-flyer programs. It's important to understand the rules and restrictions imposed on upgrade certificates. Find out how many miles you need to get upgrades and what type of fares qualify for upgrades. The references section in the back of this book offers information about the major airlines' frequent-flyer programs. For the most updated information, however, it's a good idea to check with the specific airline yourself, and this can be done through the airline's web site.

If you have frequent-flyer accounts with multiple airlines, see which account holds the most qualifying miles. If the airline with which you have the most qualifying miles will best meet your current and anticipated travel needs, then choose it as your airline travel partner. If you have miles left over in an account, don't stress too much about them. Last year I flew from Los Angeles to Vietnam earning miles with United Airlines. The trip yielded me about 22,000 miles that I knew I would not use. So I opted to redeem a free night award with the Hyatt hotels, a regular hotel partner of mine. The reality is that orphan miles or miles left over in an unused account do not have much value to you and you'll gain far better use when focusing on your one chosen program. Remember that it is very easy to rack up miles today, so focus on the real prize. (You might also consider donating orphan miles to a charitable cause.)

A good tip is to consider choosing an airline that does not have the highest number of frequent flyers. In keeping with the contrarian travel strategy described in Chapter 4, you want to seek out the travel providers that want your business and will best meet your long-term needs. For example, American Airlines is the most popular airline with the greatest number of frequent flyers. So if you choose American Airlines, you should know that you will be competing with a larger pool of flyers. Webflyer.com has a ranking of airlines with the most number of frequent flyers. Do, however, weigh this and any other supply/demand opportunities against the risk of the airline becoming defunct because of possible financial difficulties. By the way, airline load factors (a measure of the number of passengers on a flight) are often reported in *The Wall Street Journal* and are also available from the U.S. Department of Transportation (www.dot.gov).

TRAVEL FOR WORK

What if you've chosen your airline, but your employer wants you to fly on another one? Sometimes my own travel expenses are paid by another company. If the company gives me an airline ticket on a carrier that is not my chosen airline, I always try to re-ticket with my designated carrier. Sometimes it costs me a few dollars and minimal inconvenience; other times it is effortless. But regardless, I maintain my loyalty to my chosen airline and enjoy the amenities of first-class travel. This far outweighs any inconvenience.

Something that has helped me when working with companies that pay my travel expenses is to demonstrate that flying on my designated airline costs the same or is cheaper than what they would select for me. I was asked to speak at a conference in Europe and was booked on a flight with Lufthansa Airlines that made three stops and flew out of the less convenient LAX airport. I fired up my computer and planned an itinerary from the more convenient Orange County airport which only made two stops costing $100 less. In addition, I was able to upgrade on the Delta flight. In short, if you do some of the leg work for your travel planner you can normally get them to go along with your objectives.

If you find yourself in this situation, speak with the person in your company who is responsible for arranging company travels. If this person is unable to approve a change of airlines, try to get your manager's approval. Explain that you'd like to use your chosen airline, and stress that the airfare will not exceed what your company would normally pay.

Do understand, however, that many large companies have negotiated contracts with specific airlines, and thus it may be in your best interest to consider switching to your company's chosen airline. If you have many miles and an established customer history with another airline, follow the procedures mentioned above to transfer your miles into this new airline account. Also, if you have any level of elite frequent-flyer status with your previous airline, call up the new airline and inform them that your company has a contract with them; however, you have elite status

with another airline and would like them to match that
level of status for you.

QUICK REVIEW

- Select your chosen airline carefully so that you do not
  need to deviate from it. Base your decision on the airline's convenience of scheduling and routing, code-share
  agreements, frequent-flyer program, financial solidity,
  ability to transfer points from other airlines to your chosen airline, rules and restrictions for upgrades, and passenger load factors.

- Choose an airline and be steadfast in your loyalty.

- Be flexible. If you're tempted to fly another airline,
  remember how satisfying it will be to fly first class at
  coach prices.

- Stay loyal and you will be rewarded with upgrades and
  preferential treatment. Most major airlines have very
  similar routes and fares, so there is really no advantage
  to flying on an airline that is not your chosen carrier.

- Do the work for your travel planner providing the
  details of the flight you want.

- Re-ticket to your chosen airline whenever possible; if
  not, consider switching your loyalty to your company's
  airline.

FREQUENT-FLYER PROGRAMS

Since 1981, frequent-flyer programs have evolved into a
commonplace component of a consumer's everyday life.

The availability of frequent-flyer miles is now so wide-spread that they have almost become a second national currency. Almost everyone is involved in some sort of program that earns airline mileage. Today's consumer can earn miles through myriad methods, from credit cards to car rentals to dining out or even through paying their mortgages, or college tuition for their children. In fact, it has been estimated that about 60% of all frequent-flyer miles are earned on the ground.

The impact of this profusion of miles is manifold. First, many travelers today have become desensitized to the lure of frequent-flyer miles and have begun to perceive those miles as only a small motivator to fly with one airline. This is mostly because there are approximately 5 trillion miles out there in about 130 loyalty programs, and about 500 billion miles being added each year.

The sheer number of these miles and the amount earned each year have diluted the value of frequent-flyer miles. They have simply become a means to an end, which is obtaining upgrades and other forms of preferential treatment. Conventional wisdom used to hold that each mile was worth about $0.02, but these days I believe that each mile is worth about $0.01–$0.005.

Most important, this profusion of miles has created a situation where there are too many miles chasing too few awards. The vast number of consumers attempting to exchange miles for tickets has prompted the airlines to restrict the number of award seats available, and with good reason. A Wall Street analyst recently said that if all the air miles held by consumers were cashed in at once, a year's worth of industry revenue would be wiped out.

The key here is to use your miles wisely.

USING YOUR MILES WISELY

The average traveler looks at air miles as a means to a free airline ticket, which is by far the worst use of miles. It can be more difficult to redeem a straight award ticket than an upgrade and very often the value for the dollar is not worth it. Consider that an average U.S. domestic air ticket is $275, and that at a minimum it will take 25,000 miles to redeem a round trip. That gives you a cost ratio of about 1.1 cents per mile. However, if you purchase a ticket for the same $275 and use 15,000 miles to upgrade it to a first class ticket with an equivalent price of $1,500 you now have a cost ratio of about 10 cents a mile, effectively increasing your value tenfold. As a bonus it can be easier to get the first-class upgrade and you are using fewer miles.

Another mistaken approach taken by many travelers is trying to book your award tickets as far in advance as possible; this is usually 365 days prior to the first flight. This strategy fails for a few reasons; foremost is that most people find it difficult to plan that far in advance. Secondly, if you do book your award ticket that far in advance you risk losing the reservation or paying penalties for changes. Another overlooked fact is that many airlines limit award inventory until the actual flight date approaches. What I mean by this is that airlines hope to sell a seat and their chances of selling a seat are better 300 days before a flight than they are 3 days before a flight. If an airline sees that there is available inventory 3 days prior to a flight and their inventory and revenue managers feel that the seat will go unsold, they are more likely to open that seat up to award inventory. Therefore, I recommend trying to get your seats later rather than sooner.

I advise forgoing complex and burdensome methods of exchanging air miles for tickets which are so popular on many travel blog sites and stick to simplicity. Just purchase easily obtainable discounted coach tickets on your airline of choice. Then, position yourself as the right customer and use your mutually beneficial relationship to get upgraded to first class. Not only will you accumulate additional miles in the process, you will earn the all-important qualifying miles necessary to increase your heights of loyalty and reap first-class rewards.

Travelers also fail to realize the benefits of using double the points. Most airlines have gone to a formula where you can use a premium number of points to get an anytime award (although recently a few airlines have reduced the number of anytime seats). Under this scheme you simply opt to use a higher number of miles to confirm a seat or upgrade at any time. When these awards first started to come out a number of travel writers debased them for taking advantage of travelers. In reality it is giving travelers greater freedom of choice. I believe that these are good for the traveling public because it opens up what can be otherwise expensive seats at the last minute. Increasingly I've come to realize that I have friends because I have tons of air miles and can get them great airline seats. Routinely, I'll have friends call from the East Coast seeking a ticket to the West Coast that would cost over a $1,000 to book last minute, but for between 45,000 to 50,000 miles I can get them a nice first-class seat. When you think about all the various outlets for earning miles, 50,000 is really the new 25,000. On average, I probably average about 125,000 miles a month from my flight activity, credit cards, and other miles incentives.

HOW TO GET UPGRADE CERTIFICATES

Redeem miles in your frequent-flyer account for upgrade certificates. Again, this is where the true value of ancillary miles lies. Transfer as many miles as you can from ancillary programs into the frequent-flyer program of your chosen airline. Incidentally, the more ancillary points you earn through affiliate programs, the more value you bring to the airline and yourself. Today the selling of airline miles is big business and the revenue airlines receive from the sale of miles has been instrumental in keeping them afloat. So when you are positioning your loyalty with airlines remember to bring up the business you conduct with their mileage partners. This is something that they can look up in your account. If you are redeeming the minimum number of miles required by your airline for an upgrade certificate, ask the airline if there are any restrictions associated with this upgrade. You may be told that there are indeed restrictions, such as blackout dates or a limited number of available first-class seats. If this is the case, ask your airline if you can trade in a larger number of miles for the upgrade in order to waive any restrictions. If you attach a high value to flying first class, it may be worth trading in the extra miles for that upgrade.

Many airlines will also offer books of upgrade certificates or upgrades for individual flights for a nominal fee. Often these books of certificates will cost as little as $125.00 for five upgrade certificates. Each certificate allows the user to upgrade one flight to first class. Currently most of the major airlines have a program where you can upgrade to first class on the day of your flight based on the length of the flight. Keep in mind that many airlines require that your fare basis (what you pay for the ticket) be higher than the lowest available fares classes, which normally are categorized as L, T, or U fares. However, as stated earlier, you can often bump up to the next fare class for a few extra dollars and then purchase a "same-day upgrade" for $50 and all of a sudden your $300 turns into a $1,500 ticket. Some airlines will allow you to do this online 24 hours before your flight, while others require it to be done at the airport, so it's best to check with your airline before your flight, since airline rules are constantly changing.

Another way to get upgrade certificates is to ask your friends and associates if they have upgrade certificates that they will not be able to use before the expiration date. Most of the free certificates I receive expire in a year, but they can also be transferred to another person if I'm unable to use them before the expiration date. I give most of my extra certificates to friends and family. One more thing: Never buy or sell an upgrade certificate—this is against the rules, and you could lose all your frequent-flyer benefits with your airline.

When using an upgrade certificate, try to confirm your upgrade before you arrive at the airport. When you book your ticket, make a reservation for the lowest available fare. Ask if there are any upgrade restrictions associated with this fare. If there aren't, confirm your coach ticket in first class, using your upgrade certificate. If the fare you've booked is restricted in terms of upgrades, ask for the lowest available unrestricted and upgradeable fare. I believe you'll find that the slightly higher cost is worth it to keep your first-class history going, and for more reasons than that.

On a recent trip, I had the option to pay $267 for the lowest restricted nonrefundable fare, as opposed to $307 for an unrestricted/refundable fare. I chose to pay the extra $40 and flew first class. This is in keeping with the philosophy I talked about—it's worth it to occasionally pay a modest premium for value and big rewards. Besides, in a case like this, paying for a restricted fare might save you $40 up front, but what would happen if you had to change your plans? If you have a brief history with your chosen airline and have not yet earned the privilege of having restrictions waived, you might end up paying as much as $100 to change your ticket. This is again another part of the value equation; you want to determine what is going to work best for you in the big picture.

A few years ago I worked with a company and determined that 75% of their air tickets were nonrefundable. Their intent in purchasing the cheaper, non-refundable tickets was to save money on travel expenses. However, due to shifting business needs, 65% of the employees had to rebook a nonrefundable ticket. In many instances, employees had rebooked their tickets more than three times, often paying more in change fees than the original fare. This is a good reminder to always keep your eye on value, not price.

Another hot tip is to consider investing in a one-year membership or one-day pass in your airline's private, first-class lounge. As illustrated in the opening pages of the chapter, this is an investment that will give you access to the airline's lounge agent, the person who is accustomed to giving members preferential treatment, including seating upgrades. And once you have established enough of a history with your airline, you can earn complimentary access to some of these lounges.

Depending on what type of traveler you are and how often you travel, the price of these clubs can be very affordable. To illustrate, think about the value of having a nice quiet place to relax before your flight. Consider this simple equation: If you fly ten times a year and spend an average of just one hour per round trip waiting at airports, a $200 annual club membership costs you just $20 per hour. Spend a total of twenty hours, and the hourly cost of membership drops to just $10, a bargain for a peaceful haven with complimentary snacks and beverages, and in some cases, showers. By far one of the greatest benefits is access to preferred security lines at the airports. Perhaps one of the most disconcerting aspects of travel is going through security. Most airports have two security lines—one for preferred travelers, the other for everyone else. The difference in time can range from five minutes in the preferred line to over an hour in the regular line. Easing through security can not only reduce stress but it can give you extra time to make phone calls, have a drink, or just sit and read or watch TV.

On one of my trips to Vilnius, Lithuania, I had an early 7:30 arrival at the Frankfurt airport, however my connecting flight to Vilnius did not leave until seven hours later at 2.30 P.M. Knowing that I needed to be refreshed for my evening in Vilnius, I sought ways to minimize this time lag by having a nice place to go between flights. One choice was getting a day room at the Sheraton Hotel that connected to the airport for a cost of 135 euros. Not only was the cost unappealing but when I had breakfast there a few weeks prior I found the hotel's staff to be rude and I certainly did not want to experience that again. I then remembered that Delta had a Crown Room at the Frankfurt Airport that would cost me nothing to wait out my flight. This was by far the best alternative as the Crown Room had nice showers, fresh juice, fruit, snacks, computers, and a nice section with sleeper seats including headphones and a selection of music. After my shower, the club's agent provided me with a blanket and pillow making for an enjoyable sleep, easing my time at the airport and making my arrival into Vilnius a breeze.

Have credit? American Express Platinum cardholders and some other premium credit card members can receive free access to multiple airport lounges. Check your credit card program or airline for current program opportunities.

A full-fare coach ticket means upgrades and more. In today's marketplace, a passenger with a full-fare ticket is gold, because he or she is adding the most value to the airline at that time. Even if you have never flown that airline before, purchasing a full-fare coach ticket is equivalent to having a first-class ticket in hand, and you should expect a number of amenities to follow. For example, you should get complimentary access to the airline's private lounges, preferred seating (such as no one in the seat next to you or not being in a middle seat), and some airlines will even have a driver take you to and from your home to the airport.

Most important, be sure to ask for an upgrade. Most people are not aware that the airlines will upgrade full-fare ticket holders upon request. In fact, many airlines will automatically upgrade full-fare ticket holders. The only possible exception to being upgraded to first class is if the whole first-class cabin is filled with passengers who actually paid a first-class fare and it is extremely rare for that to happen. Incidentally, when you travel overseas on a full-fare coach ticket, some airlines will not only upgrade you, they will also give you a free companion ticket, allowing you to bring someone along without any additional charge. So whenever you pay a full coach fare, invest a bit of time and seek out the extra benefits, and do the math.

It's also important to look like a first-class traveler. A study by Cornell University concluded that well-dressed travelers received better service than their lesser-dressed counterparts. The way you dress will have an effect on how travel companies treat you. If you dress in a professional manner, you will have a greater likelihood of being upgraded to first class. Airlines like to think of their first-class cabin as a special area for VIP flyers. Therefore, if you approach a gate agent wearing a faded tank top and torn jeans, unless you are a major recording artist or movie star your chances of a free upgrade will be weaker than if you have a more professional appearance. By the way, this same approach holds true for hotels. If you arrive at a five-star hotel with a disheveled appearance, your chance of being upgraded to a more luxurious room will also lessen. Of course, a well-dressed look does not mean that you have to arrive in a Brioni suit or an elegant dress. Dressing for success can range from a business suit to nice slacks and a polo shirt. The key is to take care in your appearance and to look like someone who deserves to be upgraded.

ExpertFlyer.com: It Can Serve You Well

Deciphering airfares is almost as difficult as understanding Peyton Manning's offense. You have fare bases, fare codes, and buckets; refundable tickets, nonrefundable tickets, upgradeable tickets, and not. And, oh yeah: A fares, B fares, Y fares, and blackouts. Well, you get the point.

ExpertFlyer.com is changing all that. Normally, I'm reluctant to embrace web sites that promise a better travel experience than you can get on your own, but this one I cannot resist telling you about.

ExpertFlyer has been around for a couple of years, providing information by subscription on airfares, upgrades, award tickets, seat availability, and other things that frequent flyers care about. When the company asked me to review the service a year ago, I said no. But recently, after hearing some success stories, I decided to take it on a test flight. Unwittingly, I tested the system to its outer limits.

The program works with almost every major airline, though award and upgrade information is limited to certain cooperating carriers, notably Northwest Airlines and American Airlines (for awards and upgrades) and Delta Air Lines (for upgrades). My particular quest was to search the availability of international upgrades on my preferred airline, Delta. Only after meeting with ExpertFlyer's president, Chris Lopinto, did I learn that this is the program's most daunting task, due to a quirk in how Delta provides information.

In technical terms, I was looking for flights that had "Z" availability, i.e., seats in the Business Elite section which would allow me to use Delta PMU certificates or frequent-flyer miles. Before using the program I spent a few hours on the phone with a Delta representative searching for a flight from Orange County, California to Santiago, Chile. I tried every imaginable option, switching dates, flying into Buenos Aires—even connecting through Sao Paulo.

Not getting anywhere, I powered up ExpertFlyer to see if it was up to the task.

What I found amazed me. Right there on the screen I saw
"Z2"—meaning that two Z seats were available on the
flights I wanted. Immediately I called Delta, this time with
the information I needed. I specified the flights I was interested in and this time the answer was, "Yes, sir."

"O.K., lucky break," I thought. So I did a search on another route. Again, ExpertFlyer listed seats with upgrade availability, and Delta confirmed the result.

But the real payoff came when I decided to change my
flight. This time one of the flight segments came up ineligible
for an upgrade, so I enabled a nifty feature called "Flight
Alert," which sends you an e-mail when the system determines that a desired booking class has become available. Two
days later, which by coincidence was the deadline for booking
the ticket, an alert came through informing me that an
upgrade seat was available. I checked the availability again.
Still there.

Still a little skeptical, I called Delta and asked if an upgrade
had come through for my flight. The answer was "No." When
I reported that ExpertFlyer was showing a G fare available (G
is the international equivalent of a Z fare on domestic routes),
the agent cleared up the confusion. She thought I had wanted
a "segment upgrade," a complimentary upgrade that clears a
certain number of days before your flight, depending on your
membership level. The segment upgrade was not available,
but the G fare was mine.

This trial underscores the importance of having good data.
If I didn't have ExpertFlyer's detailed information, I would
not have been able to press the agent to look up the proper
upgrade code. With all due respect to reservation agents,
there are the occasional few who either don't understand your

request, don't really understand their reservation system, or are just plain lazy. But I had my arsenal ready and I was determined to get that last upgrade.

The ExpertFlyer program does have a learning curve. For example, you have to know what class category to enter, but that is easy enough to find with the quick "Look Up" feature. You also need to understand such things as "hidden codes," and I found the program to be more accurate when I entered a specific time instead of the default time (5 A.M.). And remember that the availability of award and upgrade information is limited to certain cooperating airlines, so check the list on the site's Help/FAQ page before signing up.

Overall, ExpertFlyer is a good tool that gives consumers unfettered and transparent access to travel intelligence, eliminating the need for third-party intervention and keeping them on the do-it-yourself track. It can serve you well. I, for one, will not fly without it.

QUICK REVIEW

♦ Communicate your present and future loyalty to airline agents when seeking first-class upgrades or making special requests. The possibility of your future business is what gives infrequent travelers leverage.

♦ Express your intended loyalty and be honest in your intentions. Don't lie your way into an upgrade. The airline employees who can upgrade you have seen and heard it all, and they document your conversations as well as your customer history on computer.

- Communicate your loyalty when seeking an upgrade, but don't demand one. Be realistic about the strength of your bargaining position if you are just starting a history with your airline.

- Fly first class as much as possible, using upgrade certificates. Exchange your frequent-flyer miles for upgrade certificates, pay the nominal fee if necessary, and ask your friends to give you certificates they cannot use.

- Try to confirm your upgrade before you get to the airport. Check to see if your fare or upgrade certificate has any restrictions. It's worth it to pay a little extra for an unrestricted fare and to trade in extra miles for unrestricted upgrades.

- Consider investing in a membership in your airline's private first-class lounge. This will give you access to key airline representatives who are used to giving passengers preferential treatment.

- Make sure you get upgraded to first class if you have a full-fare coach ticket. This is almost always automatically available at no extra charge.

THE MOST VALUABLE SECRET OF ALL

The airlines reward those travelers who provide them with value. Therefore, airlines do not look at your total point accumulation when assessing whether they will make special accommodations for you. They consider qualifying miles that include a combination of your actual flight miles, bonuses based on the value of your ticket price, and special limited earning opportunities based on ancillary spending on such things as credit cards or other travel partners.

In short, decisions are based on your overall profitability. Therefore, to be a first-class winner in today's frequent-flyer game, you need to pick your airline carefully, position yourself as the right customer, and remain loyal in order to earn those qualifying miles.

The good news for infrequent travelers, and something that has changed considerably since the last edition of this book, is how airlines view ancillary revenues. The secondary market of airline miles has become big business to airlines. I attended and spoke at the first ever ancillary revenue conference in November 2007 which was widely attended by airlines, vendors and mileage partners such as car rental companies, hotels, and credit cards, among others. One thing was clear: The industry is relying on this revenue stream and those consumers who provide it will increasingly be privy to the enhanced perks their profitability brings to the companies.

This strategy is particularly useful for those of you who are first starting out a flight history and have not yet accumulated enough qualifying miles to earn automatic upgrades.

This is how you establish a strong, mutually beneficial relationship with your airline.

TRACKING YOUR MILES

As discussed earlier, today airlines track every aspect of their passengers' histories. That includes qualifying miles flown versus other sources of miles, the amount of revenue you provide the airline, and the cost to serve you as a customer. This information apprises a gate agent as to whom they should upgrade to first class when the coach section is full, whom they should assign a priority position on a wait list, and for whom they will waive restrictions and penalties. If your frequent-flyer account contains only qualifying miles and you trade in some of your miles for a first-class upgrade, you will not diminish your leverage. The airline will still retain a record of how many qualifying miles you've earned with them throughout your history with the airline.

QUICK REVIEW

◆ The overabundance of air miles has diminished their value and placed a greater importance on earning qualifying miles to build loyalty.

◆ Qualifying miles—the miles you earn by flying—are your key to obtaining first-class upgrades and preferential service. Remember, the airlines offer the biggest rewards to those travelers who provide them with value.

◆ The best way to use your frequent-flyer mileage is to buy discounted coach tickets for yourself, get upgraded, and continue building your qualifying mileage to earn elite status. It is O.K. to use your miles to buy free tickets and upgrades for family members.

NOT ALL MILES ARE THE SAME

Back in 1999 when the first edition of this book hit the shelves, all miles were basically the same. Today program managers have become much more sophisticated in managing their programs as tools of profitability. Along the way managers have calculated incentives that benefit both the consumer and the airline. The good news is that passengers can earn more miles with higher-priced tickets while the not-so-good-news is that some lower-priced tickets receive a lower threshold of qualifying miles (the miles that count toward elite status). With that said, most airline tickets receive at least a one-to-one earnings ratio. (One qualifying mile for each flight mile, usually with a minimum number of miles per segment.) In some cases the lowest discounted fares, such as L, T, and U fares, do not earn miles. I have found that for most travelers this is not a disadvantage as those who have a high number of L, T, and U fares do not fly that often and typically are not in a position to take full advantage of a frequent flyer program.

The harsh reality is that airlines do not care much for those who only fly on the lowest available fares. As two managers told me at a conference in Vancouver, "If a customer is flying L/T/U, we don't want them!" This might sound offensive at first but keep in mind that the airlines are businesses and they do return perks to those who bring them profitability. The best news is that it is usually only a nominal fee to go from the lowest available fare to one that brings you and the airline greater value.

Today, travelers already find a happy medium between seeking price and value and for those reading this book and able to take advantage of the perks of loyalty, this is not much of an issue. The benefit of these new programs is that when you are faced with paying a higher ticket price you get the added reward of extra qualifying miles which builds your loyalty faster.

Since programs are consistently in flux, it is best to review your program rules to determine what tickets earn what type of miles. Incidentally, this is another reason for limiting your choice of airlines as the process of under-standing multiple programs has become too complex.

Why You Should Fly the Big Airlines

The future of American air transportation rides in the cab-ins of the nation's big airlines. For more than seventy years, airlines like American Airlines, Delta Air Lines, and United Airlines have proudly served the interests of American travelers. Along the way, they have helped busi-nesses earn trillions of dollars, worked with the govern-ment to secure our borders, and given travelers a way to explore the wonders of the world.

And what have they gotten in return? Travelers have taken advantage of airlines' willingness to maintain com-petitive fares and repaid them with fleeting loyalty and indifference. At the same time, labor unions have drained the big airlines' coffers and upstart carriers have poached their routes.

In other industries, consumers build mutually benefi-cial relationships with providers of goods and services. Wal-Mart shoppers won't shop anywhere else, just as BMW owners won't let anyone else service their $70,000 vehicles. These consumers are fiercely loyal, no matter their income bracket.

But when it comes to air travel, consumers toss loyalty aside in search of a better deal. I call this the "Southwest Effect"—the naive idea that the best deals will be found on Southwest Airlines, JetBlue, and other low-budget car-riers, as well as on third-party web sites. Not only do these better deals not exist, but this strategy is wreaking havoc with the U.S. air travel industry.

WHY SHOULD WE REWARD THE MAJOR U.S. AIRLINES?

Without the major U.S. airlines, my neighbor would not be able to visit her brother twice a year in Israel; she would not have been able to explore Central and South America, taking time to become fluent in Spanish. Without the major airlines, many Americans would be unable to share Thanksgiving and Christmas with their families.

During the past ten years, the airline industry has been in turmoil. In that time, we lost several great American companies, including TWA, Pan Am, and Eastern. Chock it up to competition—that's the American way. The remaining big airlines have answered their challenges with innovation and reinvention—that's also the American way. Responding to market conditions, the airlines have whittled their cost structures and profit margins to the lowest in any industry.

At the same time, the full-service airlines have continued to serve the American public with pride, especially in times of trouble and hardship. When America was terrified by the events of 9/11, the big airlines responded quickly and got passengers on their way. When winter storms pummel the northeast, the major carriers still take you anywhere in the world. When Americans become displaced by harsh hurricanes, the major U.S. airlines offer their services and ferry those in need to safe ground.

During such difficult times, major airlines also waive their usual change fees, rebooking rules, and refund policies. Unlike other businesses, the big airlines typically forgo opportunistic practices in order to serve their customers' needs.

Think about it. At a time when gas prices make it more expensive to drive than to fly, airlines have done their best to maintain low fares (and they have high fuel costs, too). In fact, today you can fly from coast to coast *and* stay in a five-star hotel for less than it costs to drive the same distance.

The major airlines are big contributors to charity, too—and not just in times of national tragedy. In fact, they routinely donate miles and services to such causes as the Make-a-Wish Foundation, the American Red Cross, cancer victims and their families, and many other worthy causes.

WHERE IS THIS ALL GOING?

To those who think that the new low-cost carriers like Southwest and JetBlue are the future of the U.S. airline industry, I say: Think again. Will they get you to Des Moines to see Grandma at Christmas? I think not. But Delta will.

In fact, the major airlines have maintained many unprofitable routes to responsibly serve their customers. Southwest and JetBlue cherry-picked their routes, offering limited service and poaching customers from the big carriers. With the major U.S. airlines, you can fly anywhere in the world. Southwest and JetBlue take you only where *they* want to go.

The reality of the current U.S. airline industry is that the big airlines are shrinking their operating costs while the so-called low-budget carriers are increasing theirs. David

Neeleman, CEO of JetBlue, expects JetBlue to operate more than 275 planes by 2010; those planes will include many new Embraer 190s to go with JetBlue's current fleet of Airbus A-320s. This plan will more than triple JetBlue's fleet and workforce.

My advice? Commit to one major airline and let their planes fly you anywhere you need to go. You'll be better off for it, and so will America.

ELITE FREQUENT-FLYER LEVELS: A GOAL WELL WORTH ACHIEVING

To the elite-level frequent flyer, preferential service is second nature. Qualifying as an elite-level frequent flyer is the most effective means of obtaining free upgrades and other luxury services when you fly.

To qualify for elite-level frequent-flyer status, you must earn the requisite number of elite-qualifying base miles over the course of a year. That requisite number varies from airline to airline. Recently airlines have made qualifying for elite membership easier by offering limited incentives with their travel partners that can boost your qualifying miles account. For example, Delta Air Lines occasionally offers qualifying miles with certain hotel stays and car rentals. Basically what the airlines are trying to do is get travelers in the habit of using their partners. So in order to change buying behavior they offer bonuses that can reap nice benefits for you. Another example, as mentioned earlier in this book, is Delta Air Lines relationship with American Express SkyMiles Card. Cardholders can earn 10,000 qualifying miles for their first $25,000 dollars of qualified purchases and another 10,000 qualifying miles when spending $50,000 annually. This means that a cardholder can earn 20,000 of the necessary 25,000 elite qualifying requirements just by using their card.

Spending $50,000 on one credit card might seem like a lot, and when I wrote about this in an MSNBC article a number of readers wrote to me saying they were not able to spend that much, but one reader really put things into perspective. He told me that he spends $15,000 a month by funneling all of his expenses to his card. He pays his mortgage on the card, car payment, utilities, school tuition, groceries, gas and all other monthly expenses. I bet that if you think of all the monthly bills you pay, you can see how you can rack up the points on a card.

Elite-level passengers represent only 7% of the flying public. This means that if you reach elite level by flying the required number of miles, you will be ahead of 93% of all other flyers. This is the best way to stay ahead of the game in this era of too many miles chasing too few rewards. At the highest levels of elite membership you began to reach the fractional numbers. Although airlines don't publicly state their membership figures, I have been told that the highest levels of elite qualification membership are about 1% to 2% of the population while those earning 150,000+ qualifying miles are in the .05% bracket.

Whenever airline representatives access your records on a computer, they will immediately see your elite status and unquestionably extend preferential service to you. Therefore, you should go out of your way to qualify for at least the minimum elite-level status with your chosen airline, even if it means taking an extra trip at the end of the year.

Once you qualify for an elite level, you receive elite benefits for the duration of that year and throughout the entire next year. And only one member of your family needs to be at the elite level for all family members to benefit. If you are commencing a history with an airline, try to qualify for the minimum elite level as soon as possible.

THE BENEFITS OF ELITE STATUS

Most airlines have two to three levels of elite status. It pays to achieve the highest elite level you can, but you will still reap tremendous benefits from even the minimum elite status. Some of these benefits include free domestic upgrades, which you can book at the last minute. Elite status also allows you to waive many restrictions, such as blackout dates on free tickets and change fees, even on discounted coach fares. And if a restriction still applies, your high level of loyalty as an elite-level passenger can give you greater leverage. You can push a bit harder for what you want, citing that you have developed a mutually beneficial relationship and loyalty as valid grounds for granting a request. Although your elite status is printed on the flight manifest, be sure to point out any elite status you might have when making your requests.

Most of the airlines offer special toll-free lines for their elite-level passengers as well as special lines at check-in, so you can avoid the long wait in the general check-in lines. Many of the airlines also allow elite travelers special access to their luxurious private lounges without charge, depending on the passenger's level of loyalty. And most airlines provide elite-level passengers with tier bonuses that can increase your qualifying mileage and point totals automatically by

25% to 100% every time you fly. For most travelers, this means you can earn 20,000 qualifying miles for flying only 10,000 miles. And you can trade these extra miles in for a few free tickets to give to family members and friends.

QUALIFYING FOR MINIMUM ELITE STATUS IS EASIER THAN YOU MIGHT THINK

Since most airlines have two or three levels of elite customer status, each requires a minimum number of qualifying miles. Most airlines require 20,000 to 25,000 qualifying miles over the course of a year to qualify for the minimum elite level. The highest level of elite status can range from 50,000 to 100,000 qualifying miles per year depending on the airline.

If you don't fly many miles per year, some airlines offer an alternative way for you to achieve elite status—by flying a certain number of flight segments in one year. You can also earn a portion of your qualifying miles through ancillary outlets, as I described with the Delta SkyMiles card in the previous section.

While formerly only attainable after flying a minimum of 20,000 to 25,000 miles over the course of a year, the minimum Gold elite status with American Airlines is now obtainable through a little-known program in which you earn only 8,000 points in a ninety-day period. Their Platinum elite status is obtainable by earning only 16,000 points in a ninety-day period. Just ask American to enroll you. This special program is only for flights flown on American Airlines and does not include flights on any of their alliance partners.

Here's what to do if American Airlines is not your chosen airline: Earn elite status with them under this special program and then contact your chosen airline and ask them to match the elite status you have with American Airlines. Matching of elite status is a little-known but common practice that airlines use to win over customers from competitors. Keep in mind, however, that airlines are constantly tweaking their programs in search of the best value. Therefore, you must always keep current with what your airline is doing. The best way to stay current is by checking the airline's web site periodically, calling them to see if they are offering any special programs, and by reading your frequent-flyer statement. This is another reason why I prefer to build a mutually beneficial relationship with just one airline; it takes a lot less time to stay on top of changes.

MAINTAINING YOUR ELITE STATUS YEAR AFTER YEAR: A CONTACT SPORT

Each October, you should review your qualifying mileage for the year to see where you stand in relation to achieving elite status. This will allow you to plan the next three months and seek out discounted airfares to achieve the prized elite levels. My friend Carver, a frequent traveler with American Airlines and a steady flyer of 100,000 miles annually, found he was short nearing the end of 2007. Being a friend of mine he knew not to wait until December to figure out how to exceed the 100,000 mile threshold. Starting in October he planned inexpensive trips that accumulated big miles in a short period of time. By watching the American Airlines web site for advertised specials or calling reservation agents and inquiring about specials, he was able to find great routes that padded his account and pushed him over the 100,000 mile mark before the holidays. Incidentally 5,000 of the needed qualifying miles came from hotel stays and car rentals. He describes frequent flyer programs as a contact sport and didn't want to get all bruised up for Christmas by taking last minute flights at the peak of the season.

TRANSFERRING YOUR ELITE STATUS
TO ANOTHER AIRLINE

If you find that you have to frequently fly another airline because of your company's travel or business policies, do not be afraid to inquire into transferring your elite status to the other airline, as in the American Airlines story discussed in the previous section.

On one occasion while waiting for a flight in Delta's private first-class lounge, I overheard a conversation between two businessmen. One of the men said his company just changed his territory, and now he was flying routes that were more convenient with United Airlines. He had already reached an elite level with Delta and was very reluctant to give up his elite status. He called the corporate office of United and explained to their marketing department that he was an elite-level frequent flyer with Delta. He offered to give his business to United if they would start him off with elite status in their frequent-flyer program, and they agreed. He also talked about a United Airlines gate agent he befriended who was so eager to make flying United Airlines an enjoyable experience that he upgrades him every time he flies. Similarly my friend Wanda fell short of the necessary miles to re-qualify with Alaska Airlines top elite status.

She did not realize this until she received a letter from Alaska Airlines granting her upgraded status to their top elite level due to her past loyalty.

QUICK REVIEW

- Unquestionably the airlines give preferential treatment to elite-level passengers, who represent only 7% of the flying public. If you are just starting a history with your airline, you should go out of your way to qualify for at least the minimum elite status, even if it means taking an extra trip at the end of the year.

- Qualifying for minimum elite status is easier than you might think. You can qualify on several airlines with as little as 25,000 qualifying miles, and accomplish this in as few as three to five flights. Some airlines also allow you to qualify based on the number of flight segments you fly rather than on the number of miles.

- Higher-priced tickets can earn you more qualifying miles accelerating your path to elite membership.

- The higher your elite level status is, the more benefits you will receive. But even at the minimum elite level, you will be privy to free domestic upgrades, restriction waivers, special toll-free reservation lines, and fast check-in at the airport. And depending on your level of loyalty, you can have access to the airline's luxurious private lounges and tier mileage bonuses.

- Review your qualifying mileage for the year each October to see where you stand in terms of achieving elite status. You can then plan your travels for the next three months and seek out discounted airfares to achieve elite levels.

♦ Always maintain your loyalty, but if business or other concerns necessitate a change in airlines, ask the new airline if they will transfer over your elite status. Many airlines will be willing to accommodate you in order to secure a loyal customer.

♦ Frequent-flyer programs are a contact sport requiring your constant involvement.

EASIER SECURITY CHECKS

One benefit that elite-level frequent flyers are sure to find appealing is the ease with which they can navigate through security conscious airports. Unlike many travelers, I do not dread arriving at the airport for my flight, because I know that since I maintain an elite level of frequent-flyer status I can bypass the long check-in lines and proceed directly to a special and shorter line for passengers in first-class and those holding elite status. In addition, at most airports I am able to bypass those long security screening lines with a dedicated and again short line for elite-level flyers. By upgrading or maintaining elite status, you too will find that this slight advantage will greatly reduce your travel anxiety and certainly help to make your trip more pleasurable.

Key Points

➤ *Make the choice for first class by being the right customer of one airline.*

Because the airline industry is fiercely competitive, your chosen airline will reward its most loyal customers with first-class seats and preferential treatment. Choose your airline wisely, and be rewarded for your steadfast loyalty.

➤ *Use your frequent-flyer program wisely.*
Regardless of how often you fly, earning ancillary miles helps you generate greater value to an airline. Airlines provide preferential treatment and first-class seats to the passengers who provide them with income and added value. That means you should concentrate on building qualifying miles—those miles that count toward elite membership. If your airline follows the emerging trend of calculating qualifying miles on the price and class of your ticket, you will need to factor that policy into your purchasing decisions.

➤ *Purchase discounted (upgradeable) tickets and use miles for upgrades.*
Trade in your ancillary miles for free first-class upgrades and for free tickets for your traveling companions. Buy discounted tickets for yourself and continue building qualifying miles to receive a vast array of benefits.

➤ *Fly at the elite level; it is a worthwhile goal.*
When you become an elite-level frequent flyer, you will be in an enviable position that wields the most leverage when seeking special treatment. It's worth the effort to achieve even the minimum elite frequent-flyer level with your airline.

6

Getting Those Upgrades

Additional Techniques for Flying First Class at Coach Prices

Always Befriend Gate Agents

Although air carriers have automated much of their upgrading process—which is often based on a formula that considers the level of loyalty membership, price of ticket, and date of ticket purchase—the folks who check you in at the gate counter and who take your ticket as you board the plane (also known as gate agents) still wield supreme authority. Automated upgrading will be discussed later in this chapter, but for now understand that a willing gate agent can upgrade you from the lowest priced coach ticket on a domestic or an international flight to a superior first-class seat. One gate agent I befriended upgrades me two levels of service (from coach to business class to first class) on a flight I frequently fly. She also watches out for me. When a flight I was taking from Orange County to Atlanta was canceled she rebooked me on another airline in first class even before a flight cancellation announcement was made. In return when I see her I go out of my way to say hello and when her mother passed away I brought her flowers, but most importantly, I treat her with dignity and respect.

There have been times when I've been placed on a wait list for a first-class seat on a crowded flight, and gate agents I've befriended have bypassed other passengers and placed me in first class. One smart traveler I know named Sam has developed a very strong relationship with one gate agent at his local airport. This gate agent upgrades Sam's entire routing before Sam even arrives at the airport. And whenever Sam flies with a family member, this gate agent automatically upgrades his family members as well.

Another traveler named David told me how his favorite gate agent helped him out when David was flying to Hawai'i with his family. It seems that David had left his tennis racket at the security checkpoint and did not realize it until after his flight had taken off. When he stopped to change planes, he tried calling the airport and spent a half hour getting nowhere. But when he asked to speak to his friendly gate agent, the agent not only found the tennis racket, he also had it express shipped to David's hotel in Hawai'i.

Make friends with the gate agents at your home airport. Introduce yourself to them. Tell them you're an enthusiastic customer of their airline. Tell them how you look forward to being a loyal flyer long into the future. Ask them if they will assist you in building a solid relationship with the airline. Then, the next time you are at the airport try to seek them out and cordially greet them. Although the words here may sound corny at first, don't worry, you will find your own way to express the sentiment, and it will pay off.

BE AWARE OF GATE AGENT'S INTERNAL HIERARCHY

Try to establish your strongest relationships with the lead gate agents, for they have the most power and authority to give you preferential treatment. The lead gate agents of most airlines usually wear a uniform or coat that is a different color from those worn by the agents of lower rank.

TAKE NOTE OF THE NAMES AND WORKING HOURS OF THE GATE AGENTS YOU MEET

I have befriended many of the lead gate agents at my home airport and at the airports I frequent. I ask for their business cards, learn their names, and ask what hours they work. This way, when I require special assistance, I know whom to ask for. Even if that individual is unavailable, I give whomever I'm talking to the valuable impression that I'm familiar with their airport, experienced with their airline, and therefore a more valuable customer. This results in my being offered preferential service in the form of bumping me up on a wait list, upgrading me from coach to first class on international flights, or whatever else I might request.

BE HONEST, DIRECT, AND RESPECTFUL TO GATE AGENTS WHEN SEEKING A FIRST-CLASS UPGRADE

On any given day, gate agents deal with numerous individuals, many attempting to mislead them. If you're not completely up front and respectful of the agent's authority, they'll know it.

On one occasion, while I was in the beginning stages of building my loyalty with Delta Air Lines, I was flying from Los Angeles to London on a coach ticket. In my attempt to get an upgrade to first class, I approached the lead gate agent. I politely introduced myself and said, "Hi, I am flying with you today. Your airline is the only airline I fly, and I was wondering if there's any possibility of being upgraded. I know that occasionally you will upgrade some of your frequent flyers if upgrades are available prior to departure." I then handed him my ticket, saying, "As you can see, this is a discount ticket, but if you can assist in any way, I would greatly appreciate it." I also asked for his card and expressed my willingness to write a complimentary letter to the airline about how well he did his job and when I got home, I did as promised. I'll go into more detail about the effectiveness of writing such letters later on in this chapter.

While passengers were checking in for that London flight, I left the gate agent to go about his work. Meanwhile, I patiently waited near his podium, remaining within his view at all times. As the London flight was boarding, I again politely inquired into the possibility of being upgraded. The gate agent then handed me a first-class boarding pass. And he upgraded my return flight as well. I was not pushy or demanding and came right out and showed the agent that my ticket was a discount ticket. In any case, the gate agent will know exactly what fare you paid and the type or discount level of the fare. Gate agents respond best to those who are polite and forthright.

When trying to get a gate agent to upgrade you, it has been my experience that the adage "out of sight, out of mind" holds true.

As the previous example illustrates, you should not go ahead and board the plane, hoping the agent will come back and upgrade you. This seldom happens. If you stay within the agent's view, he or she is less likely to forget about you, and you are more likely to get the upgrade.

Not that there aren't exceptions to every rule, as I discovered one day while waiting for a flight. I was waiting to board the plane and had overheard a conversation between a gate agent and a passenger. The passenger approached the gate agent and asked him if there was any way the agent could upgrade him to first class. The gate agent told the passenger, "I'm not sure, but I'll write your name down and let you know." After hearing this, I boarded the plane, and as I was waiting for the rest of the passengers to board I saw this particular passenger walk past me and go to the coach section of the plane. About five minutes later, the gate agent came onto the plane and quietly moved the passenger who had asked for the upgrade into the open first-class seat next to me. (This was a particularly nice gate agent, because typically once you board—that's it.)

I told the man that I had overhead him asking for the upgrade and wondered why he boarded the plane before being upgraded. He told me that he did not fly that often, but his brother-in-law who does told him to try asking for an upgrade on his next flight. "You'd be surprised what you can get just by asking for it," the brother-in-law had said. The passenger, however, told me that he did not think he would be upgraded, which is why he went ahead and boarded. He also expressed his surprise that the gate agent actually came back and took him up to first class. "You know," he said, "from now on I'm flying this airline." As this passenger's experience illustrates, it never hurts to ask, and don't assume you're not going to get what you ask for.

Although it is important to remain within sight and to follow up on your request, do be aware that gate agents are busy. Try not to disrupt their work. Passengers who needlessly consume a gate agent's time or behave rudely will

usually be ignored. Gate agents will appreciate your courtesy and will reward your thoughtfulness with their assistance. They, like all airline employees, can get very stressed
out during their day. They have deadlines to meet, people
complaining, and to top it off they do not have too much
job security. So being kind and courteous is always very
much appreciated.

BEAR IN MIND THAT AN AIRLINE DOES NOT LIKE TO MAKE A PUBLIC DISPLAY WHEN IT UPGRADES PASSENGERS

This could create an unfavorable impression with passengers who do not receive an upgrade. However, when first-
class seats are available prior to departure, airlines will
upgrade those loyal passengers who have developed strong,
mutually beneficial relationships. The costs to the airline
are negligible compared to the goodwill it creates.
Remember what the passenger who was upgraded after
already sitting down in his coach seat said—"From now on,
I'm flying this airline." So when you request upgrades and
ultimately receive them, take care to behave discreetly and
do not flaunt your success.

Understanding how airlines view passengers and play
favorites is what allows a traveler to be upgraded consistently.

ANOTHER TYPE OF UPGRADE

By this point in the book you should be well on your way
to getting upgraded to the premium cabins. And if you're
like me and your batting average gets up to 100%, you
might be asking what's next? One nice benefit I've found,

especially on international flights, is having an empty business class seat next to me. This allows me to stretch out, place my books, headphones, and personal items on the empty seat. What's more, there isn't someone snoring loudly next to me while I'm trying to sleep. My technique for getting an empty seat next to me is to book the bulkhead aisle seat (the bulkhead window seats seems to be the most unpopular seat on the plane), then I approach the gate agent before boarding and ask if the seat next to me is still empty. About 85 percent of the time it is. I then gently remind them that I'm Platinum Medallion/Million Miler and ask if they can keep it open. They usually tell me that they'll do their best, and often it remains open.

Quick Review

- Gate agents wield supreme authority when it comes to handing out first-class seats. Befriend them whenever possible, especially the lead gate agents, and ask them to assist you in building a solid relationship with their airline. Learn their names and find out what hours they work.

- Always be honest and respectful when negotiating with gate agents. If you're not completely up front and respectful of the gate agent's authority, they'll know it—and deny your requests.

- When seeking an upgrade, it pays to be persistent, but do be polite and considerate of the fact that the gate agent is handling passengers other than yourself. And remember, "out of sight, out of mind," so stay within the agent's view. She'll be less likely to forget about you, and you'll be more likely to get the upgrade.

♦ Behave with discretion if you receive an upgrade. The
   airlines do not want to make a public display of upgrading passengers.

GETTING OTHER AIRLINE EMPLOYEES
TO UPGRADE YOU TO FIRST CLASS

Although gate agents are the most important people for you
to know, other airline employees can also give you first-
class seats and preferential service. Essentially, you are
always selling yourself as the right customer, and you
should negotiate with whomever it takes to accomplish
your objective. This could be the reservation agent on the
phone, the counter or ticket agent at the airport (the person
who sells you your ticket and/or checks your baggage), and
even—as a last resort—the flight attendants.

When I first started to fly and my customer history was
not firmly established, I often relied on the flight attendants
to upgrade me.

Keep in mind that this is a delicate procedure. Discretion
and tact are essential. Like gate agents, flight attendants are
busy during boarding and deny requests from rude or
inconsiderate passengers. If you've already boarded the
plane, you'll need to have a compelling and honest reason
to ask for an upgrade. I have requested and received first-
class upgrades from flight attendants because of a bad back,
traumatic event, and excessive traveling in a short period of
time. Legitimate reasons combined with your loyalty as a
customer can be an effective formula for reaching the first-
class cabin. Your objective is to be resourceful yet honest.
Give a compelling reason why you should be upgraded to
first class, but do not make up reasons. Normally it is best

to approach the highest-ranking flight attendant or the friendliest. Like gate agents, flight attendants do not want you to advertise your good fortune when they upgrade you. Although approaching flight attendants is the most difficult method of obtaining an upgrade, it is your last chance, so don't be afraid to ask for what you want.

Did the Grinch Steal Travel?

I have come to think that America's favorite pastime is complaining about airline service—especially service on the network carriers. It amazes me how long we hold on to the misadventures that occur during our travels, yet how quickly we forget the times when a gate agent straightened out a missed connection or a flight attendant went beyond the call of duty to ensure a comfortable flight. Like rubber-neckers at the scene of a grisly accident, travelers become transfixed each time they hear stories of evil airlines treating a customer badly.

Of course, sometimes there are real lapses in service. Just the other week, a reader told me about a trip with five family members to the Big Island of Hawai'i on a network carrier. According to the writer, both the outbound and return flights were utter chaos. Not only did the cabin smell of urine (both times) but his Thanksgiving Day flight also served no meal (he was offered a turkey sandwich, but it would cost him $3).

Worse, the fellow's return flight was canceled, which involved hours waiting at an airport then boarding a bus to an unknown hotel without any guidance from airport agents. When the traveler finally returned home, he found his luggage was damaged; his claim for compensation was denied because the damage involved the handle and another attachment on the bottom of the suitcase.

O.K., this flight deserves criticisms. But is bad service the norm?

Well, maybe. According to the Department of Transportation, complaints about U.S. airlines have jumped more than 29% this year, due mostly to canceled flights and baggage problems. One explanation for this increase is that more people are flying—more than 481 million people this year, a 3% increase over last year.

So I wondered: Is it really the big network carriers that are doing a bad job, or is it all kinds of carriers? According to the DOT's "Air Travel Consumer Report," Southwest Airlines and JetBlue had 0.18 and 0.29 complaints per 100,000 passengers while every network airline except Continental Airlines (0.94) was in triple digits, from Northwest Airlines at 1.00 to US Airways at 1.91.

Convincing evidence? I don't think so. I think we just like to complain.

The disdain for network carriers that is evident in the press and among many people stems from past experiences when travelers felt they were being gouged by airlines with high last-minute fares and excessive fees. To this, I offer a simple observation: Airlines operate in a free and open competitive marketplace. If the market supported such fares in the past, then it was pure economics working—not the evil airlines gouging customers. They charged the prices the market would bear at the time. Thanks to discounters, airlines are now adjusting prices to meet new market conditions.

It also seems that those who complain the most are the ones who fly the least.

That makes sense if you think about it. If you took only one flight this year and it was a bad experience, you'd be more likely to complain than would the traveler flying thirty flights with three bad experiences. In one case, you've got 100% trouble, while in the other, you have a bad experience only 10% of the time. People who have good experiences 90% of the time have a better understanding that travel is not always perfect.

This still leaves one wondering why the complaints are more common with network carriers.

I believe it's all about perception. When flying a network airline, travelers have grander expectations than they do when they fly a budget carrier. When flying Southwest or JetBlue, people adjust their attitudes to lower expectations. Psychologists call this the expectancy value.

I think travelers still expect United Airlines, Delta Air Lines, and American Airlines to give them red-carpet service even while the passengers are paying unprofitable fares. Moreover, when something goes wrong, travelers expect a free first-class ticket anywhere in the world, even if they've paid less than $200 for their flight. I hate to sound unsympathetic, but there is a disconnect here.

The only path to getting better service is through a longstanding relationship of loyalty with an airline. Of course in situations of really terrible service, everyone should be compensated, but for common events, the fact is this: People who get compensated are those who have a vested stake in the company.

Think about it: With limited resources, airlines are most likely to make their best customers whole. As mercenary as it sounds, those who contribute more to the airline's bottom line will get first dibs on goodwill gestures when things go wrong.

From a business perspective, this is sound practice. If you're already giving customers loss-leading prices and you're teetering on the brink of bankruptcy (or are already there), your limited resources have to be used wisely. If you know that one customer has only a 1% likelihood of returning to your business, while another has a 90% likelihood of returning, you are going to take care of the customer with the higher expected rate of return.

Remember the fellow with the truly terrible trip to Hawai'i? He was a loyal customer of the airline—a frequent flyer and a member of the airline's preferred-customer club. In the end he got his due: a personal letter of apology in his mailbox and 20,000 miles in his frequent-flyer account.

Even if you're new to the loyalty game, you can still win with a smile. Last week I was rerouted to an American Airlines flight because of mechanical problems on my regular carrier. Now, I have only flown American Airlines once before, but I noticed that the gate agent working three flights was harried. I told her with a smile that this is only the beginning of her troubles, as Christmas is just around the corner. I then expressed my appreciation for her help. At first she handed me a boarding pass for a middle seat in the back of the plane, but then she glanced at it and said, "That's not a very good seat. Try this one." It was a first-class seat, won through simple sympathy and courtesy.

When it comes to air travel, we like to blame other people when what we really need to do is take responsibility for our own travel experiences. You can do this by managing your expectations, by funneling more of your business to one travel provider, and by extending simple courtesies. Loyalty will give you the leverage you need to guarantee quality service, and a smile will win you friends.

Last year I took my daughter to London for her eighteenth birthday. I booked my customary bulkhead aisle seat knowing that the window seat was going to remain open. I made a deal with Brittany telling her that if I could not get her upgraded to the premium cabin that I would take her coach seat. This put me on the line, and things started getting dicey as we boarded the plane without her upgrade in hand. I made my way to my seat and she to her coach seat, while I was getting settled I introduced myself to the lead flight attendant making small talk. I mentioned that my daughter was back in coach and no sooner than I could get the words out she retorted that I could not bring her up. I told her I knew the rules, but I just wanted her to be aware in case she needed anything. During the pre-departure and first twenty minutes of the flight I built a rapport with the flight attendant and when she came over to take my drink order she asked what seat my daughter was in because she would move her up to the empty seat next to me. The key point I like to make here is that patience and tact are necessary, as flight attendants don't want to feel like you are taking advantage of them. However, when they become your friend, they'll move mountains.

BEATING THE UPGRADE COMPUTER: CLEARING WAIT LISTS FOR FIRST CLASS

In an effort at fairness and to save gate agents from being bombarded with upgrade requests, airlines have automated how flight upgrades clear. This is actually a benefit if you've reached the heights of your loyalty program and know that your place in the queue is high enough to clear each flight—as is the case with me. However, if you're not in this position, don't fret. As I wrote on the first page of this chapter, the upgrade computers base your upgrade position on a few factors which typically includes your level of loyalty, the price of your ticket, and when you purchased your ticket. However, you can fool the computer into giving you a higher upgrade by purchasing a ticket that has a little higher value and doing so as far in advance as reasonable. (You don't want to purchase a ticket too far in advance and risk having to make a change that could end up costing you money.) As already discussed, the difference from one fare category to another might only be $25 to $50 but that extra category can pay off if it means getting the upgrade. The best strategy here is to ask the reservation agent what fare type is most commonly booked on the flight. You might have to dig for this information as many reservation agents won't understand you or won't want to give you the information. However, when you find a willing agent you can ask them if purchasing the next fare level will increase your chances for an upgrade. You can also ask what type of fares those on the waitlist currently hold. Again some agents won't want to provide you with this information but keep trying, as you'll find someone who will. If you come across a difficult agent, tell them that you're just trying to get the best value for yourself and you're willing to spend a little more money which helps them! It keeps them employed.

The key here is to balance the equation in your favor. If you don't have a high level of loyalty you can compensate with price and timing of your ticket purchase. Do keep in mind that the computer is not the all-telling seer of upgrades and all the tips in this book as well as the following do help.

UPGRADE CERTIFICATE

If you have an upgrade certificate or a free award ticket and are told that seats are not available, ask to be placed on a wait list. You can ask to be wait-listed for first class with or without an upgrade certificate in hand.

Whenever you are placed on a wait list, you need to exhibit a considerable amount of persistence and flexibility.

Your foremost objective when you are on a wait list is to be cleared from the wait list and receive whatever benefit you are seeking. Keep checking on your status. Prior to your day of departure, call the airline and ask how it looks for clearing the wait list, especially if you are waiting to confirm a free ticket.

I have been very successful in getting reservation agents to clear my wait-list status when I call back and ask for their assistance. If my flight is full and it doesn't look favorable for me to clear the wait list, often the reservation agent can recommend an alternate flight or routing that can be confirmed in first class. Using ExpertFlyer is also handy when you're on a waitlist because you can check the status of upgrades on their site and call the airline as soon as an upgrade opens up.

Often when I travel with a family member, they fly using one of my free award tickets or a free first-class upgrade certificate. When I make the reservation, I am frequently told that there are no more free first-class seats available in inventory. However, by calling back a few times, I finally get an agent who is willing to make a concession and open up seats for my family members. Airline agents have a wide variance in the rules they can override. Therefore it pays to call back and find the agents who are most receptive to your needs.

If you are persistent on the telephone, you will usually clear wait lists before you arrive at the airport. However, if you have not cleared wait-list status prior to your arrival, arrive at the airport early and again, talk to whoever can assist you. Try to get the ticket counter agent to clear your wait-list status.

If the ticket counter agent is unable to clear you, make a second request in the private first-class lounge. If you are still on a wait list, make sure you inform the lead gate agent and ask if he or she will clear you. With a little persistence, you will usually find that being on a wait list is not a hindrance.

If you arrive at the airport without being on a wait list, be friendly and engage the ticket agent in light conversation while you are checking in at the ticket counter. Try asking the agent some friendly, open-ended questions. For example, you might ask:

"How does the flight look today?"

"Is this flight very full?"

"How does the first-class cabin look?"

"What do my chances look like for being upgraded?"

"How do you recommend that I get upgraded?"

Then ask directly to be upgraded. They may say yes; they may not. If they say they can't upgrade you, be sure to say, "Would you put me on a wait list for first class in case I get lucky?"

Once you're wait-listed for first class, introduce yourself to the next agent (either in the private lounge or at the gate). Be friendly and make small talk if they're not too busy. Say to the agent, "I'm on the wait list for first class. Could you tell me how it looks? Do you think you can clear me?" If he cannot, tell him that you will wait patiently to see if the situation changes. Make sure to stay within his view while you're waiting.

LEVERAGING YOUR ELITE STATUS

I often board planes that have three classes of service: coach, business class, and first class. Because of my Platinum Medallion elite status with Delta, I automatically receive a one-class upgrade to business class when I book a flight that has three classes of service. Business class is more desirable than coach, but I want to be in first class at all times. Here's how I get a first-class seat on these particular flights.

When I arrive at the airport for a flight with three classes of service, I ask the counter agent to upgrade me. Usually this is enough to accomplish my goal. When it is not, I ask the counter agent to put me on the wait list for first class. Then I go to Delta's private lounge. I explain to the agent assigned to the lounge that I am wait-listed for first class and ask her to help me obtain the first-class seat. This almost always works. If it doesn't, I proceed to the lead gate agent in charge of the flight and inquire into my wait-list status. This is an effective tactic, because the lead gate agent will look up my customer history on the computer and see that I have established a mutually beneficial relationship and how loyal a customer I have been. Usually the lead gate agent clears me at that time.

LEVERAGE YOUR ELITE STATUS WITH OTHER AIRLINES
AS WELL AS YOUR OWN

On one of my trips, Delta had a cancellation and re-ticket-ed me on an American Airlines flight. I went to the American ticket counter and told the ticket agent that this was my first time flying on American Airlines, since I have always flown Delta in the past. I also mentioned to the agent that I had achieved an elite level with Delta. Eager for the chance to court my loyalty to American, the ticket agent upgraded my entire routing to first class and gave me two complimentary passes to their first-class lounge. When I checked into the lounge I made sure that the receptionist saw my elite-level Delta flight tags. As a result, she went out of her way to be courteous. She told me how I could get a complimentary one-year member-ship in their lounge. When dealing with another airline you will need to let them know that you have elite status with a competing airline. I usually do this by letting them see my luggage tags or I simply tell them. Incidentally, when I asked Delta to credit my frequent-flyer account for the qualifying miles I would have received if the Delta flight had not been cancelled, they were more than happy to honor my request.

FLYING FIRST CLASS WITH YOUR FAMILY

When traveling with your family, it is a good idea to try to reserve as many seats in first class as possible. On occasion you will only be able to reserve a few seats in first class prior to your flight. If you have at least one or two of your party already confirmed in first class, you can use this as leverage to secure additional seats there. You can tell an airline phone representative, counter agent, gate agent, or club room representative that you are traveling with your family and have already reserved a few seats in first class but would like the entire family to sit together. Usually these airline personnel will upgrade the rest of your family members to first class, as was the case with my daughter on our flight to London.

QUICK REVIEW

◆ When seeking preferential treatment, negotiate with whomever it takes to accomplish your objective. This could be the phone reservation agent, the airport ticket counter agent, the gate agent, and the private first-class lounge agent.

◆ If you are wait-listed for an upgrade to first class (with or without an upgrade certificate) or for a seat on a flight using a free ticket, keep calling the airline prior to the date of departure to check on your status. If you are still wait-listed on your departure date, enlist the aid of ticket agents, gate agents, and first-class lounge agents.

◆ If you have elite frequent-flyer status, be sure to leverage that status to obtain two-class upgrades instead of just the automatic one-class upgrade, as well as to obtain other forms of preferential treatment.

◆ When you are flying first class with your family, do not be discouraged if you cannot confirm all first-class upgrades in advance. Use the existing first-class reservations, as well as your loyalty, as leverage to obtain the remaining confirmed upgrades.

How the Contrarian Traveler Reaps Luxury
and Lower Prices

One of the main contrarian principles is flexibility. When you are willing to be flexible, not only do you increase your chances of getting upgraded, you are also more likely to enjoy lower airfares.

Many airlines offer discounted fares for a Saturday night stay. However, what they do not tell you is that you do not have to actually sleep in your destination city on Saturday night. When I need to travel for a Monday morning meeting, I depart on a late Saturday evening flight, arriving early Sunday morning. Not only does this flexibility give me a lower discounted Saturday night fare, it allows me to spend Saturday at home, and on Sunday I get to enjoy the city to which I've traveled. In addition, I save the cost of a hotel for Saturday night. Usually, if you call in advance, most hotels will allow you to check in early on Sunday morning.

Most important, it is usually easier to get a first-class seat when you travel overnight. Since many airlines use capacity controls on free tickets and certain upgrades, it is imperative that you maintain a level of flexibility in order to receive preferential treatment.

Pro and Cons of Code-Share Agreements

Being flexible also means making use of your airline's code-share agreements. If you make a reservation and are told that your airline's flight cannot accommodate you with an upgrade, ask the reservation agent if an upgrade can be made available on a code-share flight. This usually works, although for some reason reservation agents seldom investigate this option unless you ask for it.

Recently Delta Airlines entered into a code-share agreement with Northwest and Continental Airlines. Many pundits see this as a bad thing. I say look at the positives. I now have three times as many flight opportunities, more flights to select from, and the ability to earn more elite-qualifying miles.

Beware that some airlines will not allow you to use your elite membership credentials, upgrade certificates, or mileage points to upgrade with a code-share partner. I regularly receive e-mails from many travelers asking how they can upgrade with a code-share partner after they've purchased a ticket. As stated, you typically cannot do so. In this case you might redeem your points for a first-class ticket or try to stay with your preferred airline. During a recent media tour I had flights crisscrossing the United States. On one route I needed to take a flight that Delta did not offer, therefore I opted to fly Continental. To snag a first-class seat I combined my routing with my Delta flights but used a fare code for a discounted first-class seat that was about $65 more than a coach seat. The benefit: I had a confirmed first-class seat and also received the bonus qualifying miles. This was a unique situation and in most instances I advise going with your chosen airline as it is easier to upgrade, but for those occasion such as the above, keep in mind that the code share agreements provide an extra layer of benefits and fast track toward building loyalty with your preferred airline.

PERSISTENCE AND FLEXIBILITY ALWAYS PAY OFF

The smart traveler knows that persistence always works best when coupled with flexibility. For example, if you are trying to confirm seats in first class and come across an airline representative who is less than helpful, simply end the call politely and call back. I was traveling through Atlanta recently and wanted to return home to Orange County, California on an earlier flight. The first airline representative I spoke to on the phone completely shut me out and insisted that there were absolutely no first-class seats available on any flights that day. Undeterred, I hung up and called right back, and sure enough, the next representative confirmed first-class seats for me on an earlier flight. This is one reason it's often better to make your own travel arrangements rather than go through a travel agent, and this will be covered in more detail in a later chapter.

The earlier flight I took also flew a route that was different from the one I usually travel: it flew from Atlanta to Salt Lake City to Orange County instead of through Dallas. However, this new flight was just as convenient as our previously booked flight and allowed me to return home earlier. This is also why it is important to be flexible. You are more likely to get those discounted first-class seats.

Getting the Best Seat on the Plane

Having the seat I want is important to me when I fly. It ranks right up there with getting my first-class upgrade. Many travelers leave their seat assignment to chance. That just makes no sense to me. Flying is, after all, mostly sitting. You might as well be comfortable.

Is there a best seat in the house? Not really. There are good seats for different purposes, so people have different preferences. I prefer a bulkhead aisle seat, usually 1B or 1C. This puts me near the bulkhead galley. I get served first, and I'm usually the first off the plane. This works for me—so well, in fact, that when I sit somewhere else, I feel out of place.

Other people swear by window seats, which are good for sightseeing and sleeping (the window provides a nice place to rest your head, especially if you've snagged a pillow). Veteran window-sitters take careful note of the flight plan, deciding which side of the plane to sit on according to where the sun will be. Aisle seats have different considerations. They let you stretch your legs once in a while without disturbing your seatmates, but you risk getting bonked by other people's elbows and carry-ons.

Front or back? There are advantages to both. On most flights, passengers in the back rows board first, so they get first grabs at overhead bin space. On the downside, there's usually a long wait to get off the plane, food choices can be limited by the time the cart gets to you, and the line for the lavatory can be distracting and noisy. Front-seat passengers usually deplane first, but not always: Some short-haul commuter flights (such as Delta's shuttles between New York, Washington, and Boston) use both ends of the plane for deplaning, so you can make a quick escape front or back.

There are other, more particular considerations. For example, bulkhead seats are a good choice for kids who tend to be climbers and kickers, and seats near the emergency exits really must go to competent adults who will take the time to figure out how to use them. And every would-be Lothario knows that the back of the plane is where the flight attendants hang out.

How to get what you want? What most people don't realize is that seat inventories are in constant flux. Ticket cancellations and upgrades affect seat availability. So does airline policy; airlines can reserve or release a portion of their inventory to meet their own needs. The key to getting the seat you want is vigilance and persistence.

To check on seat availability, you can call your airline or your travel agent, or you can use your airline's online seat locator (a map of the plane that shows not only how the seats are laid out, but also which seats are taken and which are still available). Most airlines allow you to use the seat locator to choose or change your seat directly online.

You don't have to buy a ticket to see what's available. When I am waitlisted for an upgrade on a flight I've already booked, I go onto my airline's web site and make a second, mock booking for a first-class seat. I don't actually reserve or confirm the seat, but during the booking process, I am given the opportunity to select a seat. That's my eye into the first-class inventory. If I see that half the seats are still available a week before my departure date, I know I have a good chance for an upgrade. Having taken a peek, I just log off. Of course, you can use the seat locator in the same way to decide which flight to book in the first place.

Don't despair if you can't get the seat you want in advance. Just bring your determination to the airport. Talk to the ticket agent or, better yet, the gate agent in charge of your flight. If all else fails, you can try to trade seats with another passenger after you've boarded the plane. People generally make room for gimpy passengers and families who've been split up. And, believe it or not, some people really don't care where they sit.

Get a guru. If you have yet to heed my oft-repeated advice to put all your air travel with one airline, or if you're just not familiar with the design of your next aircraft, check out SeatGuru.com. This handy web site offers cabin maps and seat plans for all the aircraft used by most major carriers, providing useful information about seat width and pitch. It also has the inside scoop on such things as which seats have extra legroom, misaligned or partial windows, restricted reclining, tray tables in the armrests—even which seats are especially noisy or cold. SeatGuru also tells you about the availability of in-seat entertainment options like satellite TV and MP3 players. It's a really good site all around.

From the front of the plane to the back, airplane seats are not all the same. Know which one you want, go after it with persistence, then just fasten your seat belt and have a nice flight.

Here is a list of some basic rules to follow when traveling by air:

- Before you pick up the phone to call your airline, ask yourself just how flexible you are willing to be:
  - Are you concerned primarily with price, fast routing, or an upgrade?
  - Are you prepared to change planes to earn more frequent flyer miles and perhaps increase your chances of an upgrade?

- Are you willing to pay a small premium on your ticket price for extra frequent-flyer miles and/or an upgrade?

- Did you remember to check out the airline's web site beforehand to acquaint yourself with any special fare offerings?

- When making your reservations, ask the following questions:

  - Are there any other flights that I can take that will give me a better fare?

  - Would I save any money flying on a different day?

- If you know the airline has a special fare or a bonus program, but the reservation agent says it doesn't exist, insist he or she check it out further, or ask for a supervisor.

- Ask "what if" scenarios. For example, "What if I took this flight into this city and changed planes to get to my destination? Would I have a better chance at an upgrade? A better fare?"

- Take time to learn the most advantageous times and routes to travel, and to know which cities have the most accommodating gate agents.

- Be flexible, choosing a flight with a low passenger load, and you will be more likely to get an upgrade. Tuesday, Wednesday, Thursday morning, and Saturdays are the best times to travel first class at coach prices, as you will be avoiding the business travel crowd. Late Friday night can also be a good time to fly.

◆   Try to avoid stopovers in major hub cities. You are less likely to be able to use free tickets and get upgrades on heavily traveled routes.

◆   If you've experienced less than accommodating airline personnel in a particular city, try re-routing your flight to avoid that city.

◆   If you need to travel for a Monday morning meeting, you can take a Saturday night red-eye flight and still get the airline's low Saturday overnight stay fare. Also, it is usually easier to get a first-class seat when you travel overnight.

◆   If your airline does not have an upgraded seat available for you, ask the reservation agent if it's possible to book you on a code-share flight that does.

◆   Writing a complimentary letter is an excellent way for you to show your appreciation for an airline employee's exemplary service—and reap first-class rewards for yourself.

When you offer to write letters praising airline representatives for their efforts, be sure not to give them the impression that you will specifically write that they upgraded you; this is not what they want in their employee files.

Most airlines prohibit employees from accepting monetary compensation from passengers, so your letter substitutes for tipping. Whenever a customer writes about an airline employee, the letter is documented in the employee's personnel file. Many airlines base merit increases and promotions on comments received from customers. Recently some airlines have allowed flight crews to receive tips for bringing drinks and offering excellent onboard service. The rules are still unclear and it is best to ask those you wish to reward what guidelines the airlines have. Alternatively you can call the corporate headquarters of your airline before a flight to inquire what their policies are regarding tips.

I will usually ask the employee for the name of his or her immediate supervisor. That way I can send a copy of the letter to the supervisor as well as to the corporate personnel office. This ensures that the employee receives a copy of the letter. The next time I see that employee, I ask if he or she received a copy of the letter I sent. This leaves an indelible impression of my goodwill, which the employee readily reciprocates.

Lastly, keep in mind that letters work both ways. If you receive poor service from an employee, warn them that you will write a letter of complaint. If the employee fails to rectify the situation, make sure to follow through and write the letter. When onboard an airplane keep in mind that you are at a disadvantage and, as stated, if you are perceived as disrupting the flight you might find yourself facing legal problems. I found that it is best to keep things in perspective.

One morning I was returning home to Orange County after a trip to Iceland where I picked up a nasty bug and both felt and looked horrible. In fact I believe that this experience was a lesson in how dressing the part plays a role in the service you receive. Although I was in first class I was in a disheveled state, my hair was a mess, I was unshaven, wearing jeans and a sweatshirt while most other passengers were in business attire. During the entire flight I sat quietly with a frequent cough—I did not eat, drink, or do anything, basically I was a church mouse—a dog-sick one. When the flight headed into the final approach phase a flight attendant ask me to put my bag in the overhead bin. I told her that I was too weak and asked if she could help. She replied in the nastiest manner telling me to get up and do it now! When the plane landed I told the flight attendant how inconsiderate I thought she was. Again she tore into me, blaming me for everything that is wrong with the world. When I asked for her name she refused. Thinking that her anger was not worth the time it would take to complain I left it alone. A few weeks later I was discussing the incident with my gate agent friend who told me that the flight attendant who had berated me was fired for her abusive behavior toward passengers.

On another occasion, flying across the Atlantic, I had slept during the first half of the flight. When I awoke, the movies were finished and I asked one flight attendant when the movies would begin again. This flight attendant apparently thought that it was none of my business and told me that the lead flight attendant was in the coach cabin doing paperwork and would get to it when she could. I said, "So paperwork is more important than the movies?" "Yes," she said. As it turns out, the lead flight attendant was helping the crew pass out ice cream—a nice thing to do. When I saw the lead attendant in the first-class cabin I started to approach her to tell her that I would like to speak to her when she had time. The other attendant saw me approaching her and rudely said, "She's resetting the movies now—go sit down," all of which the lead attendant saw and heard. Later on I spoke with the lead flight attendant who apologized vigorously. About two weeks later I received a call from Delta's corporate headquarters telling me that they had investigated the incident and that disciplinary action was taken. This was all prompted without me making a formal complaint. I guess this goes to show that karma does exist.

Key Points

➤ *Reach your first-class goal with minimal effort, even if you're just starting out.*
Ask for what you want, express your current and intended future loyalty, fly first class as often as possible using upgrade certificates, invest in a first-class private lounge membership, and take advantage of getting upgraded when you hold a full coach fare.

➤ *Make the gate agent your best friend.*
Get to know your gate agents, especially those at your home airport. They have the most power to upgrade you from the lowest-priced coach ticket to a prime first-class seat.

➤ *Ask and you shall receive, when seeking upgrades or other special concessions.*
Be creative in enlisting the aid of anyone who can help you. Reservation agents, ticket agents, gate agents, first-class lounge agents, and even flight attendants can upgrade you and grant your requests.

➤ *Use the Contrarian Approach to achieve first class by traveling against the grain.*
You are more likely to get upgraded if you travel less busy routes and at off-peak times. Be flexible enough to schedule your travels accordingly, and you will not only have a better chance of traveling first class, you will also be able to secure a lower airfare.

➤ *Write an appreciative letter to your airline whenever you receive preferential treatment.*

Let employees know of your willingness to write a complimentary letter about how well they do their jobs. This is a powerful motivation for them to grant your special requests.

FIT FOR A KING

Sleeping at Five-Star Hotels at a Fraction of the Cost

Once you arrive at your destination, having enjoyed incomparable comforts as a first-class air passenger, there is no need to start compromising now by settling for a less than luxurious hotel room. In fact over the years I have come to believe that if you need to focus on one aspect of your trip to turn it into a memorable event, it is with hotels. More than ever hotels play a role in making your trip a dream come true or something you'd rather soon forget.

For many, air travel has become a means to an end, and despite the handy tips in the previous chapter you might still experience some of the discomforts of air travel but when you stay at the right hotel all will be forgotten. I still have fond memories of past hotel visits, with one of my favorites being on a trip I took in the fall of 2000 to Zurich, Switzerland. I stayed at the Baur au Lac Hotel, which is located in a private park on the lake on Zurich's fashionable Bahnhofstrasse, home to famous stores and cultural attractions. Following one of the suggestions I offer in this chapter, I contacted the manager of the property in advance and informed him of my impending arrival. During our conversation, I asked if the hotel had car service from the airport. As a result of this question, the hotel provided me with a complimentary ride from the airport to the hotel.

When I arrived at the airport, I expected some sort of van or perhaps a town car to be waiting for me. After I cleared customs, I saw a well-dressed gentleman holding a small sign bearing my name. He cordially introduced himself and assisted me with my luggage. We then proceeded toward an area where service cars were parked. When the driver opened the door to a brand new Rolls Royce, I could hardly believe it. Inside the car were chilled bottles of Evian and an assortment of treats, including some fine chocolates. I figured this had to be some sort of mistake, because even in my longtime experience as a luxury traveler, I had never received such royal treatment.

When we arrived at the hotel, another well-dressed gentleman escorted me to a private table and asked if I would like some tea as I awaited my room details. While I sipped my tea, a young Swiss woman handled the check-in process. At this point I was almost too embarrassed to ask if I was being charged for the airport transport; however, when I did she said, "Certainly not, this is a service we offer to our fine customers."

I was then escorted to an enchanting room with a bath area that was almost the size of my master bedroom at home. In addition, my room had a terrace overlooking a canal that led from Lake Zurich, which was also visible from the terrace.

Why did I receive such superior service? There were two main reasons. First, before my trip I enrolled in a complimentary membership program offered by The Leading

Hotels of the World (LHW) (www.lhw.com), a collection of luxurious hotels, one of which is the Hotel Baur au Lac. I had been a guest at many of the LHW in the past, and I mentioned that fact when I made my reservations. I was also flexible in terms of my plans. I called the hotel directly and asked when their slow period was. In keeping with the contrarian traveler's principle of "profit when they are not," I booked my reservation for that time period.

YOU NEED NOT BE WEALTHY TO ENJOY THE FINEST HOTELS IN THE WORLD

Right now the best opportunity for finding luxury travel bargains is within hotel brands such as the Hyatt, Hilton, or Starwood Group, where you can leverage your loyalty into luxurious nights. As mentioned earlier, some of the best values for your loyalty points are with hotels stays. For a trip to the island of Kauai I booked a regular room at the Grand Hyatt Kauai Resort and used a paltry 6,000 points to upgrade my four-night stay to a suite. Upon arriving at the hotel I found myself in the 2,700-square-foot presidential suite with a magnificent ocean view, a room that at time of this writing sells for over $3,000 a night. This was a good deal indeed, as I earned over 35,000 points for that one visit and paid about a tenth of what the room normally would have cost.

The hidden value in most hotel loyalty programs is that their brands span from ultra luxury to the conservative. For example, the Hyatt group of hotels ranges from the ultra posh Park brand to the affordable Hyatt Summerfield Suites with many in-between. Likewise the Hilton, Starwood, and Marriot brands all offer diverse properties in a selection of price ranges. When I'm traveling on a quick business trip and know that I will be in and out of the hotel without requiring much, I find the lower-level brands to be an affordable means of building loyalty and points that I can then later use at ultra-deluxe properties. This is similar to airline code-share agreements, but here the points are readily transferable to any brand within the company's group of hotels.

Unlike the airlines, it is difficult for hotels to reduce their capacity. An airline can reduce routes and retire planes, thus decreasing the number of available seats. A hotel, however, is not going to shut down when it has only 20% occupancy. Instead, it is going to go out of its way to attract more business and to satisfy the guests who do check in. That means more chances at luxury rooms for the penny-pinching luxury traveler.

If you think negotiating a beautiful room at a luxury hotel is not worth the effort, I hope that by the time you finish this chapter you will have reconsidered!

Get the Service You Deserve

The world is not wanting for world-class museums, historical churches, or breathtaking views. Nor is it lacking in companies providing planes, trains, or automobiles. What the discerning traveler does *not* find often enough are travel providers offering high-quality service.

To my mind, travel *is* service. Wherever I travel, the quality of service I receive is what makes a trip memorable or a disaster. Price is not the issue. I believe service should be excellent whether you are staying at an ultra-deluxe Four Seasons Hotel or a value-orientated Hilton Garden Inn. In fact, I have stayed at the crème de la crème of hotels whose service was terrible and at value hotels whose service far exceeded expectations.

It is important to differentiate between true service-oriented travel providers and those whose commitment to service is only a facade. Let me use a few examples from recent hotel visits to demonstrate my point. With the exception of the hotel in Vietnam, none of the hoteliers knew I was a travel writer. Ironically, the Vietnam hotel is my example of poor service.

The Hôtel de Paris in Monte Carlo is one of the pre-eminent hotels in the world, and my first visit there, in 2001, was an exceptional experience that has probably spoiled me. On a recent visit, however, a few hiccups occurred. Nothing serious, but a collection of small things like having to call twice to have my cell phone brought up from my car, and having to make more than one call to get ice and an international adaptor brought to my room. All in all, not a big deal. But when I checked out and mentioned that the service was not as great as it had been on my previous trip, the front-desk clerk notified the general manager, who came to the desk, personally apologized and then took care of my bill. (Now this was way beyond the call of duty, as my daily rate was 520 euros per night!)

On another occasion, I was checking into the Hotel Palace in Barcelona when my colleague noticed that the rate was 15 euros higher than what he thought we had been quoted and that breakfast was not included in the rate as he had expected. As it turns out, my colleague was wrong on both counts, but come Monday morning, the

manager approached us during breakfast to say that he had
adjusted the rate and that breakfast would be included
after all.

Now the Vietnam story. This one is instructive because
it illustrates what I've found to be a common combination:
gorgeous view, lousy service. When I was in Vietnam in
October, I had the opportunity to visit Evason Hideaway
& Six Senses Spa at Ana Mandara, a resort located on its
own island—arguably one of the most picturesque settings
in the world. But I found the staff to be unwelcoming, for-
getful, slow, and indifferent to its guests. (I got not so
much as an apology when the gift-shop clerk gave my purchases to another guest.) Of course, service often takes its
cue from leadership, and this resort is run by an arrogant
general manager who (among other things) failed to
return phone calls when I inquired about a pair of shoes I
had left in my room; he later answered my complaint that
it had cost me $40 in phone charges to reach him with an
abrupt "I can't do anything about that."

Don't get me wrong. Quality service doesn't mean you get
a refund every time you have a bad experience. This past
summer, I visited The Four Seasons Hotel Gresham Palace
Budapest. I must have had a bad flight, because I got all
upset over something silly like having to wait for a minute
before the front desk picked up the phone. When I complained (and I had no right to), the hotel manager personally apologized and gave me his direct number should I need
anything else from the hotel. Here I was whining, and yet
the hotel showed me respect and demonstrated care for my
experience. This hotel manager made his guest whole.

The Park Hyatt in Washington, D.C. takes an equally
respectful and proactive approach toward customer service,

placing complimentary bottles of Voss water in every guest room. Many hotels offer bottles of water, of course, but they typically come with a tag saying you can enjoy the water for a $15 extra charge! The Park Hyatt also offers two empty slots in the mini-bar for your own beverages. Nice touch. Another nice touch: When I called the operator to get the room service department, he did not transfer the call but instead promptly took my order himself.

Commitment to service is also expressed as a willingness to listen to the customer and change business practice. During a recent trip to Ethiopia, Green Land Tours led me through the many wonders of northern Ethiopia. On the last day of my trip, I spoke to the owner of this tour company and told him that his buses were not up to par and that I couldn't recommend the company to other travelers because of it. Well, between the language barrier and my boorish attitude, we had a clashing of Titans (mind you, the buses weren't *awful*; I'm just a tough critic). Later that evening we cleared up our misunderstanding, as Dario, the owner, explained to me the difficulty of obtaining financing for tour buses and how they can cost more than $60,000. I apologized for my ignorance—and arrogance—and we made friends. The very next day, Dario sent an e-mail saying that despite the large investment, his company was expanding its bus fleet to better serve its customers. Hearing the customers and acting on their feedback is the highest proof that a company cares about you.

Finding hotels with good service can be tricky. You can't rely on the ratings of peer-to-peer sites such as TripAdvisor, especially if you have high standards for service. Instead, I recommend that you call the hotel yourself and get an idea of how they treat their guests by asking questions about the property. You might also ask how long the manager has been there. A new manager does not necessarily signify trouble, but if someone new is on board, you might ask what happened to the last manager. Finally, go with well established hotel groups. The Hiltons and Four Seasons of the hotel world work hard to keep their brands up.

Travel is service. When you come across a travel provider that offers value and quality service, you are certainly in for a good ride.

THE IMPORTANCE OF HAVING YOUR OWN OASIS

An upscale hotel is an oasis away from the bustling streets. It provides you with much-needed pampering after a long day of business meetings, sightseeing, or shopping. Having traveled throughout the world, I have spent the night in all sorts of hotel beds. And let me tell you, there is no substitute for a spacious, elegant, and quiet room with a spectacular view and a comfortable bed with ultra-soft pillows and a fluffy down comforter. When speaking with travelers, I often hear them say, "The type of hotel you stay in doesn't really matter, since you're hardly there," or "it is only a place to sleep." I then ask them to look back at their last few trips and think about how much time they really did spend at the hotel, and what they did while they were there. Usually they say waking up in the morning, getting ready for the day, eating breakfast, returning in the middle of the day to take a break from sightseeing, to have a business meeting, or to take a nap, and they usually say they are in the hotel room at night. I think that many people do not really take into account the benefits and added value of a luxury hotel, and how it truly can enhance an entire trip.

The hotel you choose will have a crucial impact on the psychology of your trip. Having a nice doorman acknowledge you each time you enter or leave the hotel and a pleasant staff that greets you by name are just a couple of the small but significant differences that can make you feel special and add satisfaction to your trip. A fine hotel will give your journey an overall feeling of luxury, because your hotel is the number-one place to experience quiet indulgence and VIP treatment.

THE VALUE OF PAYING A LITTLE MORE FOR LUXURY

There is an old adage that is resoundingly accurate when traveling—you get what you pay for. That is what I experienced in August 2000, when I traveled to Vienna in a vain attempt to learn German. I had signed up for a four-week program of morning classes, leaving my afternoons free to explore that magnificent city. I knew from experience that the hotel where I stayed would have a significant impact on my trip, so I booked a reservation for three days at the Hotel Bristol, which is part of the luxurious Starwood collection of hotels, a group with which I have built a mutually beneficial relationship over the years. This way I would spend my first few days in the city at a luxury hotel where I would continue to build my loyalty and initially get a good rate. I figured that I would be able to seek out other options once I was in Vienna if the Hotel Bristol proved to be too expensive for such an extensive stay.

During my first three days in the city I did check out other housing options, the worst of which was a deal through the language school at an inexpensive, dormitory-like accommodation in a geographically undesirable part of Vienna. I was already being spoiled by the luxurious service and central location of the Bristol, which had turned out to be one of the best hotels in Vienna, so I was reluctant to go elsewhere. I sought out the manager and explained my situation.

Not only did he offer me a fair deal for a suite overlooking Vienna's famed opera house, but he also provided me access to the hotel's private lounge, where I was able to get coffee and pastries each morning. The hotel also had an arrangement with a good gym, so I was able to maintain my exercise program as well. I did pay a small premium to stay at such a fine hotel versus what I would have paid for student housing, but after taking a look at the big picture, I decided that the value for what I received outweighed the minor additional cost of about 15%, which included my breakfast and access to the gym. The hotel was even more affordable because at that time the dollar was strong against the euro.

QUICK TIP

- If you are traveling to a city that you are not familiar with, it can be a good idea to book your first night in a well-known hotel. Not only will this offer you security while you get to know the city, but it will also give you a chance to look at other hotels and see what kind of bargain you can create for yourself.

Over the years I have gotten to know the travel industry quite well. Besides a first-class sleeper seat on a transoceanic flight, my favorite part of traveling is getting a great upgrade at a great price at a luxury hotel. It's easier than you might think.

My proven, five-step method for getting the best rate for an upgraded room at the most luxurious hotels:

1. Make the Most of Frequent Guest Programs
2. Research Your Way into Luxury
3. Call Directly, and Don't Forget Your Contrarian Strategy
4. Seek Added Value for Your Hotel Stay
5. Maintain the Value Principle

STEP 1. MAKE THE MOST OF FREQUENT GUEST PROGRAMS

What makes it possible to enjoy a luxurious five-star hotel while paying discounted prices? The simple answer is the competitive nature of the hotel industry. Like most other kinds of travel companies, the hotel industry is a highly competitive business that is vulnerable to certain economic cycles. To get through tough economic times and to build up a loyal customer base, the hotel industry has designed frequent-guest programs that are similar to the airlines' frequent-flyer programs.

Most of the major hotel chains, including Hilton, Starwood Hotel Group, Hyatt Hotels, and Marriott Hotels, offer frequent-guest programs. And although some of the very upscale hoteliers such as The Leading Hotels of the World and the Four Seasons do not actively promote a frequent-guest program, they do track their guests' customer histories and make special accommodations and upgrades available to their most loyal guests.

Here is how customer loyalty can enable you to secure the best rooms in the most luxurious hotels at a discount price. During my frequent trips to New York, I've found one hotel to meet my needs at a reasonable price (not an easy task in New York). I stay at the Grand Hyatt New York, which is admittedly not The Plaza or St. Regis, but it is conveniently located and since I am a frequency member of Hyatt's loyalty program and have gotten to know a number of the staff members at the hotel I tend to get great value. I am always upgraded to their Regency level that serves breakfast and offers water, juice, coffee, and snacks throughout the day. This is a big cost savings as breakfast alone in the city can cut into anyone's budget. Further, I often get a suite with a wonderful view of the city that makes my stay even nicer.

Like the airline frequent-flyer programs, the hotel industry's frequent-guest programs provide the average traveler with an entrée to a world of benefits. However, you will need to follow a strategy that is somewhat different from the strategy outlined for the airline frequent-flyer programs. Rather than stick to one particular hotel chain, you should join a few select frequent-guest programs and remain loyal to those few programs. The main reason for this is flexibility. Enrolling in the frequent-guest programs of a select few hotels will provide you with the flexibility you need to ensure first-class hotel accommodations every time.

Unlike the major competing air carriers, who tend to offer similar services and rates, hotels are not always so consistent. When you travel on your chosen airline there is only one choice you need to make, flying first class. But when it's time to select a hotel, you are faced with a multitude of options.

These options vary from low-priced, low-service hotels to luxurious, full-service resorts—with an array of choices in between. To add to the confusion, hotels offer a rate structure more challenging to understand than the airlines' rate structure.

Recently, a few hotel chains have consolidated and now offer different brand names under one group, much like the airlines' practice of code-share agreements or alliances with other airlines. This is a beneficial change, in that it allows you to build mutually beneficial relationships with a broad range of hotels and have more geographical coverage while maintaining a higher level of loyalty to that group brand during your travels.

Like Air Miles, Not All Hotel Points are Rewarded Equally

As mentioned earlier in this book, some hotels are beginning to deny loyalty program points and other benefits to guests who book their hotel stays through discount, third-party travel web sites. For example, effective August 1, 2003, Hilton HHonors members will not receive HHonors points, airline miles, or have their stay credited toward tier (elite) status for stays booked through third-party online sites. To ensure you receive your HHonors benefits when you book online, make your reservation through the Hilton's 800-number or on their web site, www.Hilton.com.

Make sure you stay current on the rules and restrictions for any hotel loyalty program you join. These rules are always subject to change. Be sure to check the hotel's web site before you make your booking.

HOTEL POINTS CAN TRANSLATE TO AIRLINE POINTS

Many hotel frequent-guest programs are aligned with airline frequent-flyer programs, which gives you the option of transferring accumulated hotel points into those programs. In past editions of this book I advised that it was worthwhile to transfer hotel points into airlines miles. That is no longer the case. These days I find it advantageous to keep your points in your hotel program to maximize your awards. This is how I was able to get the presidential suite at the Hyatt in Kauai.

YOUR LOYALTY CAN PAY OFF IN OTHER WAYS AS WELL

As mentioned above, hotels track their guests' customer history. Hotels do this tracking to ascertain which guests bring them the most value. The finest hotels will also typically track their guests' travel habits, special needs or requests, likes and dislikes, and personal preferences. This information allows the hotel to personalize the guests' hotel experience and encourage them to keep coming back.

If you are establishing a loyal history with quality hotel groups, be sure to make your preferences known. In the finer hotels, you only have to state your preferences once. If you tell the hotel you are allergic to down pillows, you should expect that on your next stay you won't have to make that call to housekeeping again. Or if you tell the hotel's spa director, as I did, that you prefer a quiet massage, you can be sure that on your next visit you won't be given a spa appointment with the most talkative massage therapist on staff.

STEP 2. RESEARCH YOUR WAY INTO LUXURY

One technique that hotels have used in the past years is a yield management program that adjusts rates in line with occupancy and anticipated demand, similar to what the airlines have been doing for years. Since the hotel industry has a unique pricing structure and methodology in determining room type, it is very important to do your homework.

HOTEL DIRECTORIES

The best way to research your hotel is to use the internet. You can also refer to sites such as TripAdvisor.com to read past guest reviews, but as the sidebar articles demonstrate, take the reviews with a grain of salt.

Travelers' Hotel Reviews: Are They Helpful?

The internet has certainly been a boon to travelers, especially those looking for a place to stay. Countless web sites offer hotel searches and price comparisons, and many also offer pictures of hotels, online reservations, package deals, and even travelers' reviews. The pictures usually tell an unbiased tale, but you need to exercise caution when you read those reviews. They are often biased, sometimes out of date, and may not serve your interests at all.

First, there's the question of taste and priorities. How do I know that the reviewer and I want the same things from a hotel? Perhaps the reviewer wants a pool and a sports bar, while what I want is timely room service.

Then there's the problem of the reviewer's motivation. The more reviews you read, the more you notice how they tend to cluster at the extremes of opinion. On one end, you have angry reviewers with axes to grind; at the other, you have delighted guests who lavish praise beyond believing. You will probably not be surprised to learn that hotels sometimes post their own glowing reviews, or that competitors line up for the chance to lambaste the competition. So, how can you know which reviews are authentic, or whether one traveler's experience is representative of many others'?

Here's what I suggest:

- **Look for balance.** The best reviews are the ones that focus on both the good and the bad, providing an objective picture of the hotel and of the reviewer's experience there.

- **Look for recent reviews.** Last year's stellar hotel might not be operating with the same zest for service this year. Changes in management, or in behind-the-scenes ownership, can almost instantly affect a hotel's performance—especially when the changes also involve budget cuts related to service. Even a new general manager with a different management style can render older reviews obsolete.

- **Call the hotel.** The best way to learn about a property and its service is to call it directly and judge the staff's responsiveness for yourself. How long does it take for a clerk to answer the phone? Does the operator answer your questions? If you are transferred to another department, how long does it take? Are you disconnected?

How do the various employees treat you? Do they seem friendly? Also ask some basic questions, such as how long the current manager has held the position, whether you can make dinner reservations before you check in, or whether you can speak to the spa manager.

- **Ask around.** Have any of your friends, co-workers or colleagues ever been to this hotel? What was their impression? Do they have the same taste and interests as you? How long ago was their visit? Would they go back?

- **Talk with a travel agent.** But find one who has actually been to the property or has sent a number of long-term clients to the hotel. If the agent tries to direct you to another property, find out why.

Whether you travel for business or for pleasure, the right hotel can make a big difference. To increase the odds that a hotel will meet your exceptions, be a proactive consumer. Take a select look at travelers' reviews, but don't stop there. A few extra steps can save you from some nasty surprises.

RESEARCHING RATES

The amazing flexibility in the rate structure within the hotel industry is a key reason to call directly. Moreover, this rate flexibility requires you to be persistent in exploring all available discounts when making hotel reservations. Keep in mind that your objective is to get the best room at the lowest price.

Here's how I research hotel rates:

- First, I look on the hotel's web site for special rates and to get an idea of their room types. Sometimes I will check rates with third-party vendors, such as SideStep.com or Kayak.com, but as mentioned previously, it is inadvisable to do your booking through them if you want to position yourself as the right customer.

- Then I check with my preferred airline's web site to determine if they are offering any special incentives such as price discounts or qualifying mileage bonuses.

- Next I call the hotel's 800-number to find out what rates and specials they are offering. Lastly, I call the hotel itself directly to confirm the best room and rate, armed with the knowledge from my research. If the hotel reservation agent does not offer me a particular low rate or special, I know to ask for it.

- When I speak to the reservation agent at the hotel, I attempt to ascertain what discounts are available for the specific property. Even though a hotel might be a member of a major chain, many individual hotel properties offer discounts for specific groups and organizations. By finding out in advance what discounts the hotel offers, travelers who are affiliated with those groups and organizations can cut through the higher rates and save time as well as money.

It is not uncommon to encounter numerous rate discrepancies. For example, last spring I had to travel to San Diego during a busy spring break week. My initial call to the

Sheraton resulted in a rate quote of $250 per night; however, on my fourth call the reservation agent informed me of a special MasterCard rate of $95 per night. And even though I did not have a MasterCard, he secured the special rate for me anyway. One thing to remember is that often when you check into a hotel, the front-desk representative only has access to your rate and not what type of discount is associated with the rate. As a result, hotels seldom ask for corporate ID or any other membership cards or credit cards associated with a discount. Remember that many hotels offer a broad range of corporate rates and special discounts, which can provide savvy travelers the opportunity to enjoy upscale hotels at discount prices. The following are just a few of the possible affiliations that can earn you hotel discounts: AAA, AARP, airline frequent-flyer programs, credit cards, U.S. Embassy discount (especially when traveling overseas), special weekend or promotional rates including corporate discounts.

Once you have secured the lowest-priced room, it is time to try to secure a free upgrade. If you cannot, ask what an upgrade to the next level of room will cost. Most people are happy to obtain a low rate and leave it at that, but you can also travel in style without being a spendthrift. Therefore, find out how much it will cost to secure an upgrade, a suite, or to get access to the club level. And remember, many of the hotels that have frequent-guest programs also offer confirmable upgrades for either no additional charge or only a nominal charge. Sometimes you can redeem points to obtain confirmable upgrades as well. This is the real advantage and strength of hotel programs—it takes only a few points to upgrade to readily available suites.

PUBLISHED RATES, ALSO CALLED "RACK RATES"

"Never pay the rack rate at hotels" has become a kind of mantra with me and with many other travelers, and rightly so. Everyone should be able to save between 10% and 20% off the published rate at most four- and five-star hotels. At the very least you can usually get some kind of corporate rate (a caution, however: corporate rates are not always the lowest rates) just by just calling or asking at the desk.

QUICK REVIEW

◆ Build loyal relationships with a few select groups of hotels. If the hotel group offers frequent-guest programs, be sure to join them. Mention how much you enjoy being a return guest of the particular hotel or hotel group whenever you make your reservations and whenever you check in.

◆ Research on the internet to find out as much as you can in advance about the quality of the hotel, the amenities offered, and the available discounts.

◆ Make the flexibility of hotel rates work for you by exploring all available discounts, using the internet, and calling 800 numbers.

◆ When you cannot secure a free upgrade, find out how much it would cost to upgrade to a more luxurious room. Often, the cost is nominal.

QUICK TIP

◆ Ask that your reservation record be marked with a request for an upgrade. If you have this done, especially by the general manager or his or her staff, the front desk is more likely to upgrade you upon arrival.

STEP 3. CALL DIRECTLY, AND DON'T FORGET YOUR CONTRARIAN STRATEGY

While planning a trip to Puerto Rico, I initially encountered costly hotel rates through LHW's 800-number reservation service. I was told that the lowest rate for the location and time period I desired was $525 per night. Because I was not satisfied with this rate, I called back a few minutes later and was quoted a rate of $350. This was still too high, so I followed one of my cardinal rules and directly called the front desk of the hotel I was interested in visiting. Just by calling the hotel directly, I was able to obtain an $525-per-night room for only $175 per night. That was quite a difference, and it was well worth the cost of a long-distance call to Puerto Rico.

QUICK TIP

◆ When calling an overseas hotel, check out their local time zone and call when it will be early to late evening at the hotel, and the hotel staff will be in a lull period, which will enable them to spend time with you getting the best deal.

The best way to maintain control of your travel arrangements and make that personal connection with a hotel is by calling directly. Calling directly accomplishes three important goals necessary to secure first-class accommodations at discount prices:

- You can establish a relationship with the front desk staff;

- You can find out when the hotel will be at a low occupancy level; and

- You can directly inquire into discounts and upgrades.

In my case, when I called the hotel in Puerto Rico, I was able to speak with the front-desk representative on the actual hotel property, instead of dealing with a remote hotel reservation service. This enabled me to establish an all-important rapport with that front-desk representative. Also, he was in a position to most accurately tell me when the hotel would have its lowest occupancy. Booking at a time when the hotel would have low occupancy helped me confirm the lower rate and get the best room.

During our conversation I told the front-desk representative how much I enjoyed being upgraded and how, when I am given preferential treatment, I reciprocate by being very generous. That was my way of telling him that I would tip him handsomely for upgraded accommodations. Do be aware, however, that you must be careful how you approach a situation like this. Some employees do not understand the value of service, and you will be able to tell by talking to the employee. If an employee does not respond to your stated intention to be generous when treated well, do not push the issue. Instead, wait until you arrive at the hotel, then feel out the situation and perhaps ask the bellman to upgrade you. I will explore this option in more detail below. In this particular case, I was fortunate to be talking to a front-desk representative who fully understood my suggestion.

As a result of my direct call, I received much more than a low room rate. This particular front-desk representative upgraded me to the best oceanfront suite in the hotel, tagged my reservation as a VIP guest, and showered me with gift baskets. The hotel staff, which frequently deals with stars, treated me with distinction and exceptional courtesy. The front-desk representative also provided me with two complimentary golf passes for five days, a cost savings of $95 per person per day. In addition, he gave me daily breakfast coupons. In return for this preferential treatment, I tipped him $100. At first glance this may seem excessive; however, considering the free golf and breakfast, I saved more than $1,200, stayed in the best room in the hotel, and was treated like a VIP. I'd say that is a bargain for $100.

During the fall of 2007 I found myself needing to take a trip to London. As discussed, this was not the most advantageous time for travel to London as the dollar was at an all-time low and hotel prices where at an all-time high. I tried book a room at the plush Four Season's London but came up with rates hovering over 300 pounds (about $600 U.S.). Undeterred, I called the hotel directly and they offered me the same rate I paid in the past—150 pounds per night. This was much lower than most average hotels at the time.

Calling your hotel directly usually enables you to negotiate the best deals, especially when you call upscale hotels. During a conversation I had one day with a high-level executive of the Four Seasons Hotels and Resorts, I was told to always call a hotel directly. This is because many upscale hotels are reluctant to advertise low rates, as they do not want to be grouped with lower quality hotels in the mind of the consumer. However, by asking questions on the phone, you will know when they are experiencing low occupancy. Most hotel representatives will have no problem answering your questions about what their occupancy level is and when to book in order to have the best chance for upgrades.

The personal contact and ability to make in-depth inquiries will allow you to find hidden offers. Just as American Airlines has that little-known elite-qualifying program I mentioned in Chapter 5, hotels have promotions and specials that they do not advertise. Just ask whether there are any such unadvertised specials or programs, and you may be pleasantly surprised.

The benefit of calling directly applies not only to hotels, but also to car rental agencies, airlines, and any other travel company. Remember, a brief phone call can often yield a luxurious trip at a fraction of the cost.

TIME YOUR CHECK-IN

The best time to negotiate an upgrade with a front-desk representative is when he or she is not busy. Therefore, you should try to arrive at a time when all the other guests of the hotel are not trying to check in. For example, late afternoon is perhaps the busiest time for check-in, so if you know you are scheduled to arrive during this time period, try to call the front desk in advance and request your upgrade before you even get there. If the front-desk representative is not too busy, he or she will be more likely to offer you preferential treatment, listen to your needs, and search for the best room.

In December 2007, the house I was staying at in Malibu developed a gas leak, so I called the Four Seasons in Westlake Village, California, during a busy weekend when the PGA tour was playing a tournament at a local course. Although the likes of Tiger Woods and other golf luminaries were in-house, I was offered the 2,500-square-foot Presidential Suite due to my loyalty and they even offered late check-in! As it turned out, all the golf professionals and television personnel were in standard rooms, leaving the plush suite open for me.

Also, take into consideration the following factors:
Transitional Time—this is the time after most guests have checked out, and before most guests have checked in. During this time period, some rooms are probably being serviced or cleaned. So if the front desk does not have upgraded rooms available at that moment, ask if there is a room that is being serviced that you can have.

Late Night—this is the time when most of the hotels' guests have checked in, and the hotel still has available rooms. There are two things to do at this point. 1. Negotiate for a discounted rate, since it is unlikely those rooms will be filled that night. I have been able to have a $275 room reduced to $95 using this technique. 2. Get an upgrade. If any of the nice suites or upgraded rooms are open, ask if you can have one.

PRE-CHECK-IN STRATEGY

If you are unable to advantageously time your arrival, you should try the hotel's pre-check-in procedure. Some hoteliers permit all guests to do a pre-check-in on the day of arrival by calling an 800-number. This is usually a good idea for several reasons. You can bypass the long lines to check in, and usually upon your request the pre-check-in phone representatives will upgrade your room. Therefore, you will know in advance that you have been upgraded to luxurious accommodations. If you are unable to obtain an upgrade at the time of pre-check-in, you can follow one of the other methods to obtain an upgraded room, such as making friends with the bell staff.

TWO DAYS FOR ONE

Want a quick weekend getaway? I've found that it is often hard to get away early on Friday and by the time you get to a hotel for a weekend jaunt on Friday night you're just ready for bed. So instead of leaving Friday night I call the hotel and request an early check-in on Saturday and late check-out on Sunday. This way I pay for one night but get two days for the price of one.

QUICK REVIEW

- Book the lowest-priced room during the periods of low hotel occupancy to have the best chance of getting free or low-cost upgrades.

- Hotels have a fixed number of rooms, so when their occupancy rates are low, the prices of the rooms will drop and luxurious suites will be more available.

- Call directly to maintain the highest level of control over your travels and to seek out the best deals.

- Arrive at the hotel when the front desk will not be very busy. If you cannot arrange this, try to arrange for a pre-check-in and secure your upgrade in advance.

STEP 4. SEEK ADDED VALUE
FOR YOUR HOTEL STAY

During the last recession, some hotels sold rooms at pretty well any price they could get—the theory being that some income is better than none. Basically, hotels were trading higher occupancy rates for lower profits or for a reduction of their losses. This time around, luxury hoteliers are enjoying high occupancy and it is more difficult to get a rock-bottom price—which is why I advocate using your points for upgrades or free nights at luxury hotels. Today instead of lowering prices to those previous rock-bottom levels, hotels are adding on the perks. Extra enticements can range from room upgrades or spa services to welcome fruit baskets, champagne, buffet breakfast, late check-outs, and airport limo transfers—just be sure to ask.

One of the most attractive packages of guest incentives I have found is with the Shangri-La Golden Circle, available at all its hotels and resorts in the Asia-Pacific region. The program works this way: you make a reservation for a non-discounted room. For your trade-off of paying a slight premium, you receive the following benefits: airport limo transfers, guaranteed room upgrades, unlimited laundry and dry cleaning services, breakfast, tea and coffee all day, fax and phone calls at cost, free local calls, and a 6 P.M. check-out—all in all, a very good value.

Whether a package of guest incentives adds good value for you depends, of course, on your needs and priorities. Do you need the fruit basket, or would you rather have a special spa treatment? Or do you just need a basic room for the night and breakfast at the café?

◆ It is always wise to call a hotel in advance and ask if
   they are offering any such packages of guest incentives.
   If so, you can tell them that you would prefer a spa service instead of a bottle of wine and fruit plate in your
   room, or vice versa.

STEP 5. MAINTAIN THE VALUE PRINCIPLE

As I have said many times already, there are times when it is
worth it to pay a little more for better value. For example, I
took a trip to Cancun, Mexico and reserved a regular room
at a discount rate of $95. While checking in, I asked the
front-desk clerk if they had a club room. (I had already
found out in advance that they did, but the lowest rate I
had found for the club level was $165 per night.) Sure
enough, the front-desk clerk confirmed that they did have
a room available on the club floor. I then inquired if he
would upgrade me to this floor. While he scanned his
computer, I asked for his name and told him that I would
like to write a letter to management praising his service.
That was enough of an incentive for him to offer me an
oceanfront room on the club level for an extra $15 per
night. That extra $15 was well worth it, because on the
club level I had access to sodas, bottled water, fresh fruit,
and coffee in the morning, afternoon, and evening snacks,
including chocolate chip cookies and milk. The $15 was a
bargain in comparison to what these extra amenities
would have cost me in the restaurant or from the
mini bar.

QUICK TIP

- If given the choice, many service employees, such as front-desk representatives, have told me they would prefer a complimentary letter to their manager rather than a small cash tip. A letter lasts a lot longer than a few dollars; it becomes a permanent part of an employee's file and has a dramatic effect when the employee is seeking a promotion or a new job. You can combine monetary tips with complimentary letters or write a letter in lieu of a tip if the employee cannot accept money; use your own judgment and discretion.

MORE TIPS FOR LUXURY HOTELS:

MAKE FRIENDS WITH HOTEL PERSONNEL FOR PREFERENTIAL TREATMENT

Just as flyers who seek preferential treatment should make friends with the airport gate agents, hotel travelers should acquaint themselves with the front-desk representatives and the bell staff. A good relationship with the bell staff and front-desk representatives can mean the most luxurious rooms in the hotel and the most valuable amenities. I have already discussed how the front-desk staff can be instrumental in helping you obtain the best room at the lowest price. Occasionally, however, a front-desk representative will be unreceptive to your needs. When faced with this predicament, befriend the bellman when he escorts you to your room. If your room is unsatisfactory, ask the bellman to call the front desk in an attempt to arrange a new room.

When I stayed at the Hotel Bristol in Vienna, I made a special effort to get to know the hotel employees because I was there for four weeks. Soon members of the housekeeping staff were making sure I had a fresh vase of flowers and fresh fruit in my room. Whenever I entered the hotel, the front-desk staff was at the ready to hand me my room key. On the weekends I would rent a car, which the hotel concierge would always arrange to be delivered to the hotel. At the end of the weekend, all I needed to do was hand him the keys and everything was taken care of.

Another story exemplifies the benefits of befriending hotel employees, even on the phone. A Florida couple who spent their honeymoon back in 1948 at the Waldorf Astoria Hotel in New York wanted to celebrate their fiftieth wedding anniversary there. The wife was in for a shock, however, when she learned that the least expensive room was $435—quite a difference from the $15 per night rate she and her husband had paid fifty years before. When she told the reservation agent what her rate had been in that bygone era, the agent was so charmed by her story that she put them on hold and secured permission from her supervisor to offer the couple their $15 per night rate plus tax for seven nights. This is my favorite story about getting luxury at a discount.

GET INTO THE HABIT OF LUXURY

When dealing with front-desk representatives or the bell staff, act as if it is an everyday occurrence to be treated in a preferential manner. Do not act like an unsophisticated tourist and gawk at the niceties of a fine hotel. Without acting arrogant, anxious, or pretentious, behave as if it is no big deal to receive this preferential treatment. This piece of advice is related to my suggestion that you dress the part when seeking an upgrade to a first-class airline seat, you will be much more likely to receive preferential treatment if you look the part, act the part, and believe you deserve the best. Remember, the very rich and famous expect luxury as their due, and so should you. Do, however, be genuinely appreciative of the people who give you preferential treatment.

Despite my usual adherence to this principle, I must admit that on one trip to Rome it was difficult to maintain my poise. I stayed at the St. Regis Grand, Rome, which is within walking distance of the Spanish Steps, the Trevi Fountain, and Via Veneto. Upon walking into this majestic hotel, which had recently undergone an extensive restoration and renovation, I could see that everything about it was matchless. This hotel truly awed me, and it was very difficult for me not to "ooh" and "ah" like an inexperienced tourist.

ULTRA LUXURY IS NOT ALWAYS THE BEST

Dubai is a city known for its hotels and over-the-top service. Their landmark hotel, the Burj Al Arab, is ostensibly the world's only 7-star hotel. While the hotel has 7-star prices, in my opinion it does not have 7-star or even 5-star service. The hotel is a product of a much-publicized machine that touts its fine qualities but upon my visit it was sheer disappointment. During my stay in Dubai, the lowest-priced room at the Burj Al Arab sold for $2,000. Now you do get a nice suite with an ocean view, but I found the view to be plain and rather unremarkable. Likewise the service seemed to be detached and hardly on the friendly side. It is a property that relies more on its location and hype rather than an ethic of hard-earned service. On the other hand, while in Dubai I also visited the Park Hyatt where I had a room for $225 that I found to be warm and inviting. The Park Hyatt also offered a nice view of the Dubai Creek and wonderful architecture combined with a very accommodating staff. About the only thing that the Burj Al Arab had on the Park Hyatt was that they offered chauffeur rides in a Rolls Royce. The Park Hyatt had a late model 7-series BMW which was readily available to take me to my meetings, and for a cost savings of $1,775, I think that a sporty BMW is just fine.

The key here is that often you can find great luxury at an affordable price when you follow your instinct and avoid the much-hyped latest trends, such as is the directive of the contrarian theory.

WHEN YOU ONLY NEED LIMITED SERVICES

Sometimes a larger room and special perks might fit your needs, while at other times a simple room will do. For example, there are times when I travel to a city and arrive at the hotel around 6:00 P.M. or as late as 9:00 P.M., and check out of the room the next morning by 8:00 A.M. In these instances, I am not that interested in being upgraded to a grand suite. This is a type of situation where all I need or want is convenience and a good room at a fair price. (Of course, I only do business with the finest travel providers, so even a basic room will almost always be of high quality.) On these occasions it is not worth the effort to try for a big upgrade or some special service. On the other hand, if I am staying at the hotel for a few days or on a vacation, I seek the best value by getting a nice room upgrade. Keep the big picture in mind. If you're only going to be in the room for a few hours overnight, save your leverage for the times that you really want to receive preferred services.

SPECIAL EVENTS OR ATTENDING CONVENTIONS

Many people who travel to conventions or a special event such as a wedding might not travel a lot. So here are a few special tips to help you on your way. It is commonly assumed that when you book a group rate or convention rate that you are getting the best price. Sometimes this is not the case.

While planning a trip to attend a professional psychology conference I discovered firsthand how hotel conference rates are not always the best deal. The conference organizers had negotiated an attendee rate of $235 a night, which required that a one night deposit be paid in advance and was non-refundable in event of cancellation. Instead of opting for this high-cost restricted program, I made my reservation at the famed Drake Hotel in Chicago for a rate of $195. This lower rate did not require an advance deposit and I could cancel up to 24 hours prior to arrival. Upon arriving at the hotel, I was upgraded to a picturesque lakeview suite, due to my loyalty with the Hilton chain (the conference hotel was not part of a chain I have built loyalty with). In addition, the conference hotel was only a short walk along Chicago's beautiful Lakeshore Drive.

With the multitude of travel resources today, especially on the internet, many people use sites like Expedia and Hotels.com to search for cheaper hotels. Often they can find cheaper rooms that are some distance away. There are trade-offs to consider when choosing a different hotel than the one designated by the group or convention. Some disadvantages include:

- Being charged a higher rate for your convention fees.

- No access to the airport shuttle bus intended for convention attendees.

- Reduced opportunities to network with colleagues.

- Paying cab fare back and forth to the convention.

Those who stay at the preferred hotel often get good discounts on a wide range of services, such as spa services (or even a free spa service), meals in the restaurant, or the gift shop, to name a few. This takes us back to the value equation, where the traveler needs to weigh any potential savings with the inconvenience of staying at another hotel, including not having the convenience of quickly running to your room even if it is for a twenty-minute power nap.

Always, however, call the preferred hotel to make a reservation as an ordinary person to see if the hotel does indeed offer lower rates. This way you will save money while still receiving all the perks of being at the convention hotel. One industry trade group reports that group rates in 2006 averaged $187 a night while other travelers paid approximately $125 to $150.

There might be times when the convention hotel is not part of your preferred group of hotels, and your preferred hotel is close enough to endure the difference. For example, at the Anaheim Convention Center in California, there are two main hotels directly across from each other. It is common for multiple hotels to be located around a city's large convention center. In Anaheim, the Hilton and the

Marriott are almost a stone's throw from each other. If the Hilton was your preferred hotel, then it could be wise to forgo the convention's designated hotel, the Marriott, to continue building your mutually beneficial relationship.

QUICK REVIEW

◆ Get into the habit of luxury. If you look the part, act the part, and believe you deserve the best, your travel providers will treat you accordingly.

◆ Go for the perk when needed—at other times, such as when your hotel stay lasts only a few hours, it may not be a priority for you to negotiate for an upgraded room. As long as you pick a fine hotel to begin with, a basic room may provide everything you need.

◆ Do not assume that convention or group deals are a travel bargain; in some cases they are not.

FINALLY, IF YOU ARE UNSATISFIED, CHECK OUT

This strategy is based on the principle of using the competitive nature of the market to your advantage. If you are faced with a stay in an unsatisfactory hotel property, I recommend that you do the following. First, call the front desk and tell them why you feel the hotel is not satisfactory. If they cannot improve the situation, then speak with the hotel's general manager. When speaking to the front desk or manager, explain your situation in a positive manner. For example, you could say, "I know this is an excellent hotel, but this time something went wrong. And I find this thing unacceptable." Remember, be polite and diplomatic; never act pushy or aggressive. Explain your dissatisfaction in a caring and concerned manner. However, if you are still dissatisfied, check out of the hotel and go somewhere else. Do not stay even one night in an unsatisfactory hotel.

Before you check out, be sure to follow these steps:

1. Contact the front desk and ask for the manager on duty.
2. Tell the manager of your intention to check out, and explain your reasons.
3. Make sure it is clear that you are not going to pay any room charges.
4. Let the manager attempt to make amends.
5. Gracefully accept a reasonable solution.
6. Tactfully decline an unacceptable offer.
7. Before checking out, call a hotel that will better fit your needs.
8. Explain what happened at your current hotel and ask them if they have any rooms.

For your efforts you will either receive a nice enhancement at your current hotel, or you will most likely receive preferred treatment at your new hotel. Generally, the staff at the new hotel will be very accommodating, as they will view this as an opportunity to win a new customer.

HERE ARE SOME REASONS TO CHECK OUT OF A HOTEL

- Inadequate Hotel—the hotel is not what you expected. You were told that you were booking a charming and authentic oceanfront hotel room. However, it turns out to be a dilapidated building across the street from the ocean.

- ◆ Unsafe Circumstances—the hotel is not located in a safe part of the city. There are no doormen or security guards on the premises.

- ◆ Shabby Service—you expected a congenial hotel with a courteous staff. Instead you find an indifferent staff that seems clueless or indifferent to your needs.

- ◆ Substandard Room—when you check into the room you find unexpected extras, such as hair in the shower or on your pillow.

As a travel consumer striving to build mutually beneficial relationships, you have the leverage to make sure your preferred travel providers are meeting your needs. And once you get used to the experience of staying in a luxurious, charmingly decorated hotel, you will consider it to be one of your needs. For me, hotels such as the St. Regis Grand in Rome and Zurich's Baur au Lac hold precious, unforgettable memories that are an integral part of the best in travel.

Key Points

- ➤ *Select a few hotel companies with which you will build a relationship, and cash in on your loyalty.*
  There is inconsistency in quality and service among hotels. Therefore, to have the flexibility necessary to secure first-class rooms at a discount every time, choose a select few hotel companies and stick with them.

➤ *Take advantage of the tremendous flexibility in rates in the hotel industry.*
Explore all available discounts, and be persistent.

➤ *Take control of your hotel bookings and reap the biggest rewards.*
Call directly, do your research, ask questions, and time your travels and check-ins using your contrarian strategy. Be wary of convention or group rates; they are not always the best deals.

➤ *Make friends with the hotel staff.*
Build relationships with front-desk representatives and the bell staff; this can mean the difference between an average room and the most luxurious suite in the hotel.

➤ *Seek out access to the concierge or club levels.*
These floors can save you money and are an oasis of amenities.

➤ *Do not hesitate to check out if you are dissatisfied with a hotel.*
Use the competitive nature of the hotel industry to your advantage.

8

The Mercedes Mentality

Driving a Premium Car at Discount Prices

While traveling to Denver recently, I passed the Hertz rental counter. What I observed confirmed my opinion about the necessity of this book. Lined up were at least fifty people waiting to contract for their rental cars. Although I, too, was renting a Hertz car, I was permitted to bypass that fiasco and proceed directly to the shuttle bus, where I was the only passenger. Everyone else was still waiting in line. I was dropped off directly at my car, where the engine was running and the trunk was open and ready to accept my baggage. As usual, I had paid a discounted rate yet received a complimentary upgrade to a luxury car. All in all, I was off to my meeting in less than five minutes and enjoyed the conveniences of premium service.

My experience in Denver is not based on good fortune; it is based on a solid knowledge of how to obtain fast, upgraded car rentals and preferential treatment. For me, hassle-free, low-cost upgraded and luxury car rentals are an everyday occurrence when I travel. And they can be for you.

THE IMPORTANCE OF UPGRADED
OR LUXURY CAR RENTALS

Car rentals are a small yet important part of luxury travel. With an upgrade and a low rate, you can have the opportunity to spend a few days driving a car you can't afford to purchase, or you can simply add a delightful experience to your trip. If you're in Southern California, you might want to experience driving a convertible with the top down on a beautiful day. Or if you're in a ski area, you might want the added comfort and fun of a nice four-wheel drive. For me, the ultimate car rental experiences are in Germany and Switzerland, where I can drive the autobahn with an upper series Mercedes or BMW. I still clearly remember driving a BMW through the winding roads of the Swiss Alps—a real adrenaline rush. Memorable experiences like these can be yours, too.

When you have the opportunity to drive a low-mileage, clean, upgraded vehicle such as a Cadillac DeVille, Lincoln Town Car, or Ford Explorer while on vacation, you will enhance your overall travel experience. And even if you only have a chance to drive a roomier four-door car that will accommodate your bags and passengers rather than a two-door compact on your business trips, it will make your journey that much more pleasant. After all, by now you are flying first class and staying in five-star hotels, so why not drive a more spacious or more luxurious car, especially when you need not pay more than the average cost of an economy-size rental? Although there will be some occasions when you might choose to pay the price of a mid-size rental to receive an upgrade to a higher class of car, the price difference is often negligible.

The benefits of knowing the secrets to renting cars also go beyond upgraded vehicles. In addition to saving money, you will be able to save time and the usual hassles associated with car rentals. No longer will you have to wait in those long rental lines, because you will be escorted directly to your car in advance of all other renters. And for the most part, obtaining a premium rental car at a discount price is a relatively simple procedure.

FREQUENT-RENTER PROGRAMS

Like airlines and hotels, major car rental companies track the rental history of their customers and offer preferential service to those who are loyal. Most of the major car rental companies offer frequent-renter programs that are similar to the airlines' frequent-flyer programs and hotels' frequent-guest programs. By participating in these programs, renters can earn free car rentals, discounts, and upgrades. Therefore, similar to your approach with the airline and hotel industries, you will want to build a strong history of loyalty with select car rental companies.

A STRATEGY OF LOYALTY

When you are choosing a car rental company, you will want to follow a strategy similar to the one recommended for selecting hotels. In other words, instead of choosing just one car rental company, you will need to select at least two different companies. Like the hotel industry, you will find that rates and the availability of vehicles can vary somewhat according to location. However, for the most part, car rental companies offer similar rates, and most major car rental companies have locations at airports throughout the world. There will be occasions when one company offers a grossly overpriced rate while another company offers a rate that is more reasonable. Likewise, on occasion you will find that one company will offer a special while another company might not. This is especially true when you rent in primary resort locations, such as Hawai'i, Orlando, ski resorts, and in Europe.

Therefore, to maintain flexibility, choose at least two rental companies—one as a primary company, the other as a secondary company—with which to build a loyal customer relationship. However, as in selecting hotels, you do not want to spread your business among too many companies, because you will want to establish a strong, loyal relationship. Furthermore, many of the car rental companies offer "partner points" with many of the airlines. So in addition to earning car rental points you can also accumulate points in your chosen airline's frequent-flyer account. Usually you can also transfer your car rental points into a frequent-flyer account to earn more miles for upgrades. Therefore, consider choosing the car rental companies that offer points in your chosen airline's frequent-flyer program. And not only will you earn additional airline miles, but your airline will also offer special car rental discounts and car upgrade opportunities.

I use Hertz as my primary car rental company and Avis as a secondary company. Both of these companies offer excellent frequent-renter programs. My experience with these companies has been very favorable and, in my opinion, both of these companies offer attractive, new, clean, low-mileage cars along with very good customer service.

They also offer enhanced services to frequent renters and have fairly good global coverage.

Quick Tip

◆ Some car rental agencies will charge or levy a special fee for earning airline frequent-flyer points. So if the airline points are not that important, tell your car rental representative that you prefer not to receive them. However, you will still be earning car rental points at no charge. Also, the car rental points you earn can often be transferred into your airline frequent-flyer account for a small fee or for no charge.

Preferred-Renter Clubs

Along with frequent-renter programs, most major car rental companies offer what is known as preferred-renter programs or clubs. When you belong to one of these preferred-renter clubs, you are guaranteed preferential treatment, including automatic upgrades, based on availability. The good news is that you can join these programs at any time, even if you are a first-time renter with that company.

An example of the value you can receive from these clubs is what the Hertz #1 Club offers. Their #1 Club membership saves you valuable time when making reservations because your personal data and rental preferences are on file. This membership is worldwide and free to join. Also, you can save even more time with their #1 Club Express service, which eases you through the check-out process.

Hertz also offers its #1 Club Gold membership, which allows you to go directly to your waiting car and bypass the long lines of renters, like the lines I saw at the Denver airport. If the rental lot is outside the airport, then the shuttle will drop you off at your car before any other shuttle passengers. And instead of waiting to verify your paperwork before you can leave in your car, all you have to do is show your driver's license and you're on your way.

Most Hertz rental locations also have a special canopy area that shields preferred customers from the weather. Furthermore, when you reach your car, it will have been pre-started, and you will find either the air conditioner or heater running to ensure a comfortable drive.

In addition to the benefits you will receive at the airports, you will also be provided with a private 800-number staffed by well-trained representatives who usually are very accommodating and willing to meet your needs.

Other rental companies have special clubs with benefits like the Hertz #1 Club Gold membership. Becoming a member of one of these car rental clubs is the best way to receive fast, courteous service. However, do be aware that the quality of service varies between franchises even under the same brand name, so don't hesitate to find the franchise that best serves your needs. This is one of the reasons to build relationships with two or three major car rental agencies.

HOW TO JOIN PREFERRED-RENTER CLUBS

Ordinarily, car rental companies will charge a fee for the highest level membership in their preferred-renter clubs. Consequently, many consumers refrain from joining, because they believe that it is not worth the expense. What they do not realize, and what you, the well-informed traveler will now know, is that it is possible to join these clubs without paying a fee. By writing or calling your car rental company, you can usually get them to waive the membership fee. It makes sense for these companies to waive that fee, because in so doing they will secure you as a loyal patron of their company. Like most other service industry companies, the car rental industry is very competitive, and they want your business.

Here is how I got both Hertz and Avis to waive my annual membership fees. I called these companies and informed them that I was a frequent flyer of Delta Air Lines (which is a mileage partner with both of these companies) and that I would give them my car rental business if they would waive my membership fee in their preferred-renter clubs. As a result, both companies waived the fees, and each year they send me a letter stating that they have waived the fee for the upcoming year.

A special note: Most of the rental companies that maintain frequent-renter programs track your customer history or complete rental record exclusively on their central computer system. Consequently, most of the on-site rental locations will not have access to your complete rental history. However, your reservation will make note of your preferred-renter club membership. Therefore, by virtue of being a member in these preferred renter clubs, the rental locations will treat you as a high-frequency renter, even if you're not.

I recommend researching the various car rental companies to see which ones will best meet your needs, and contact them to become members in their preferred clubs. If for some reason your first choice does not offer you a free membership, which probably will not be the case, go to another company. Thankfully we are in a competitive market that offers a broad range of choices.

ELITE STATUS

In addition to the preferred-renter clubs that are available to the general public, car rental companies also offer a very elite level of service that is reserved for CEO and business executives who can influence the car rental decisions of their companies. If you happen to fall into this category, do look into this status. These elite renters are greeted at the airport gate, escorted directly to their cars, which are waiting curbside at the airport, and are always given the most luxurious car available on the lot. Upon their return, these members are escorted directly back to the airport. However, this type of elite status is difficult to obtain. When I called the corporate office of Hertz to inquire into their President's Circle status, they informed me that if I qualified, they would know. Their policy is to contact those who they feel deserve this status.

Hertz recently loosened their entry into their prestigious President Circle by offering mid-tier renters such as myself the opportunity to pay an annual fee of $250, for the following benefits:

- Guaranteed availability during their busiest periods on just two hours' notice

- Guaranteed one-car-class upgrades

- Preferred parking space assignments

- Free Rental Day after every 15 qualifying Hertz rentals

- A 25% Bonus on Hertz #1 Awards Points on your Hertz rentals

- At most airports, a lot attendant will drive you to the curbside check-in, avoiding a long trip on the shuttle bus

I took Hertz up on this offer and so far have found the added bonuses more than paid for the annual fee. If you're interested in this program contact Hertz directly and ask if they will enroll you as a President Circle Member.

QUICK REVIEW

- Driving an upgraded or luxury car will enhance your overall travel experience.

- Choosing at least two car rental companies (a primary company and a secondary company) with which to build a loyal relationship will give you more flexibility.

- Joining the frequent renter programs and preferred-rental clubs will help you receive preferential treatment, and you can get your club membership fees waived.

OBTAINING UPGRADED AND LUXURY CARS AT A DISCOUNT

After you have researched and selected the car rental companies with which you wish to do business, gained access to their preferred-renter clubs and, if available, joined their frequent-renter programs, you will want to obtain the highest quality of car at the lowest possible rate. Again, the car rental industry parallels the hotel industry very closely. When searching for the best price and highest quality of car, you will need to call the car rental companies directly, sometimes making several phone calls to get the kind of car at the rate you want. Similar to calling hotels, it is not uncommon to speak with one rental agent and be offered one rate and then call back a few minutes later and get another rate.

My friend Rob has a sure-fire method for getting a rental car upgrade. By exclusively booking the lowest available rate from smaller companies such as Alamo, Dollar Rent A Car, and Thrifty Car Rental (which he says have smaller fleets), he consistently receives an upgraded luxury vehicle. It seems that by the time Rob arrives to pick up his rental, the economy cars are already gone.

QUICK TIP

* Bear in mind that many car rental agencies will have certain restrictions (such as having a return air ticket) when using check-debit cards, even those that have the Visa or MasterCard logo. If you want to pay with such a card, call or ask about debit cards at the time of making your reservation.

Gotta Get Me a Cool Car

On a recent trip to Spain, I rented a BMW 3 Series car with Hertz's NeverLost GPS system and unlimited mileage for 92 euros a day. Yes, I could have saved 30 euros a day with a subcompact model, but since I was planning to drive from Barcelona to Bilbao and on into southern France, I figured the extra 120 euros (the total for my four-day rental) was little enough to pay for the thrill I would get hugging the curvy roads through the Pyrenees, along the Bay of Biscay, and on through Toulouse and Bordeaux. To this driver, a snazzy car makes driving a rental a joy rather than a chore.

Car rental companies have been quietly sprucing up their fleets with cars designed to give travelers a little extra. One beefy example is Hertz's exclusive special-edition Ford Shelby GT-H Mustang, which is sure to please the muscle-car crowd. Adventurous types might find a Hummer fits their needs when they head out to explore the red rocks of Sedona or to ski in the Rocky Mountains. Want to impress your business associates, or cruise Rodeo Drive or South Beach in luxury? Try a car from Hertz's Prestige Collection, which offers Audis, Jaguars, and Cadillacs.

Sometimes what you want from your car is something fun or out of the ordinary. While planning a rental for a recent visit in Hawai'i, I was pleasantly surprised to find that Hertz's Fun Collection features unusual and sporty cars like the Mazda Miata, Nissan 350Z, and PT Cruiser Convertible. And Avis recently launched a line of Cool Cars, including the new Cadillac CTS, Volvo S60, and Hummer H3. Avis has also expanded its fleet with more convertibles, including the Chrysler Sebring and Ford Mustang, and more sedans and coupes, including the PT Cruiser and the Chevy HHR.

Most of these special-collection cars come equipped with Sirius satellite radio and GPS systems, and in many cases, you'll get special services like free pickup, delivery, and dedicated customer service agents.

Here are a few tips for getting the most from your car rental:

* **Join the club.** Most major car rental companies offer memberships that allows you to book online and bypass rental lines. Just print out your contract and go directly to your car.

* **Book direct.** The best rental deals are found on the company's own web site. Look for limited-time specials, which can save you big money.

* **Use your membership.** Being a member of AAA, AARP, and other organizations can often save you 5% to 10% on the cost of a rental.

* **Look beyond the lowest rate.** Sometimes cheapest is just, well—cheapest. There is a lot to be said for comfort, special features, and a fun drive.

* **Think safety.** Special-collection cars typically have added features like side air bags and enhanced braking and stability systems that increase your chances of walking away from an accident.

With customers looking for vehicles that are more fun and entertaining to drive, car rental companies have made great strides in improving vehicle selection and their customers' overall driving experience. In some markets, Hertz even lets you select the exact make and model of your car—which really gives customers something to get excited about.

Look past the jalopies the next time you rent, and you will drive away happy.

SEEK OUT ALL AVAILABLE DISCOUNTS

The best method of getting the lowest rate is to seek out all available discounts. Similar to the hotel industry, car rental companies offer a myriad of discounts, ranging from corporate discounts to those affiliated with airlines and hotels. Often I have found that AAA has special rates with many of the car rental agencies, as does American Express, and often your airline will include information on car rental discounts and upgrade opportunities with your monthly mileage statement. Go onto the car rental company's web site and look for any special deals or promotions, including those they might offer when you do your booking directly on the internet. In addition, individual rental locations will occasionally offer their own specials and promotions, so you should ask at the counter if they have any special deals for that day or week.

GO LOCAL

A number of car rental companies offer local or in-town rental centers. Often these can save you money, as you will often avoid surcharges and special taxes imposed at airport locations. In addition, local edition rental centers normally offer lower overall rates. It can also be easier to snag an upgrade because many of the rentals from local centers are from insurance claims which are highly discounted and therefore not normally upgradeable. So if you come along with a regular cost-saving rate you'll be the likely candidate for an upgrade. Very often I have found that I can get a good deal by taking a taxi to my hotel and renting my car from a local center and then returning the car to the airport on my way out of town. This gives me a lower rental rate and saves me the fees imposed by airport locations.

WEEKLY RATES

One of the oddities of the pricing structure of car rentals is that contrary to what you might think, the weekly rate for renting a car is often a better deal than renting the same car on a per-day basis for the number of days you need it. However, before you make any assumptions, be sure to ask what constitutes a rental week; it's not always seven days! Some agencies consider a car rental week to be four days, while other agencies consider it to be six days. This is important information to have, because if you return the car too early, your rate will revert back to the highest daily rate.

OBTAIN UPGRADES THROUGH YOUR OTHER TRAVEL PROVIDERS

Frequently, you will receive car rental upgrade certificates or special promotional code numbers from your airline or other travel providers. When you do have one of these certificates or code numbers, make sure to mention it to the reservation agent, so that he or she can note it in your electronic record. For example, as a Delta Air Lines Platinum Medallion member, I have a "PC Code" that allows me to receive special car rental upgrades. Be aware that some agents may not know how to enter these codes into your reservation. When this happens to me, I just call back and the next agent usually knows how.

CASH IN ON YOUR LOYALTY

Usually if you are a member of a car rental company's pre-ferred-renter club and/or frequent-renter program, you will automatically be upgraded one or more car levels based upon availability. However, it helps to remind the reservation agent that you would like to request an upgrade. Ask what kinds of upgraded vehicles are available in inventory, and put in a request for the vehicle you want. Types of cars vary according to location. If you arrive at your car and would prefer a different model, you can also, subject to availability, successfully request a change of vehicle at the car rental lot.

QUICK TIP

♦ When making a car rental reservation, have the reservation agent document in your record your request for an upgrade upon availability. This will greatly increase your odds of being upgraded.

LUXURY CAR UPGRADES AT RESORT LOCATIONS

A resort location is usually one of the best places to confirm a luxury car upgrade. This is because many car rental agencies at resort locations have an inventory of luxury vehicles that regularly go unrented, especially during the off-season, since most people do not want to pay more for a luxury car and are unfamiliar with how to obtain one without additional cost. With this in mind, make sure that when you travel to a resort area, you use your established relationship with the car rental company to obtain the highest level vehicle without additional cost or for a nominal charge that can run you as little as $10 a day or $25 for the week. And again, this is yet another reason to adhere to the contrarian strategy of luxury travel.

If you are traveling to a resort location and were unable to confirm a luxury rental when you made your reservation or would like a higher level luxury car, go to the special line or lounge designated for members of their club, identify yourself as a club member, and express your disappointment with the vehicle allotted to you. Try to speak with the manager or the lead person of the car rental location and request an upgrade.

Another way to increase your probability of being upgraded if you were unable to confirm one through the reservation service is to consider calling the on-site manager in advance of your arrival. Tell the manager that you rent often from their company and would appreciate any special accommodations they can provide. This technique is especially helpful for those times when you want to avoid having to take any additional steps to secure an excellent car. It has been my experience that most on-site managers are very accommodating and will usually upgrade you to a higher level of car, especially when you are a member of their preferred-renter program.

Another thing to consider doing if you are traveling to a resort location is to ask the hotel where you will be staying if they offer a package rate that might include a rental car. Sometimes you can package a rental car into your hotel reservation for a few additional dollars and receive an upgraded class of car. If your hotel will not arrange to upgrade your car, call the rental agency. In most cases they will accommodate you. One good example of this is a program offered by The Four Seasons Hotel, which offers high-end Mercedes Benz cars when you reserve rooms at select hotels.

NON-SMOKING CARS

As a side note, no matter where you travel you will increase your odds for a newer, cleaner car when you request a non-smoking car. This is a necessity if you are a non-smoker, for there is nothing worse than a car that emits cigarette smoke from the air conditioner. Further, you will increase your chances for an upgrade, because if a non-smoking car (the most requested car type) is unavailable in the class of service you booked, you will be upgraded to accommodate your non-smoking needs.

CHECK OUT THE DIFFERENCE IN COST

It is also worthwhile to look into the difference in price between an economy-size, mid-size, full-size, and luxury car. Customarily, the difference in price is only a few dollars a day, and sometimes it will even cost less to rent a higher level of car! For example, while planning a trip to Hawai'i I was quoted a mid-size car rate of $250 per week. However, upon further inquiry, I found out that there was a special luxury rate of only $215 per week. Therefore, I was able to confirm a luxury Cadillac, which is three to four levels above a mid-size car, for $35 per week less than what I would have paid for a mid-size vehicle.

Likewise, one day when I was quoted the usual rate with Hertz for a mid-size rental car, I asked what my rate for a full-size rental would be. It was the same. Then I asked about the rate for an economy size and again it was the same. As a result, I now book a full-size car at the same price as the economy, but since I am always upgraded at least one class size because of my preferred-renter club membership, I am now upgraded based on a full-size rental. Very often the rate difference between the class sizes is inconsequential, a few dollars a day. However, most people ask for the lowest-priced rental, which is the economy-size, and fail to inquire further. Be sure to investigate all possible rate options.

QUICK TIP

◆   Ask the reservationist to calculate the total cost of your rental. This will leave you without any surprises at the end of your rental period. Often you are quoted a rate without the added extras, such as airport fee, city tax fee, license fee, and more. (And if you're wondering about whether you should pay extra for rental car insurance, I'll be exploring that point a little later in this chapter.)

Summer Vacation: Fly or Drive?

Summer is always a popular time to travel. In summers past, families would load up the station wagon, pack a cooler, fill up the gas tank, and head down the road for hours of quality family time on the way to Grandma's, a national park, or some faraway historical attraction. But the annual road trip doesn't make as much sense these days. For one thing, the old highway pastimes—license plate contests and family sing-alongs—have given way to the more private enjoyments of iPods and Game Boys, so there's less real family time on the road. But the biggest problem is skyrocketing gasoline prices. Which raises a question for all summer travelers: Should you fly or should you drive?

Let's consider a few scenarios that are typical of many family summer trips:

The Price family, two adults and two children, wants to visit the historic city of Philadelphia from their home in Miami, a distance of 2,404 miles round trip. That's a big trip and it sounds exciting—until the Prices do the math. Their SUV gets only 17 miles per gallon, so gas will cost them $411. Then there's the cost of food and lodging. It's a 19-hour drive, so figure three days, two nights, each way, allowing for a couple of stops on the way. Let's say the Prices can get hotel rooms for around $125 a night (everyone in one room), and they can keep their food costs to $50 a day. That means $411 for gas, $500 for lodging and $300 for food, for a total of $1,211. How much would it cost to fly? As of this writing, $138 per person, round trip on American Airlines, or $552, for a savings of $659.

The Anderson family of four wants to head out from Chicago to visit Grandma and Grandpa in Salt Lake City. The drive is a total of 2,800 miles. The Andersons have a minivan that gets about 24 miles per gallon, highway, so their gas will cost about $340. Since it is a long trip and the kids are small and squirmy, they plan to spend six days and nights driving round trip. This puts their total driving cost (using $175 for hotel and food per day) at a whopping $1,390. To fly they would spend $198 per person on the American Airlines 2007 summer fares for a total of $792. For the Andersons, air transportations saves $598.

The Portillo family wants to take their dream trip to southern California. They are a family of five living in Austin, Texas, which is 1,400 miles from Los Angeles. Their fuel-efficient car gets about 26 miles per gallon on the highway, so they would spend $313 on gas round trip. Not bad. Since Mr. Portillo is heavy on the pedal, he figures he will spend only four days and nights on the road. Like the Prices, the Portillos are thrifty and willing to sleep in one room, at $125 a night, but their food costs average $75 a day because the family is bigger and the kids are older. Here's the math: $313 for gas, $500 for lodging, and $300 for food for a total driving cost of $1,113. How much would it cost the Portillos to fly to Los Angeles? $270 per person round trip on American, or $1,350 for the family. For the Portillos, driving is the cheaper alternative by more than $200. But what's really going to cost them is the dead time they spend on the road. Staring out the window mile after mile isn't much fun (ask the kids). The Portillo family can maximize their vacation time by spending the extra $237, flying to Los Angeles and getting a two-day jump on their vacation.

Three families, three different calculations, but in each case flying is clearly a good alternative to driving. Sure, there are other things to consider. The fares I quote today may be gone tomorrow. The price of gasoline may go down. There are airport taxes and fees to add on (but there's vehicle depreciation if you drive, too), and if you fly, you may need to rent a car at your destination (and that will cost you about $20 a day from Hertz if you rent a compact). The point is: You need to think carefully about transportation for your summer vacation. To me, flying is almost always a no-brainer. It gets me where I want to be faster and with far less hassle than driving. I get to spend more time sightseeing, relaxing, and enjoying my companions. Plus it saves me money.

It's your vacation. You do the math.

On one occasion while traveling in Europe, I found it necessary to travel to Frankfurt and Brussels. After researching the fares for inter-European flights, I decided that it would be more economical to drive. While researching rates and availability of cars, I came across a "Drive Europe" special that allowed me to rent a luxury car for what I would normally pay in the U.S. for a mid-size car. Upon further questioning, I found that I could upgrade to a premium Mercedes Class for less than $10 extra per day, and that rate included insurance, whereas the lower rate did not. Even with the upgrade to the Mercedes, my rate was effectively lower than it would have been had I rented a mid-size car in America with insurance. For this excellent price, I was able to drive a beautiful Mercedes Benz, which was equivalent to the U.S. version of an E-320, on the pristine, open road between Frankfurt and Brussels. Pure pleasure!

To obtain your own upgraded and luxury car rentals at a discount, remember to be persistent and ask the right questions. Ask about all available special offers and discounts, price differences between luxury cars and lower classes of cars, prices of all available upgrades, and whether insurance can be included in the price. It definitely pays to research all available options of rates and cars with the car rental companies you have chosen.

You Deserve the Best

As with all other aspects of your luxury travels, be a stickler for quality. Any time you arrive at your car and it does not meet your standards, let the manager know. If the car is not clean, has high mileage, or is not the type of car you want, request a different car. I have never had my request to change a car denied. Of course, use this technique judiciously. For example, if you are only using the car to drive a short distance to a meeting and then back to the airport, it is probably not worth your time to exchange your car. Just be sure that the next time you make a reservation, you mention that you were not satisfied with the last car, and most likely the reservationist will make a note to upgrade the current rental for you.

Quick Review

- When you are unable to confirm a luxury upgrade at a resort location through the reservation service, try to obtain one when you arrive, or call the on-site rental agency manager in advance.

- In some cases, the quoted rate for a luxury car could be less than or the same as a mid-size or even an economy car.

◆ When you are not happy with your car, request a
   new car.

CAR RENTAL INSURANCE

Another thing to bear in mind in terms of cost is car
insurance. Before renting a car, check with your personal
automobile insurance to see what type of insurance coverage it provides for rental cars. Likewise, ask your credit
card company about this; many will provide rental car
insurance coverage when you use their card for car
rentals. If your credit card does not offer this coverage,
consider using a card that does. Usually the gold and platinum cards issued by Visa and MasterCard offer good car
rental coverage. You can also get pretty good rental insurance coverage from American Express and Diners Club
cards. These options will allow you to save money by
refusing the expensive coverage that rental companies
aggressively promote.

When renting overseas, you need to take a few extra precautions. First, if you're unsure whether your credit card or
personal insurance covers you, then take the insurance,
especially if you are renting in a country where you have
never driven before. Usually you are safe with just adding
the loss damage waiver (LDW). However, do take extra care
to check what coverage your personal insurance provides
outside the United States, as it can often be difficult to
resolve problems overseas.

Renting a car is one of many elements that enhance your
overall luxury travel experience. So treat yourself well and
drive the finest cars available at discounted prices.

FIND YOUR WAY

One of the best upgrades I have found for a rental car is getting a GPS system. Hertz has what I think is one of the best with their Never Lost system, but others also have great systems that can save you a tremendous amount of time getting around a strange city. I put Hertz's system to the test in the very difficult-to-navigate city of Florence, Italy. Anyone who has been to Florence (those who have not—take a look on Google Maps) knows small meandering streets can be difficult to get around on foot, let alone in a car. I simply dialed in the address of where I needed to go and instead of burning fuel on a lost quest, I was guided directly to my destinations. Another handy feature is that the system will tell you how long until you arrive and how many miles are remaining in your journey. I also like the extra features they offer, such as searching for local attractions, gas stations, restaurants, shopping, and hotels.

Overseas Car Rental Tips

If you're traveling internationally, should you spring for the extra car rental insurance? Determining whether that friendly agent is offering you an optional policy for your protection, or just for the commission, can be a trick. In the U.S., it's usually an easy call. If you already have personal auto insurance or are renting with a major credit card, you're probably covered. But it gets a little complicated once you cross the border. Here are three easy questions you need to ask yourself before you sign on the dotted line:

1. What are the country's insurance requirements? If you rent an economy car in France, certain companies only accept Visa Gold and American Express. In Australia, the basic rental rates usually include collision and damage waiver. When in Italy, theft insurance is mandatory. Most Italian rental agencies offer a discounted comprehensive policy, but it's only available at the rental counter.

2. What is my liability if I'm involved in fender bender (or worse)? A simple accident in some countries could land you in jail, require a large deposit on your credit card, or delay departure until the matter is settled. If you bend fenders in Ireland and don't have the proper insurance documentation you'll need to pay a deposit of 2,000 euros. Get into an accident in Germany without collision coverage and you'll pay a 750 euro deductible.

3. Where am I driving? Drivers outside the U.S. can transverse multiple international borders in hours. Unknowingly, laws can significantly differ from country to country. I learned this lesson when I took a weekend jaunt from Vienna to Prague. Renting a Mercedes Benz in Vienna was no problem. Getting it out of the Czech Republic was another matter. In attempt to make a Monday-morning meeting in Vienna, I left Prague at 12 A.M., more than enough time to get to the city and prepare for the day. It turns out that many former Eastern European countries have a high incident of auto thefts, and that the Benz was a hot car. So when I arrived at the main border crossing, the Czech Guard turned me away. Thinking that it was no big deal, I went to a secondary crossing, where again I was turned away. With time running short, I pleaded and begged for permission to cross, only to be met with a

monotone "No!" With the Austrian boarder two feet away, I pondered making a run for it, although the guard's large rifle made me think otherwise. The guard told me I could leave the car there and walk across the border. Finally, I found a small town on the map about 120 kilometers away with a border crossing. In a last ditch effort, I drove through the rural winding streets, coming upon a sleepy guard. I approached him with my passport in hand, and was promptly waved through.

The moral of the story: Be well-informed. Rental rules are in constant flux, so it's best to know before you go.

Key Points

➤ *Car rentals are another opportunity to add pleasure to your travels.*
Drive a spacious, upgraded car or premium luxury vehicle, and get the most enjoyment from your time on the road.

➤ *Follow a strategy similar to the hotels.*
Choose a primary and a secondary car rental company. This will allow you to maintain loyalty while having the flexibility to ensure the best car at the lowest price.

➤ *Join the Special Preferred Renter Clubs for free.*
These special clubs will provide you with preferential treatment, discounts, and upgrades. If you call your rental companies and pledge your loyalty, they will usually waive the membership fee.

➤ *Join the Frequent Renter Programs.*
These programs will allow you to earn points that can
be traded in for upgrades and discounts, and often they
will earn you points in your airline-flyer programs.

➤ *Seek out all available discounts and special offers.*
Ask the right questions, be persistent, and you will be
rewarded with luxury cars at discounted prices.

➤ *Check your personal auto insurance and credit cards for
rental insurance.*
Many personal auto insurance policies will cover
domestic car rentals, and many credit card companies
offer rental car insurance as well. However, some companies offer only domestic coverage. When renting
overseas, it may be wisest to pay for the rental company's insurance coverage or negotiate it as part of the
rental package.

9

CREDIT CARDS

Spending for Rewards

More than any other topic, readers fill my inbox with questions about credit cards. And for good reason, because when traveling you will have a variety of options for handling the money you've set aside for your trip. Although travelers' checks are still a poplar alternative to cash, I recommend credit cards as the best choice for cost-conscious travelers. Aside from being easy to use, credit cards offer several clear advantages. You can:

1. Avoid carrying large amounts of cash.
2. Obtain favorable exchange rates.
3. Receive enhanced travel amenities and travel protection from many of the premium credit cards, such as gold and platinum cards.
4. Earn points in your frequent-flyer accounts by using certain cards.
5. Dispute erroneous charges.
6. Replace your cards if lost or stolen.

OBTAINING FAVORABLE EXCHANGE RATES ON CREDIT CARDS AND INTERNATIONAL TRANSACTION FEES

Please note that if you are traveling overseas, you will be charged a transaction charge (also sometimes called a "currency conversion fee" or "convenience charge") on all charges you make with a credit card, and on all purchases you make with your debit card. All credit card issuers assess a minimum of a 1% fee for international transactions, which is often buried in the currency conversion transaction. Since this fee is 1% over the wholesale exchange rate, it is still a very good deal compared to using cash or other forms of payment. Recently, some issuers have boosted this 1% fee to 3%. Likewise, many of the major co-branded airline cards charge a 3% fee. American Express and Diners Club generally charge a 2% fee.

Despite the exchange rate for using credit cards outside the U.S., they are still your best bet for making purchases and obtaining cash through ATMs. Generally, exchange rates at a local bank or currency convenience center charge transaction fees as high as 10%. When drawing cash from overseas ATMs, try to use your bank debit card instead of a regular Visa or MasterCard credit card. For example, one of my readers recently took a trip overseas and when she used her MasterCard credit card in the ATMs for cash advances, she was charged a 4% transaction fee or a $10 minimum fee. When she used her ATM/debit card to withdraw cash from the machines, she was only charged a flat $3 fee. (NOTE: Many ATM machines charge only a $2 fee.) Check with your financial institution before you leave for your trip so that you don't have any unpleasant surprises when you receive your bank or credit card statement.

ENHANCED TRAVEL AMENITIES AND TRAVEL PROTECTION

Your gold or platinum credit card might provide you with upgrade opportunities if you use it to pay for your hotel or even your airline ticket. Some cards will cover insurance on rental cars, provide flight insurance in case of an accident, offer lost baggage insurance, or guarantee a rain check for the trip in case of cancellation (usually this applies to a cruise or a resort that gets rained out). Some cards also provide specialized overseas travel emergency assistance, such as transporting you to a hospital that maintains the same high standards as American hospitals, or providing legal assistance, if needed. Your premium credit cards can also provide you with emergency cash if you find yourself stranded.

DISPUTING ERRONEOUS OR UNFAIR CHARGES

Paying for your travels with a credit card provides one advantage that neither cash nor travelers' checks can match. That is, if you have difficulties with your purchase, be it a hotel, car rental, piece of art, tour, or anything you charge on your card, you can dispute the charge with the credit card company. During one trip, I took a tour that turned out to be a big rip-off. Fortunately, I paid for that tour with my American Express card. When I returned home, I called American Express and told them that I felt I was cheated and wanted to dispute the charge. Immediately, the representative reversed the charges and initiated an investigation. There are many travel scams, and using a credit card can help you to recoup your losses.

REPLACING A LOST OR STOLEN CARD

On one of my trips to Istanbul, I left my wallet in a taxi cab. Luckily for me I usually carry my cash in my front pocket so I did not lose any cash. However, I did lose two credit cards and my driver's license. As soon as I returned to my hotel I called the Diners Club Card member services, and they immediately stopped usage on my old card, arranged for the hotel to use a new authorization number for my charges, and had a temporary card for me to use immediately.

All premium cards and many of the classic cards will replace a lost or stolen card in twenty-four hours or less. Be sure to keep credit card numbers and 800-numbers for customer service in a separate and safe place, like the hotel safe, including numbers that will be good overseas if you're traveling internationally. Call your credit card company as soon as you discover the card missing.

WHICH CARD IS RIGHT FOR YOU?

The most frequently asked questions that I receive for my Penny Pincher column at travelerstales.com/experts concerns credit cards. This is because using the right credit card can yield many extra miles. The most common question that I am asked is, *"What is the best credit card for me to use?"* To best answer this question and all questions about credit cards, you must first ask yourself: How do you plan to use the card and what are your priorities? Do you want no annual fee? A low APR? Do you want to be able to carry a balance, or do you want to pay the bill in full on a monthly basis? Do you want to earn the most reward points with a specific travel company, or would you prefer points that can be used in multiple ways?

Earning miles or points through credit cards is probably the best way to accumulate a bonanza of ancillary miles in your account. By using the right card, you can earn miles by purchasing your air ticket (in some cases double miles), by renting a car, and by staying in your hotel. Moreover, any other type of ground-based purchase will help you accumulate miles in your account.

For example, I use the Delta SkyMiles American Express card for many of my travel related purchases. Built into the card is a feature called "Open" which automatically gives me a discount on purchases with companies such as Delta Air Line (5%), Hertz Rental Cars (5%), and Hyatt Hotels (3%). This is handy, as these are the companies I have my travel loyalty with anyway. They also offer discounts with FedEx and a number of other vendors. For full information, you can check their web site at www.americanexpress.com/open. In the first ten months of 2007 I saved over $1,700 with this program and this is something that is automated— meaning you don't have to sign up for it.

While traveling overseas I often use my Visa card issued by U.S. Bank because they do not charge me an international transaction fee. However, I carefully weigh the savings I might get on other cards such as my American Express, which can offset any international transaction fees.

QUICK TIP

♦ When signing up for any credit card with a mileage program, be aware that the rewards structure and value of the points or miles you accumulate is subject to change at any time, at the sole discretion of the financial institution, and sometimes even without prior notice. It all depends on what's written in the fine print of your cardmember agreement, so be sure to read it and any updates or changes to it that arrive in the mail.

What card to use comes down to your personal needs and preferences. There is no simple answer, for there is a plethora of cards to choose from. In the next few pages I will try to clear up some of the confusion surrounding credit cards and offer my advice on what cards might fit the bill for you.

THE NITTY GRITTY OF CREDIT CARDS

The choice of rewards-earning cards is mind-boggling. Virtually every major airline, hotel, and car rental company offers a points-earning credit card. In addition, American Express and Diners Club offer cards with mileage-earning opportunities. And lastly, there are proprietary cards issued by banks that earn points you can use with just about any travel provider. Then there are Discover Card, Citibank, and others that do not earn any travel points whatsoever but do offer cash-back rewards that you can use for anything you want, including travel.

Consider the range of miles/points-earning cards as a spectrum with cards designed for infrequent to frequent travelers, infrequent to frequent buyers (those who earn most of their miles through ground-based purchases), and combinations thereof. Again, figuring out which card is good for you depends on what your priorities are: earning points on your chosen airline, earning points on any airline, paying off your balance every month, carrying a balance, having a low APR, or a number of other factors.

The main question is: Are you interested in building a long-term, mutually beneficial relationship with one airline or hotel? If so, then you may want to go with your preferred airline or hotel's co-branded card. This way you will build more ancillary miles or points to trade in for upgrades and free tickets or hotel stays for family and friends. If your answer is no, and you have no allegiance to one particular airline or hotel group, then you will probably want a card that offers more choices for using the points you earn.

I will first discuss the co-branded cards, the first type of which are commonly called airline cards. Then I will review hotel cards. After that I will discuss multi-use cards and then bank cards. You can also review the various card programs and associated costs and benefits in the appendices.

AIRLINE CO-BRANDED CARDS

Airline cards are charge cards that are specifically linked to one airline or a group of airlines with a code-share agreement. The points you earn with these cards go directly into your chosen airline's frequent-flyer account. These cards can be used with your airline and any vendor that accepts that branded type of credit card. Usually these cards will only allow you to earn a certain number of points per year, and typically they have high annual fees and high APRs. Very often airlines will run promotions where you can earn double or triple ancillary miles when using the card to purchase your airline tickets. These would be in addition to the qualifying miles you earn from the flight. My co-branded Delta Sky Miles card gives me an additional 2% discount when purchasing a Delta ticket which nets me a total of 5% savings, as discussed in the previous section.

QUICK TIP

♦ Remember, airline qualifying miles are still the only miles that will earn you elite status with your chosen airline.

HOTEL CO-BRANDED CARDS

Hotel credit cards are somewhat overshadowed by the airline credit card programs. Because of this, hotel cards often offer more generous earning and reward opportunities than the airline cards.

If flying on one airline is your main priority, then you're still better off with an airline co-branded card. However, if you remain grounded like John Madden of NFL fame, then the hotel card program can provide you with good value. To illustrate, most of the hotel cards do not charge an annual fee, and some classify you automatically as an elite member of the hotel's frequent-guest program, just for being a card member.

All of the major hotel companies offer a frequent-guest program, so even without holding a specific hotel credit card, you can earn points in the hotel's program (and use those points for upgrades) by virtue of being a customer of the hotel. The advantage of having the hotel credit card is that if you pay for the hotel stay with your hotel card, you usually earn bonus points and, as discussed earlier in the book, today's hotel programs offer strong value. (The points you earn for the credit card purchase, plus the points you earn for the hotel stay.) If you accumulate enough points, typically 50,000 or more, you can have a few free nights in some very luxurious hotels.

MULTI-USE CHARGE CARDS

Two cards fall into this category: the American Express Card and the Diners Club Card. Note that these cards are charge cards and not credit cards, which means that the balance of the card needs to be paid in full each month.

(Although American Express does offer credit cards, such as its "Blue" card or Optima card, for our purposes I'm limiting this discussion to the basic green, gold, or platinum American Express charge cards. These basic American Express charge cards do offer "Sign and Travel" and "Extended Pay" options, which make them function very much like a credit card, but the basic intent of these cards is for card members to pay their balances in full every month.)

Unlike the co-branded airline or hotel cards, both the American Express and Diners Club Card allow you to earn points that can be used with a broad range of airline and hotel programs. These points are also redeemable for merchandise.

BENEFITS OF MULTI-USE CARDS

* Flexibility for redeeming points.

* Earn points in a central account and use or distribute the points as you see fit.

* American Express Points can be converted into twelve airline programs.

* The Diners Club Card has affiliations with twenty-three airline programs.

* Excellent customer service (Diners Club usually answers on the first ring).

* Reciprocal airport lounge agreements.

LIMITATIONS OF MULTI-USE CARDS

* Monthly balance must be paid in full.

1. American Express allows approximately twenty-eight days (unless you arrange for "Sign and Travel" or "Extended Pay" options).

2. Diners Club gives you two billing cycles, approximately fifty-eight days.

• Hefty annual fees.

1. American Express Green Reward Card is $65, with a 2:1 earning ratio; Gold Delta Skymiles Credit Card is $85 per year with 2:1 earning ratio; the Gold Reward Card is $125, with an earning ratio of 2:1 on select purchases. (Please note: American Express offers additional card programs.)

2. Diners Club is $95.

• American Express points cannot be used with American Airlines and United Airlines, the two largest frequent-flyer programs in the U.S.

MERCHANT ACCEPTANCE

In the U.S., Visa and MasterCard still enjoy a much greater acceptance among merchants than American Express and Diners Club, because both American Express and Diners Club have typically charged merchants a higher rate for consumer purchases. However, American Express and Diners Club have recently made inroads, increasing the number of U.S. merchants that accept their cards. Based on my own observations, I believe that Diners Club is now as widely accepted overseas as both MasterCard and Visa, with American Express also enjoying high rates of merchant acceptance.

According to a recent Nielsen Report, the current world-wide merchant-acceptance numbers are as follows:

- Visa/MasterCard: 29.2 million

- Diners Club: 8.5 million

- American Express: 7.5 million

POINTS-EARNING BANK CARDS

Adding more confusion to the question of what type of card to use is the array of rewards cards. Looking on the information web site www.creditcards.com shows that there is an obscene amount of reward and points cards being issued by various institutions, with various benefits and fees, some with the name of the bank itself, such as Citicorp or Chase, and others that are branded with an airline or other travel provider.

There are some very distinct differences between the bank cards and the airline and hotel co-branded cards. A major difference is that the points earned are considered proprietary and therefore not combinable with traditional frequent-flyer miles. That means you cannot take those points and transfer them to any of your frequent-flyer accounts. The points you earn are redeemable on any airline, but when you want to redeem your points you must do it through the financial institution's travel service or rewards center, which actually books the travel for you or sends you the upgrade certificate you requested. In addition, you only earn points for making purchases, not for travel-related expenditures. In contrast, an airline or hotel card earns you points for your flight or hotel stay in addition to your actual merchandise purchases.

The earning ratio is typically 1:1, meaning 1 point for 1 dollar spent. Unlike airline miles, however, bank card miles are usually good for only a certain period of time before they expire. (Airline miles expiration are extended as long as you use the card within the time period established by the airline). In addition, some bank cards cap the number of points you can earn on a monthly and/or annual basis.

The benefits of the bank cards are that many of them have no annual fee, a low APR, there are no black-out periods for redeeming awards, and the points you earn can be redeemed with most airlines. However, with most of the bank cards you need to reserve your ticket twenty-one days in advance and you usually cannot redeem them for an award worth more than $500. With some cards the limited value is $300 per award.

By the way, some banks issue debit cards that offer rewards just like the bank credit card, except that money comes directly out of your linked account at the time of purchase. Examples of such rewards-earning debit cards are Citibank AAdvantage Debit Card, Continental OnePass Banking Card, and Northwest World Perks Credit Card.

DISCOVER CARD—A CARD ON ITS OWN

There is also another card that does provide good benefits from the reward perspective. The Discover Card, issued by Discover Bank, a Morgan Stanley Company, is a contrast of good and bad. The good news is that this card offers a cash-back award bonus of 1% to 2% depending on the type of card and based on your annual level of purchases. Most Discover Cards offer no annual fee, 0% introductory APR, and an annual APR as low as 9.9%. The downside of the card is that it has limited acceptance among merchants (although gaining in numbers) and is available for use only in the U.S., with limited acceptance in Canada, Mexico, and throughout the Caribbean. Despite its limitations, the card offers good service, and if you want to earn cash that you can use without any limitation, unlike the rules and regulations of miles and points, this could be the card for you.

QUICK TIP

*   The use of credit cards during your travels is a powerful ally. Credit cards provide convenience, security, and protect against fraud. Credit cards also offer favorable exchange rates, rewards and rebates, good expense tracking, and travel benefits such as no-cost rental car insurance, free upgrades, and free airline tickets and hotel rooms.

THE BEST CARD FOR YOU

In reality there has not been a card that fits everybody's needs perfectly. When considering what card to carry in your wallet, keep in mind the following:

If you are building a mutually beneficial relationship with one airline, you may want to use your airline's co-branded card to earn ancillary miles to use for upgrades and free tickets for family and friends. (But don't make a habit of carrying a balance on these cards; the high interest rates could make your free upgrades and tickets pretty expensive if you don't take care.)

If you are not loyal to one airline (or to two groups of hotels), then you might want to consider a multi-use card like American Express or Diners Club, or one of the mileage-earning bank cards. If you'd rather earn cash than points, you would want to use Discover. Also American Express recently released a new cash card called Blue Cash. It has up to 5% cash back, no annual fee, and a 0% introductory APR. The card also allows holders to pay over time. The Citi Dividend Platinum Select card earns 1% cash back on eligible purchases.

When making your decision, consider these features of the different cards:

- Superior customer service (American Express, Diners Club).
- Building loyalty with a preferred travel provider (airline cards, hotel cards).
- A variety of conversion options (Diners Club, American Express).
- No annual fee, low APR (hotel cards, bank cards).
- Carrying a monthly balance (MasterCard, Visa).
- Double miles for most purchases (American Express).
- Extensive number of merchants who accept the card (MasterCard, Visa).
- Awards on any airline (bank cards).
- Cash-back rewards (multiple cards).

The best route to take is to consider your usage and habits, follow the advice I have given above, and most importantly, do not spread your spending or points accumulation among too many cards. You want to establish value and frequency with the most limited number of card issuers that you can. By doing this not only do you build a mutually beneficial relationship with your financial institution, but you also eliminate the need for complex record keeping.

DEBIT CARDS

As an alternative to a credit card, I like to use my bank's debit card, which works like a Visa (some bank debit cards use the MasterCard logo instead), but instead of using credit, the money is pulled right out of my bank account. Again, there are some recent additions to the world of debit cards that do earn points or miles.

There are a few caveats to using debit cards, which make them an adjunct to a credit card rather than a complete replacement: You usually cannot rent a car with a debit card (there are some exceptions, but you need to hunt for them). Some hotels do not accept them, and the dispute process for wrongly purchased items can be more difficult than with a standard credit card, although I have personally found making a dispute on my debit card to be as easy as with any credit card.

The true value of a debit card, aside from its merit in helping you keep down the size of your credit card balances, is that they give you low-cost access to cash worldwide. When you travel overseas, you should always carry a debit card with you. Using your credit card for cash advances can be quite costly.

ONLINE TRACKING

Something I like with all of my credit cards is the ability to track expenditures online. This is handy if I need to submit a bill to a client or want to gauge how much I am spending during a trip. I have also found the ability to make payments online rather handy as well. There are occasions when I make large expenditures during a trip or have not been back to my office for a few weeks and find my American Express card nearing its limit. Fortunately, I can go online and instantly my available credit is increased to the amount of my payment. This is especially convenient when you're traveling overseas.

Finally, in past editions of this book I outlined various credit card programs with fancy charts of rates and earning abilities. Today the change among credit cards happens so quickly that such a chart is outdated as soon as the book goes to press. The best method for searching the variety of offerings from credit card companies is the internet. Today you're best served by doing a Google search. A few suggested terms include: "travel credit card," "credit cards." Go directly to your preferred travel providers' sites such as americanexpress.com, visa.com, mastercard.com, dinersclub.com. I have found that cardtrak.com and credit-card.com consistently offer the most up-to-date information on a wide range of credit card offerings. They also offer useful consumer articles.

"The Extra Mile" by Tim Winship

THE GREAT CREDIT CARD DEBATE: FREQUENT FLYER MILES OR CASH REBATE

For many consumers, choosing a credit card comes down to choosing a future stream of awards. And two of the most popular credit awards are frequent-flyer miles and cash back.

Although miles and cash may seem like apples and oranges, there's a fundamental similarity. A cash refund is a rebate by definition. And one traditional view of frequent-flyer miles is that they also constitute a rebate: buy a ticket, receive miles which can be combined with other miles for another ticket.

While it's always financially prudent for mile collectors to ask whether there are more lucrative rebates to be had outside the realm of travel rewards, it's even more important now, in light of the significant decline in the value of frequent flyer miles in recent years. The question: might it be a better deal to trade in your airline card for one of the available credit cards which reward users with a straightforward cash rebate?

A RANGE OF REBATE CARDS

Among the many credit cards which use cash rebates as their central selling point are the following three:

1. First, the Cashback Bonus card from Discover is a descendent of one of the original rebate cards. It takes a tiered approach to awards, rebating .25% on the first $1,500 in yearly charges, .50% on the second $1,500, and

a full 1% on charges exceeding $3,000. Cardholders can also earn a 5% rebate on purchases of merchandise in selected categories, which change quarterly. For consumers who reach that $3,000 threshold early in the year, or whose purchases happen to fall within the merchandise categories generating the 5% rebate, the card offers solid value. Otherwise it's an iffy proposition. The Discover card has no annual fee.

2. The Cash Returns MasterCard from Citibank takes a more straightforward approach, offering 5% cash back on all purchases for the first three months and a 1% rebate thereafter. As with the Discover card, there's no annual fee for the Citibank product.

3. Another variation on the cash rebate theme is the Fidelity Investment Rewards Visa Signature card, issued by FIA Card Services (formerly MBNA). The featured benefit of the card is a 1.5% rebate, which is deposited into a customer-designated Fidelity Investments account. For every dollar charged to the card, consumers earn one point. Points in turn can be redeemed in 5,000-point increments, with every 5,000 points generating a $75 deposit into a Fidelity individual, joint, trust, corporate, traditional IRA, Roth IRA, or rollover IRA account. The process is manual rather than automatic, so cardholders must monitor their earnings and go online to convert them into dollar deposits when they reach set thresholds. But the payout is generous and there's no annual fee to hold the card.

THE MILEAGE CALCULATION

The value of frequent-flyer miles has always been a moving target. Ticket prices rise and fall. Sometimes award seats are readily available; other times, they're nowhere to be found. And airlines differ in their overall award allocation policies, ranging from moderately generous to downright tight-fisted.

But to generalize—taking into account the price of paid tickets, the limited availability of award seats, and so on—my current assessment is that the average value of a frequent-flyer mile is around 1.2 cents.

That puts the rebate value of a frequent-flyer mile squarely between the payout of the Citibank and the Fidelity cards. And they all fall within a fairly narrow range between 1 cent and 1.5 cents.

But bear in mind that the valuation of miles does not factor in the value of one's time—an abundance of which can be spent, sometimes futilely, searching for available award seats. When the hassle factor is included in the calculation, even the less generous rebate cards arguably offer roughly the same value as a mileage card.

WHAT'S IN MY WALLET?

I currently maintain two credit card accounts, one for travel rewards, the other for cash. The first is a MasterCard linked to my primary airline program. The second, more recently acquired, is the above-mentioned Fidelity Visa card. When I have a trip on my wish list and need miles for a free ticket or an upgrade, I use the airline card to add to my frequent-flyer account. Otherwise, the Fidelity card is my card of choice. As much as I covet airline miles in the short run, a solid 1.5% rebate invested toward future purchases, or toward retirement, increasingly seems like the more rational move.

If significant numbers of consumers begin scaling back their use of mileage cards in favor of cash rebate cards, as I have done, it could pressure the airlines to adjust the value proposition of their programs. In particular, the airlines would be forced to increase the supply of award seats, to regain some of the value recently shed by mileage programs. And that, come to think of it, would be yet another benefit of charging my next purchase to a rebate card.

Tim Winship is a nationally known authority on the travel industry and frequent flyer programs. Tim is a contributing editor for Frequent Flyer *magazine and SmarterTravel.com. He also writes the syndicated monthly newspaper column, "The Extra Mile." Tim also co-wrote* Mileage Pro: The Insider's Guide to Frequent Flyer Programs.

Key Points

➤ *Credit cards offer travel protection.*
Credit cards provide good security when traveling overseas because you can have your card quickly replaced if lost or stolen. In addition, many credit cards also provide protection such as travel insurance, rental car insurance, or medical emergency services.

➤ *Low liability for lost or stolen cards.*
If your credit card is lost or stolen during your travels, your liability for any charges is usually limited to $50.

➤ *Ability to dispute erroneous charges.*
It is possible for erroneous charges to appear on your

card's statement, which you can dispute and have removed. In addition, your credit card provides protection when you purchase fraudulent items.

➤ *More favorable exchange rates.*
Using your credit cards overseas usually offers you the best value for conversion rates for purchases (not cash advances).

➤ *Choose the right card for your needs.*
If you have a strong alliance with a travel provider you should consider its card; if not, multi-use or bank cards might work best for you.

10

TIPS ON TIPS

*Knowing Whom to Tip, How to Tip,
and When to Tip*

It was during a vacation in Hawai'i, which also happened to be my first visit to the Ritz-Carlton in Kapalua, Maui, when I discovered the true power of tipping. After check-in, a bellman named John was taking me to my room. On the way to the room I asked John about the type of rooms that the hotel had, and he started to describe beautiful oceanfront rooms and suites. When we arrived at my room it was average, nothing very special. So I asked John if he could call the front desk and see if perhaps I could be changed to one of the nice oceanfront rooms. As I said this, I pulled money out of my pocket so that John would know I was ready to reciprocate his goodwill. Immediately, John called down to the front desk and asked them if it was possible to upgrade my room. After that brief phone call I was on my way to a beautiful oceanfront suite. In return I tipped John $40, which might seem excessive; however I received a room for a week that cost hundreds of dollars more than I was actually paying. In addition, every time John saw me in the hotel he was very attentive and always asked if he could help me with anything. On this occasion I invested $40 for a great room and at the same time made a hard-working employee very happy.

YOUR TIPS ARE AN INVESTMENT

Many of the employees who work in the travel industry derive the majority of their income from tips. Consequently, they have a vested interest in providing the best service possible, since a higher quality of service ensures that they receive better tips. Therefore, when you tip and how you tip will be important to these employees, who will go out of their way to give you preferential service. Look at your tips as an investment in your quest for luxury travel. If you tip wisely, you will be able to gain benefits far in excess of the average traveler. This does not mean you need to be extravagant to receive preferential treatment, but you do need to be prudent and perceptive.

IT PAYS TO TIP A LITTLE EXTRA
FOR PREFERENTIAL SERVICE

The derivation of the word "tips" is "To Insure Prompt Service," but I like to think it means "To Insure Preferential Service." Thus, a fundamental principle in traveling like the rich and famous is that in many situations it will be necessary to tip a little extra to insure preferential treatment. Although you might usually think of tips as a reward you give to a service employee for having provided you with superior service, in some cases your tips are given in anticipation of the future preferential service they are about to provide. That's where the derivation of the word "tips" comes into play—you are insuring the high quality of service you have come to expect. However, as you will see later in the chapter, when you are requesting special services or amenities, such as an upgraded room or access to a club floor, you should hold off on your tip until after you receive the desired service or preferential treatment in return.

When should you tip in anticipation of future preferential service? It is generally a good practice to do this, for example, when you first arrive at a hotel and drive up to the valet parking stand or after a bellman first brings your bags to your room or performs a service such as delivering your laundry to your room. By simply adding a couple of extra dollars to the customary tip indicated in the chart at the end of this chapter, that staff person whom you tipped well the first time will be more likely to go out of his or her way to accommodate you if you should make special requests thereafter.

Hotels are a common place where you will use this technique to ensure preferential service during your stay. Since hotels are the places where you will spend most of your tip money, a good deal of this chapter will be devoted to advice on hotel tipping. It has been my experience that in most hotels you will receive the most preferential service from the bell staff, valet parking staff, and front-desk representatives. Consequently, I recommended that you invest your tips in these employees in particular. In return, these individuals will go out of their way to enhance your stay.

TIPPING GUIDELINES FOR HOTELS

The ultimate decision to tip, when to tip, and how to tip is yours. As you experiment with different situations using your own judgment, these decisions will become easier to make. However, the following will provide you with some guidelines that have served me well and are based on my own extensive experience as a value-conscious luxury traveler.

Here's how it pays to tip a little extra in the beginning to receive preferential treatment. Whenever I first arrive at a hotel, I customarily tip the valet parking attendants an amount that is dependent on the regional location, usually $2 to $3. In higher priced cities such as New York, I will tip as much as $4 when I first arrive at the hotel. Then, whenever I request my car, I will tip the attendants $1 to $2. (My average tip when I request my car is $2; I only tip $1 if I am in a region with a low cost of living.) If my car has been washed or I receive some other exceptional service, I will tip $3 or $4.

As a result, whenever I request my car it is always waiting for me in front of the hotel, which allows me to bypass the long lines of guests waiting for their cars. It feels good to walk out the front door of the hotel and have your car running and waiting for you. And when I return to the hotel, the attendants rush to open the car doors for my passengers and me. Another benefit I receive from tipping in this manner is that if my visit involves a few days, most valet parking attendants will have my car washed without an additional charge. I receive this type of preferential treatment just because I invest a few extra dollars initially to ensure better service.

As a side note, usually the only time I tip the valet when I drop off my car is when I initially arrive at a hotel or if the valet assists me with my golf clubs or some other large parcels. Other than those instances, I usually only tip the valets when they retrieve my car for me. The decision as to whether to tip when you drop off your car is a judgment call; I listen to my gut feelings based on my cumulative experiences of traveling.

If you tip the bell staff wisely and add a few extra dollars to the initial tip, they will be friendly and accommodating throughout your visit, making you feel welcomed and appreciated. If you return laden with packages, they will rush to your aid, or they will quickly seek out a cab and perform any task that you might need completed. And as you can see from my experience with John, the bell staff can do a lot more for you than just carry your bags or call you a cab. Likewise, members of the front desk staff can be extremely helpful, especially when seeking a luxurious upgraded room. And as mentioned in Chapter 7, the bell staff can also help you secure an upgraded room or access to the concierge or club levels when the front desk staff cannot. These individuals should be tipped accordingly when they provide exceptional service. Also, if you plan to revisit this hotel, make sure that on your departure you graciously thank the staff and let them know that you plan to write a letter to the hotel's general manager that praises particular employees for their exceptional service.

It has been my experience that many hotel concierges (except those located on the dedicated concierge or club floors) tend to be somewhat condescending and less likely to go out of their way for you unless they are convinced of being tipped impressively. I have found most of the bell staff, valet parking staff, and front desk representatives, however, to be very appreciative of any reasonable tip. Additionally, throughout my travels I have failed in my attempts to have a concierge on the main floor or lobby upgrade me to a prime luxurious room. They can be useful in making dinner reservations, but they have also been known to send unsuspecting tourists on excursions from which the concierge receives a kickback. Of course this is not a hard and fast rule, and in some hotels a concierge will be a valuable ally. However, if you make a habit of finding helpful and enthusiastic members of the valet parking, front desk, and bell staff, you are much more likely to obtain greatly enhanced travel experiences.

Bᴇ Cᴏɴsɪsᴛᴇɴᴛ Yᴇᴛ Mᴏᴅᴇʀᴀᴛᴇ

Remember, when tipping you do not need to be extravagant or excessive. However, you'll want to tip a sufficient amount to make an impact, enough for the staff to remember you and ensure preferential service. Typically, I will tip the valet parking attendants, bell staff, and staff members in any restaurant I plan to frequent (including the hotel restaurant or any local restaurant) more upon my initial arrival, and thereafter I usually scale back to a customary tip. However, it is important to remember to distribute your tipping through-out your entire stay. That way you show the staff that you are consistent in demonstrating your appreciation for their fine quality service, which encourages them to be consistent in providing you with that service. There is also more than just thriftiness to argue against tipping excessively. If you tip excessively, you will lose the respect of the people you tip. However, remember to be fair and, most importantly, demon-strate your sincere appreciation for their efforts. Your kind words are just as valuable as a monetary gratuity. The two combined will ensure a luxurious experience.

Qᴜɪᴄᴋ Rᴇᴠɪᴇᴡ

◆　Modest yet smart tipping can pay big dividends.

- Tip a few dollars extra in the beginning to ensure future preferential service.

- Tip consistently, which means tipping when you arrive, throughout your stay, and when you leave.

- The bell staff, valet-parking staff, and front-desk representatives can be your best allies and are therefore the people in whom you should invest most of your tips.

Tipping the Right Employees is Imperative

You will want to make sure that you are tipping someone who appreciates your tips and earns your money by giving you superb service. Since this book is about traveling first class at bargain prices, I do not advocate a free flow of your money. Wealthy individuals can tip whomever they encounter freely and extravagantly, but essentially they are paying excessively for the service they receive. Our objective is to receive preferential treatment while maintaining thrifty economics. Therefore, seek out those particular staff members who are eager and motivated to assist you, instead of tipping everyone you meet.

Although I mentioned above that you will usually find the valet parking, front desk, and bell staff to be highly motivated to assist you, do not limit yourself to these individuals. For example, there will be occasions when you will find that the concierge is eager and motivated to be of service, or perhaps it might be a member of the housekeeping staff. You might even need to go all the way to the general manager of the property. With general managers, however, your best tip is to let them know that you will write a complimentary letter to their corporate office.

AVOID THE DUCKS AND SEEK OUT THE EAGLES

Wherever you go, you will always find what I like to call Ducks and Eagles. The ducks are those workers who go about their jobs only wishing for the clock to strike quitting time. Basically, they are the ones who just go through the motions. The eagles, on the other hand, are those whom you want to find, because they are the employees who are willing to take the extra step that makes your travel experience an extraordinary one. Eagles take pride in their jobs, readily offer their services, and provide exceptional service with a genuine desire to please you and meet your needs. They are the ones who will work to upgrade you to a prime luxurious oceanfront suite and make every other aspect of your stay a pleasure. Moreover, they understand the value of service, which is why you want to find these individuals and invest your tips in them.

Finding the eagles will take some practice. Usually eagles will greet you very courteously and exhibit a high level of enthusiasm about their job and their surroundings. Typically they will reach for your luggage or offer other services without your request, while emanating a positive, "can do" attitude. With careful observation and practice you should be able to readily spot these individuals. John, the bell person who helped me get an upgraded room at the Ritz-Carlton in Maui, was an eagle who went out of his way for me. From the moment he came up to me and took my bags, I could tell that John was a go-getter. His positive, enthusiastic manner said it all. This is the type of worker you want to seek out and reward with your tips.

Conversely, a couple of good examples of ducks come from a hotel I once visited. Initially, I was thinking of asking assistance from the bellman to access the concierge

floor. However, when we walked to the elevator, this bellman saw me struggling with my luggage yet failed to offer
his assistance. I decided he was definitely not the person to
ask about gaining access to the concierge floor. And when I
had checked out and was carrying my luggage through the
doors leading outside the hotel, another bellman battled me
with his bell cart for space in the doorway instead of step-
ping aside and allowing me to pass. Another example of
duck service comes from a time when I was traveling in
Prague, Czech Republic. While checking into my hotel, I
innocently asked a hotel employee whom I believed to be
the bellman to assist me with my luggage. This man retorted offensively that I should not ask someone who is older
than I to carry my luggage.

It is not advantageous to tip ducks, because they will not
provide you with decent, let alone preferential, service. Try
to spot those who seem to be unmotivated or just going
through the motions and avoid them. At the same time, be
on the lookout for eagles, those who will go the extra mile
for you. Treat them with respect and reward their exceptional service with good tips.

You will find ducks and eagles in a variety of situations.
When making a hotel reservation, you could encounter a
duck who is unwilling to search for a competitive rate, or you
might find that an airline reservationist does not put forth the
effort to accommodate your needs. The point to remember is
that you want to avoid the ducks and soar with the eagles.

IT'S BETTER TO TIP AFTER YOU RECEIVE UPGRADES
OR OTHER SPECIAL SERVICES

How you offer a tip is also key to receiving preferential service. When you are ready to offer a tip, do it in a way that

ensures that you will get your desired benefit in return. I know many travelers who walk up to employees and hand them money, without receiving any preferential treatment in return. Remember that your tips are an investment, so use them wisely. Never waltz up to the front-desk representative, hand him a twenty, and then say, "Oh by the way, do you have an upgrade available?" Most representatives will be less motivated to find you one, since you have already handed them money. Likewise, some individuals might find it offensive and manipulative that you handed them money and expect something in return that they might not be able to provide.

Instead, let it be known that you desire an upgrade, and state in a subtle manner that you would be very willing to show your appreciation. I do not directly say, "If you secure me an upgrade I will give you X dollars." Rather, I let them know that I will reciprocate their goodwill with my own goodwill. I might say, "I certainly would appreciate any special accommodations, and likewise I will express my appreciation." Or I might say, "On my last visit Tom upgraded me to a suite, and I really showed him how thankful I was." Remember that you will be dealing with hotel representatives who are accustomed to working with celebrities and a well-to-do clientele. Therefore, you will need to have a degree of sophistication in securing your extra amenities. If you bluntly or crudely request special consideration you might offend the representative.

When I am seeking an upgrade or other special amenities, I do not ever tip until I receive the goods. If you are going to invest your money, make sure that you get some sort of return for your investment. My friend Kevin's story is a case in point. Kevin, an investment banker, went on a vacation to Disney World with his family and some friends. While checking into the hotel, Kevin handed the front-desk clerk $40 and requested an upgrade. The clerk took the money and said, "I will see what I can do," then gave him room keys. Upon arriving at the room, Kevin was disappointed to discover that his room was the same as his friend's who did not waste $40 with the front-desk clerk.

QUICK REVIEW

♦ Tip the right person, and learn to tell the difference between the ducks and the eagles.

♦ Expand your search for eagles beyond the parking valets, bell staff, and front desk representatives. Sometimes the concierge, general manager, or even the housekeeping staff will go out of their way to make your travels luxurious.

♦ Offer your tips in a way that ensures you will receive preferential service. Know when to tip in advance and when to tip as a reward for special services rendered.

TIPPING OUTSIDE THE HOTEL INDUSTRY

Although hotels are where you will primarily invest in monetary tips, you might also find that when dining out at your favorite restaurant it can pay to tip the maitre d' so that on your next visit you will get a table even if you don't have reservations, be seated quickly, and be offered a nice, quiet table. Again, do not walk into the restaurant and hand over money to the maitre d' without some assurance that you will get a prime table. It is probably better to tip the maitre d' on the way out (if you plan to return to the restaurant and feel that the maitre d' will still be there) to ensure that next time you will be treated in a preferential manner.

Sometimes a nice smile is all it takes. After I coached Diane McInerney, a correspondent with the popular television show *Inside Edition*, she ventured out with a hidden camera to see how my tips worked. When Diane approached the maitre d' at New York's celebrated Gotham Bar and Grill, one of New York's hottest power lunch spots, McInerney decided to see if she and her party could get the best table in the house. Just by asking with a nice smile, they were moved to a private and spacious table by the garden—usually reserved for New York's VIPs.

Occasionally you will also receive exceptional service from an employee of a car rental agency. For example, when I return my rental car to the airport, I often ask the lot attendants if they will give me a ride back to the terminal, especially if I am pressed for time in order to make my flight. This allows me to avoid waiting for and squeezing onto the shuttle for a return trip to the airport. In return for this preferential service, I usually tip the lot attendant $5, which makes him happy and saves me the usual hassle of getting back to the terminal.

With airline employees, you must use a different strategy. Most airlines place a restriction upon their employees receiving monetary compensation from passengers. However, you can still show your appreciation and ensure preferential service by writing a favorable letter to the airline that praises the employee for a job well done. As discussed in Chapter 6, when an airline receives a nice letter from a passenger about a particular employee, that employee receives favorable treatment from the company. Telling an airline employee in advance that you will write a letter can often aid in obtaining preferential service. Just remember to follow through and write the letter!

Most importantly, remember that tipping is not limited to hotel, restaurant, or car rental employees, nor is it limited to monetary compensation. Tips can be offered in many ways and work to your advantage in receiving preferred service.

TIPPING BASICS

A reasonable formula for influencing the behavior of others through tips includes the following steps:

- Clearly signal what you would like. Express your wishes diplomatically in terms of what you would prefer to have, rather than what you demand to have.

- Do not expect perfect compliance with your wishes. Accept the fact that you might have to accept approximations of what you want. For example, you might not get upgraded to the actual concierge floor room. Instead, you might be provided an access key to the floor. Or perhaps you might be given a suite with a nice view of the ocean rather than an oceanfront room that is not a suite.

- Recognize and reward this accommodating behavior with adequate tips and expressions of gratitude.

- Be willing to reciprocate other's goodwill with your own. Your own goodwill could take the form of monetary tips, letters, or telling their supervisor how valuable that employee is to customer service.

- ◆ Skillful use of this formula will significantly improve your ability to influence but not manipulate employees to positively enhance your travel experiences.

A LAST CAVEAT ABOUT TIPPING

Bear in mind that you want your tips to be perceived as a genuine show of appreciation for an employee's fine service. Therefore, it is imperative that you do not come across as manipulative, arrogant, or a show-off. Maintain decorum in the way you tip and invest your tips with the same care you afford to your other financial assets. Remember, tipping should be tied to a specific service you desire or receive. If you freely hand over tips without expressing heartfelt appreciation or without reason, you will lose respect or be seen as trying to exploit an employee. Therefore, it is very important that tipping be closely related to the behavior it is intended to reinforce.

Note: There are different tipping customs in different countries. For example, in Europe hotels automatically charge a tip ranging from 17% to 20%. And if you have room service you often pay an additional $2 to $5 delivery charge. Therefore, you have to be careful not to overtip. One method I found to effectively deal with this potentially awkward situation is to clarify the tipping protocol. I do this by opening the check wallet, reviewing my charges, and then inquiring with the service personal if the tip is included. When they reply yes, I ask what is customary for an add-on tip. Usually, they bashfully respond with "whatever you think is fair, sir." I then give them a few dollars and everyone seems to be happy.

Recently many resorts have implemented a resort fee that can range anywhere from $12 to $25 per day. Ostensibly, the fee is to cover incidental tipping, such as valet parking, pool service, housekeeping, and bell services. If you find yourself in this situation, try to have this fee removed by telling the manager or front-desk personnel that you'd rather tip services employees on your own. If they refuse to remove this surcharge then be careful how you tip. However, do show your appreciation to employees by thanking them and asking if tips are included in the resort surcharge. Also let them know that you will write a nice letter for them.

In certain regions of the world or at some companies, employees are prohibited from taking monetary tips, so don't push one on them. Do, however, give them a warm smile and thank-you. Be sure to consult a regional guide-book for specific guidelines, and inquire at your hotel's front desk about their customary protocol.

TYPE OF SERVICE	AMOUNT OF TIP
GROUND TRANSPORTATION AND BAGGAGE	
Car-rental shuttle driver	Up to $1 per use, more if they assist you with your luggage.
Car-rental attendant for priority return service to airport	$5–$10
Hotel courtesy shuttle	$1–$2
If driver helps with luggage	$2
Taxi dispatcher	None, unless they did something special to help you get a cab, then $2.
Taxi driver	10–15% of the fare.
Car service	Gratuity included, or 15% of bill.
Airport curbside baggage handler	$1–$1.50 per bag.

TYPE OF SERVICE	AMOUNT OF TIP
HOTEL	
(Remember to add a few extra dollars the first time you tip a helpful staff member for customary services.)	
Parking valet	$1–$2 per use, more on first arrival.
Front Desk—for securing a room upgrade (tip after you are escorted to and have seen the upgraded room)	$5–$50, depending on the quality of the upgrade and length of stay (use discretion).
Front Desk—for access key to concierge or club floor	$5–$20
Bellhop —for taking luggage to room and delivering messages or packages	$1–$2 per bag or message.
Bellhop —for securing a room upgrade	$5–$50, depending on the quality of the upgrade and length of stay (use discretion).
Bellhop —for access key to concierge or club floor	$5–$20
QUICK TIP	
It is a good idea to put tips for front desk staff in an envelope with their name on it and hand the envelope to them	
Doorman for cabs and assisting with bags	$1–$2 per cab or bag.

TYPE OF SERVICE	AMOUNT OF TIP
Doorman for special services	$1–$5 per day.
Manager of hotel	Write a letter.
Housekeeper—standard	$1–$2 per day.
Housekeeper—special services (cleaning at special times, special treats in the room, turn down service)	$2–$5 per day.
Room Service	15–20% If service is included in bill: 5% or $1 min.
Message service	$1–$2 per delivery.
Concierge for theater tickets or making special accommodations	$5–$10, depending on the quality of the service and/or tickets. Use discretion.

QUICK TIPS

- Upon departure: Let the most helpful employees know that you plan to write a complimentary letter to the hotel's general manager.

- When tips are included: Some upscale hotels automatically add a tip to your restaurant, bar, room service, and poolside bill. It normally ranges from 17% to 18%. Tipping is your choice, however. If the service was not worth the amount added, cross it out and tip what you feel is appropriate. If the service was excellent, then add a few dollars.

TYPE OF SERVICE	AMOUNT OF TIP
RESTAURANT	
Maitre d' for a preferred table or any special service	$5 for two persons; $10 for four or more (double the amount for five-star restaurants)
Waiters	15–20% of bill; if gratuities are included, an additional amount is warranted for special services.
Bartender	15% of liquor bill.
Wine steward	10% of wine bill.
AIRLINE EMPLOYEES	
Gate agent, ticket agent, flight attendants, and phone representatives	Write a letter or give them a nice little gift, such as a box of chocolates.
OTHER	
Rail porter	$1 per bag.
Hat/coat check	$1 per coat or per person.

Key Points

➤ Make your tips a worthwhile investment in luxurious travels.

➤ By tipping in advance you can ensure preferential treatment. When you are seeking room upgrades or other special amenities, it is better to make your intentions known, but tip after the service has been rendered.

➤ Remember that the valet, front desk, and bell staff can do a lot to enhance your hotel stay. Spend most of your tips on these helpful individuals. However, sometimes the concierge or even members of the housekeeping staff will offer you preferential treatment and should be tipped accordingly.

➤ Tip the right person.

➤ Be on the lookout for eagles, and avoid the ducks.

➤ Tip enough to make an impression but not excessively.

➤ Be sure that you show your sincere gratitude, but do not overdo it. Otherwise you will lose the respect of employees or appear to be manipulative. And remember, tipping should always be tied to a specific service.

➤ Tip consistently throughout a trip. This will keep the staff motivated to constantly provide you with exceptional service. And when you leave a place to which you intend to return, tip the staff whom you are reasonably assured will be there to make your next stay special.

➤ Your heartfelt appreciation is as valuable as a monetary gratuity. Express it.

➤ Show your appreciation by writing complimentary letters, especially for airline employees or hotel general managers

*who cannot accept monetary tips. This will encourage them
to offer you preferential treatment and can improve their
standing with their employers. You can also write to the
hotel general manager to express your appreciation for the
fine service you received from particular hotel employees.*

➤ *Follow the Basics of Tipping.*

Tips on Tipping

When you're traveling, it seems that every service employee is looking for a handout. Your valet pauses for a moment after you hand him the keys to your car. Your luggage porter lingers after delivering your bags to your room. A server signs your check with a smiley face, hoping for a generous gratuity. Knowing whom to tip, how to tip, and when to tip can save money and help you avoid awkward situations.

The ultimate decision to tip, when to tip, and how to tip, is yours. As you travel you'll find that customs vary from city to city, country to country, hotel to hotel, making the tipping process confusing at best. Here are a few guidelines that have served me well and are based on my own extensive experience as a value-conscious luxury traveler.

- Tipping is not a requirement—it's an investment or reward for good service. Subtly let service employees know that if they take care of you, you'll take care of them.

- Be sure to see the goods before handing over a tip. My friend Kevin handed over $40 to the front-desk agent at a Walt Disney Resort and asked for an upgrade. "Sure," she replied taking his money, but poor Kevin ended up with a standard non-upgraded room.

◆ If your service is not up to par, don't leave a tip. It's perfectly acceptable to write a note on your restaurant bill, or inform a manager why you're not leaving a tip. Often you'll end up with a free meal or some other compensation.

◆ A note or letter can be more effective than money. Recently, I conducted a survey of service industry employees. An overwhelming majority, 80%, said they would prefer a written letter to their supervisor over money. The reason? A letter helps them with promotions and merit-pay increases.

◆ Carry small bills. Have a stack of $1 bills readily available so you can quickly and easily hand over your tips, without having to ask for change.

◆ In foreign countries it is perfectly acceptable to tip in U.S. dollars. The advantage to you is that you don't have to compute your tips into the local currency rates.

Many of the employees who work in the travel industry derive the majority of their income from tips. Consequently, they have a vested interest in providing the best service possible, since a higher quality of service ensures that they receive better tips. In other words, when you tip and how you tip will be important to these employees, who will go out of their way to give you preferential service. Look at your tips as an investment in your quest for luxury travel. If you tip wisely, you will be able to gain benefits far in excess of the average traveler. This does not mean you need to be extravagant to receive preferential treatment, but you do need to be prudent and perceptive.

CAVEAT EMPTOR

Know Before You Go

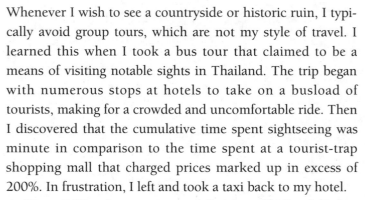

Whenever I wish to see a countryside or historic ruin, I typically avoid group tours, which are not my style of travel. I learned this when I took a bus tour that claimed to be a means of visiting notable sights in Thailand. The trip began with numerous stops at hotels to take on a busload of tourists, making for a crowded and uncomfortable ride. Then I discovered that the cumulative time spent sightseeing was minute in comparison to the time spent at a tourist-trap shopping mall that charged prices marked up in excess of 200%. In frustration, I left and took a taxi back to my hotel.

"Tours" like these are not confined to Thailand. A few years back I was with a group of graduate students traveling through Peru, and unfortunately the coordinator of the trip (my department chairperson) did not know much about these travel rip-offs. Consequently, we went on a number of tours that stopped at least every hour at some village where we were supposed to buy trinkets, and after the first stop everything was the same. I also did not like the hotel he chose, so I made my own arrangements, much to his chagrin—luckily I was almost finished with my dissertation.

On subsequent occasions, I have avoided such disasters

by finding reputable local guides who give me firsthand knowledge of the region. This has not only allowed me to avoid tourist traps, typically it also costs only a fraction of what a tour operator would charge. For example, while traveling in Istanbul, I hired a driver/guide through the front desk of my Four Seasons hotel. The guide was superb and took me to sights I would not have seen on my own or through a major bus tour. He also took me to shops where I bought antiques, prints, and a Turkish rug that would have cost me a great deal more money had I gone to the shops where the major cruise lines that come into the harbor take their guests. For a full day of riding in a Mercedes and the knowledge of a professional guide, I paid $75. I even had my coffee grounds read for free.

There are many ways to avoid misleading offers like the "tour" I took in Thailand, save money, and enjoy a totally first-class experience in the process. In this chapter we will focus on the most efficient means of touring unfamiliar regions and how to protect yourself financially and personally, particularly while traveling to foreign countries.

This is not to say that all tours operators are bad, and in some exotic countries and regions tours may be your only route. I took a trip to Ethiopia in 2006 and used a tour operator to guide me through the northern part of the country A place like Ethiopia is very difficult to get around on your own. With vast expanses of land between villages, and with a number of local sites, I found an insider's knowledge to be very helpful. When considering a tour operator, ask them for references in your country and ask if you can customize your tour to your liking. When dealing with exotic locations a travel agent can be handy. I will cover this later in this chapter.

Is Your Passport Really in Order?

I was recently in the Atlanta airport, headed for a flight to Tel Aviv, when I noticed something odd: a young man and his 3- or 4-year-old daughter were taken aside and asked to stand behind the security perimeter.

Were they carrying too many toys? Was there something wrong with their tickets? Did they fail the security screening? Could they possibly be terrorists?

None of the above. This gentleman, who was traveling from California to Israel for an important family gathering, had failed to check his passport. The passport hadn't expired. In fact, it wouldn't expire for 5 months and 22 days. But that wasn't good enough. Like several other countries, Israel will not permit travelers to enter the country unless their passports will remain valid for at least six months after their scheduled departure.

This young father didn't know the rules. Both he and his daughter were denied boarding, and they had to spend three days in Atlanta getting new documents. The airline kindly waived the customary change fee for rebooking their flights and upgraded them to business class. But, sadly, they missed their family gathering.

WHAT TO KNOW ABOUT SPECIAL EXPIRATION RULES

It's true: Some countries require that your U.S. passport be valid not only for the duration of your visit, but also for three to six months after your entry or return from their country. This means you have to check your passport expiration date carefully. For example, if your passport expires on March 1, 2007, and you want to travel this coming November, you may need to renew your passport before you go.

Here is a list of some countries that have special passport expiration rules.

* Brazil, Ecuador (including the Galápagos Islands), Indonesia, Israel, Malaysia, Paraguay, Romania, Singapore: 6 months

* Cambodia, Denmark (including Greenland), Fiji, Switzerland: 3 months (Denmark applies its 3-month rule to your stay in any of 15 European countries)

There are many others. Some countries count their expiration windows from date of entry into their country, others from scheduled departure, so be sure to ask. For further information about special passport expiration rules, check the U.S. Department of State's listing of foreign entry requirements. Other good sources of information are your airline, your travel agent, and the host country's embassy or consulate.

WHAT TO DO IF YOUR PASSPORT WILL EXPIRE IN LESS THAN SIX MONTHS

* Contact the host country's embassy or consulate to see if you can get a special visa for travel within the expiration period.

* Renew your passport. The State Department says to allow six weeks for renewal, but you can sometimes get it sooner. For example, if you apply during September

or December, when relatively few travelers apply for passports, the turnaround time is faster.

◆ Apply for an expedited renewal. For an additional fee of $60, you can get your passport renewed in about two weeks.

Only the U.S. State Department can issue you a U.S. passport. For information on all passport matters, consult the State Department's web site.

A FEW MORE THINGS YOU SHOULD KNOW ABOUT PASSPORTS

◆ Many Middle Eastern and African countries will deny entry and refuse to issue a visa if your current passport contains an entry or exit stamp from Israel. If you are in this situation, you should apply for a new passport.

◆ New passport rules are scheduled to take effect for travel to and from the Caribbean, Bermuda, Panama, Mexico, and Canada. As of December 31, 2006, a passport or other secure documentation will be required for all travel by air or by sea to or from Canada, Mexico, Central and South America, the Caribbean and Bermuda. As of December 31, 2007, a passport or other secure documentation is required for all land-border crossings to or from these countries.

◆ If you have been traveling a lot and have run out of passport pages, as I recently did, you can add new passport pages. Be aware that South Africa requires that all travelers have at least two blank pages for visas in their passports.

- In most cases, U.S. citizens planning to stay in one country for more than 90 days will be required to provide additional paperwork, such as visas, proof of financial resources, and an outgoing ticket.

- Finally, be aware that all U.S. citizens must have their own passport. Children cannot be included on a parent's passport—even newborn babies must have their own passport to travel.

Don't let your next overseas trip get tripped up by a passport fiasco. Check your passport well in advance, and make sure your paperwork is in order.

IF YOU'RE LOOKING FOR BARGAINS, AVOID TOURIST TRAPS

I discovered in Thailand the disadvantages of being lured into a supposedly "great tour," only to find out that it was nothing more than a pricey and dishonorable means of getting me to a designated emporium designed to sell me overpriced goods. This story raises some important considerations for the penny-pinching luxury traveler, beginning with the obvious: while traveling, you will find no shortage of ways to spend your money. This is certainly true if you are on vacation. There will always be enticing souvenirs to buy, tours to take, events to attend. Although many of these experiences are what make traveling fun, you will want to minimize frivolous spending. Therefore, think twice about what you are about to spend your money on. It is usually best to step back from the emotional excitement of the moment and use your best judgment.

For example, many tourists in Hawai'i visit galleries and fall in love with a piece of art. Most often that piece of art is overpriced and can be purchased on the mainland for considerably less money. That is not to say that all art in Hawai'i is an imprudent purchase. I have purchased art while traveling in Hawai'i. What I suggest, however, is to stay away from the main tourist locales when shopping for art or other regional specialty items. Seek advice from an unbiased employee at your hotel, someone like the manager or perhaps someone who works in the restaurant where you are having a meal. In other words, try to seek the advice of someone who has been there for a while and does not have a vested interest in how you spend your money.

When you are shopping for art, try to find out how long the gallery has been in business, what artists they work with, and if they have other locations. The artists they represent will give you an idea of how established the gallery is. If they only work with one artist, they may be limited in their scope. If they have multiple locations, this will indicate some stability. A single location might indicate that they are small or might not have been in business long. If you're serious, find a gallery that is well established; it is more likely to want to build a long-term relationship with its customers and would be less likely to give you a bad deal.

Do not succumb to the pressure of a gallery owner telling you that if you do not by a piece now, it will be sold. Instead, tell the gallery that you are interested in the piece but would like to think it over, and request that it be placed on hold. Sometimes the gallery might require a small deposit. If that is the case, make sure that your deposit is refundable, get a receipt that says so in writing, and put your deposit on a credit card. Placing the piece on hold gives you an opportunity to determine if this is something you really want and if you even have room for it in your home. On a number of occasions, I have gotten caught up in the excitement of purchasing a piece of art, thinking that I needed it, but after some time away from the gallery, I realized that it would not even work in my home.

You can also do a Google search for the artist or souvenir you are considering purchasing. This provides the opportunity to determine a baseline for the price, as well as lets you see if you can get the item near your home or have it shipped, eliminating the need to carry it with you on a plane.

SIGHTSEEING IN STYLE AND SAFETY

One of the best ways to determine which tours will offer you a peak experience is to consult a regional guidebook. Guidebooks are also an excellent way to discover restaurants and nice shops or galleries. You can also find out about reputable tours by asking the hotel manager, front-desk representatives, bell staff, or even the hotel's restaurant staff. As I mentioned earlier, you can also consult the hotel's concierge, but be aware that while many concierges will have your best interests in mind, some might be influenced by the percentage they sometimes earn by recommending a specific tour. Using the internet along with a good guidebook will help you to get the most out of your planning. The guidebook will provide you with a direction to head, while the internet can provide you with up-to-date information on events and maps or pictures of your intended destination, as well as independent reviews and stories of sites and travel providers.

If you would rather not take organized group tours and desire something more private and comfortable, consider hiring a local guide. You must be extremely careful about whom you select as a guide, however. In some cities it is not uncommon for tourists to be kidnapped or driven to a remote location and stripped of all their worldly goods. In Mexico City, for instance, there have been numerous cases of tourists being assaulted and robbed by taxi drivers. The taxis to avoid are usually those cruising the streets. In fact, in Mexico City you should never hail a cab on the street, but should accept rides only in taxis you have ordered by phone or obtained through a hotel.

But don't be paranoid; a trustworthy taxi driver or other local guide can significantly enhance your travels. My friend Lance found such a driver who took him on a shopping trip in Indonesia. Lance felt comfortable enough with this driver to leave his shopping bags in the taxi while he continued shopping. A few of my pleasurable journeys that were led by private local guides have been treks through Jamaica and the English countryside. To ensure my safety, I usually ask my hotel for referrals to reputable and trustworthy private guides, or I hire an off-duty hotel employee. I have found that the price is usually more reasonable than an organized group tour and always of higher quality, since private local guides will usually know the hidden secrets of your destination. In addition, you have the flexibility to go where you want to go on your own schedule. When you combine the private-tour approach with the knowledge you will gain from regional guidebooks, you will have a nice travel experience that few mass tours can rival.

ADDITIONAL TIPS ON TAXIS

If you don't have a rental car, taking taxis can be a good alternative to mass public transportation. However, when using taxicabs keep in mind the following: most cities require that private drivers, taxicabs, and motor coaches or buses have a city permit to operate. Therefore, make sure that you use a driver, taxicab, or bus that is licensed by the city to perform these services. If there is a meter in the cab, insist that it be used. Or negotiate a flat fee in advance. If there is a plaque in the cab explaining various surcharges, read it.

If you are at the airport or train station, go to the designated taxi stand and use a taxi only from that designated stand. If you have a question about transportation services, you should find an information booth at the airport or the train station. Inquire with them about the accredited modes of transportation. If you need to take a taxi from your hotel, only use the ones that are waiting in front of your hotel and will be waved forward by the hotel's door attendant. Within many cities you will find designated taxi areas; use these areas to ensure that you get into a safe taxi. If you are dining out and are not in an area where there is a taxi stand, ask your waiter to call you a taxi. By the time you have finished with your coffee and dessert, the taxi will be waiting. When you are at a museum or area where large crowds gather, be sure that you go to the taxi stand or look for a taxi that has the appropriate credentials.

If the taxi does not have a meter, be sure to discuss what the rate should be in advance. I once made the mistake of neglecting to agree on a price before we drove off and it cost me. I took an unlicensed taxi from the airport in Madrid to my hotel and paid $85. While checking into the hotel I saw a couple who were on my flight and asked them how they got to the hotel. They said they took a taxi, and it only cost them $25.

Likewise in Bucharest, I found that many taxi drivers turn their meters off at night. Leaving a club one night I had to speak with five different drivers before I could find one that would offer me the normal rate. Sometimes in foreign countries taxi drivers charge a "foreigner" fare, which is higher than the normal rates for locals. Since I had consulted with the hotel before my trip I had a good sense of what the fare should be. You can also ask your restaurant, club, bar, or the driver who dropped you off what you should expected to pay for your return trip. Bear in mind that many cities do legitimately charge a "night surcharge" after certain hours—this information should be clearly posted somewhere in the car.

AVOIDING PICKPOCKETS

Another potential threat when traveling is from pickpockets. I was in Rome in the fashionable shopping district at the bottom of the Spanish Steps. It was nighttime, and I was walking along the outside edge of a crowd of tourist shoppers. I passed by an older Gypsy woman asking for money, when all of a sudden her little girl, who couldn't have been more than eight years old, flung herself on me and held on with surprisingly strong arms. I found it very disturbing that she kept clinging to me and wouldn't let go, despite my loud protests. When she finally let go and I got back to my hotel, I realized that the wad of cash in my front pocket was gone. The mistake I made that night was walking on the outer edges of the crowd, which made me more vulnerable than I might have been in the middle. And though I had assumed putting cash in a front pocket was much safer than a back pocket, it wasn't safe enough.

Here are some ways that you can avoid becoming a victim of pickpockets and purse snatchers or, at the very least, mitigate the damage:

- Be careful when walking in a crowd. Stay in the middle of the mainstream, and don't go wandering off from the herd.

- If you must be out alone at night, stay in well-lighted areas. Walk close to streetlights and stay away from alleys and building entrances.

- Ask at the front desk of your hotel if there are any warning signs to watch out for when you're on the street. The best way to avoid pickpockets is to spot them before they target you.

- Sadly, professional pickpockets have long used children as a means of parting tourists from their money. Sometimes the children wave sheets of cardboard to distract the victim, sometimes the children literally grab onto the victim, and sometimes they use both tactics. The pickpocket or his accomplices might not be a child; he or she could be anyone who bumps into you, asks you for directions, "accidentally" spills something on you, or otherwise distracts you and/or creates a disturbance. Therefore, keep your distance from anyone who looks in the least suspicious, be aware of your surroundings at all times, and don't be afraid to set firm personal boundaries between yourself and all strangers. If anyone approaches you whom you don't know, be firm in telling that person to stay away from you, even if it's a child, a group of children, or a woman holding a baby.

- Wear a money belt or travel wallet under your clothes. If you must carry a purse, don't put anything in it that you can't afford to lose, and wear it with the shoulder strap across your chest. If you carry money in your pockets, carry it in a front pocket that is zippered.

- Don't wear flashy watches or jewelry, and definitely don't flaunt your cash.

- Carry only as much cash or cards as you absolutely need for that day or outing. In these days of credit cards and worldwide access to our money through ATM debit cards, there is certainly no reason to carry large wads of cash. Use ATMs and withdraw only as much cash as you absolutely need.

- Stay in hotels that provide a room safe or at the very least, a safe at the front desk. Leave extra credit cards, cash, travelers' checks, and your passport in the safe. This is also the place to keep a list of your credit card numbers and toll-free numbers to call if they are lost or stolen. Leave a copy of this list at home, too.

- Above all, if you are physically threatened by a thief, give up your valuables. A purse or a wallet isn't worth dying for.

A Last Word on Safety

Consult regional guidebooks and web sites for travel safety information, especially the travel warning web site for the U.S. Department of State at travel.state.gov/travel/cis_pa_tw/tw/tw_1764.html. Another good source is World Travel Watch at worldtravelwatch.com. A good guidebook or web site will warn you about the potential dangers of particular regions and how to avoid putting yourself at risk. It pays to know in advance about what precautions to take.

SOUNDS TOO GOOD TO BE TRUE? IT PROBABLY IS

"World-class offer for a free Bahamas vacation."

"Two Weeks in Hawai'i for $350!"

"You Have Won a Free Vacation, Call 1-900-555-5555 to Claim."

"You Have Just Won Complimentary Hotel Lodgings to an Exotic Location."

"Buy This Right Now and Get Free Airfare to a Vacation Resort."

Have you been approached with any of these fantastic travel bargains? Each year in this country, more than 18 billion dollars are lost to travel fraud and scams.

There are many ways the unsuspecting traveler can fall prey to mail or telephone solicitations for free or discounted vacation "deals" that not only seem too good to be true but are.

When researching travel opportunities, you will come across many tempting offers. Unfortunately, many of them may be fraudulent. Nationally, travel fraud is one of the top ten scams in the United States, with the U.S. Postal Inspection Service identifying bogus vacation offers as one of the top five. *The Wall Street Journal* reported on one air carrier that advertised an extremely low (and nonexistent) fare on a flight. In fact, the flight itself did not exist.

Typical scam operators start with an email, postcard, certificate, or phone call stating that you have been selected to

receive a free vacation—after you pay a "one-time membership fee" or "handling charge." Sometimes you might be
told about a wonderful vacation destination, except that
you will not be given any details about your trip until you
pay some sort of fee. And then when you hear those details,
they either involve other hidden costs or the vacation itself
bears little resemblance to what you were promised.
Another popular scam is to send out a postcard that will
instruct you, the recipient, to call a 900-number in order to
claim your prize. While on the line you discover (at the end
of a lengthy sales pitch) that you will have to pay some sort
of fee to claim that prize, and in the meantime the clock is
ticking away on the phone charges, as you are being
charged by the 900 service for every minute you are on the
line. Some victims of the 900 scam have paid over $100 in
phone charges.

Also watch out for fake web sites. The newest scam is to
direct consumers to sites that look professional or are a copy
of a legitimate site. For instance, it might look like a booking
site for American Express travel but in reality it is a fake site
that has nothing to do with a real travel provider. I'm told by
internet security experts that consumers should look at the
text before the dot com. For example www.jetready.com
would be real while www.flyfree4unow.com/jetready would
not. Also many scam artists misspell what otherwise looks
like a legitimate site. Try www.americanexpress.com versus www.americenexpress.com (Note the use of e after the
c and before n). The difference can mean someone offering real travel value versus someone out to part you from
your money.

It is relatively easy for con artists to scam the public,
because so many people want to take a vacation, and

understandably get excited about a supposedly great deal. However, when you arrive at your destination (if you ever do arrive), it becomes apparent why the price was so low, and quickly your enthusiasm turns to displeasure. A fraudulent brochure might show oceanfront accommodations, but when you get there you might find that there are no such rooms in the hotel. Or the hotel will be run down, old, and ugly; definitely nothing like what you were promised.

SMART WAYS TO AVOID TRAVEL FRAUD

The best way to avoid falling prey to travel frauds and scams is to adhere to the principles I have emphasized throughout this book: restrict your business to well-established, high quality travel companies, and take control of and responsibility for your own travel planning. Become a student of the travel industry. Today's travelers have at their disposal 800-numbers, the internet, and specialized travel-planning software that can easily assist them in researching travel destinations with reputable companies. When you research your travel destinations, you will know in advance what kind of value you will be receiving for your money. I cannot count how many travelers have told me crushing stories of disappointment upon arriving at a travel destination, when prior to their arrival they were excited about what they were going to get and how much money they were going to save.

Again, the key principle to receiving low-cost, luxury travel is by virtue of your history as a loyal, paying customer whose repeat business is the incentive for quality companies to reciprocate with preferential treatment. In this arrangement, you and the company benefit mutually.

That is why you need to ask yourself when faced with an unbelievable bargain from an unknown company if there is the possibility for the company as well as for you to benefit. If it doesn't seem possible, then it may very well be a fraudulent offer that will only serve to part you from your money and give you little more than aggravation and disappointment in return.

If you find yourself tempted nonetheless, be alert for the following signs of travel fraud. If a travel company or salesperson exhibits any of these signs, don't even think about spending your money with them.

- High pressure to buy now or make a large deposit—or else the offer will be gone.

- Promises of a deal that seems too good to be true.

- Inappropriate request for credit card or other personal information, including asking for your credit card number in order to reserve a "free vacation" for you.

- The use of 900-numbers.

- Restrictions against using the travel voucher for sixty days (the deadline for disputing a credit card charge).

- Agencies or companies that use P.O. boxes as an address, have toll-free numbers that go unanswered, or refuse to take credit cards.

- Unsolicited emails and fake web sites.

If you have access to the internet, search the worldwide web for reports of travel frauds and scams and make note of these companies and offers as ones to avoid. To conduct your search, type in "travel fraud" or "travel scams" in your internet search engine.

INSTANT TRAVEL AGENT

Another twist on travel scams are untrained travel agents offering travel services. Many people do not realize that it is possible for someone to become a travel agent simply by paying a fee. There are companies that offer individuals "instant" travel-agent credentials in return for this fee and their agreement to solicit friends to join the program as well. Moreover, many of these companies pressure these new travel agents to sell trips to locations where the company has bought bulk certificates. These vouchers are cheap to the company because they are laden with restrictions that are passed on to you. These restrictions can include limiting travel to certain time periods, requiring you to make reservations a certain time in advance, mandating that your stay be a certain number of days, or requiring that your stay include certain days such as Saturday night. With these vouchers it is possible that you will have a vacation, but it is seldom what you were led to expect.

A subgroup of the instant travel agent is those who are a part of a multi-level marketing program. In these schemes a sponsor signs up as many would-be travelers as they can in hope of reaping their sign-up fee. In exchange, the newly minted agent gets a web site that makes them look like a big travel retailer. Most of these agents use the system to book their own travels in hopes of getting a discounted rate and commission back on their own bookings. The disadvantage is that their sites might not allow them to book travel with all travel providers. One person I know who belongs to one of these groups tried to book a visit with a certain Hilton Hotel, and while the hotel had rooms her site would not make the reservation. My recommendation is to shy away from these pseudo-agents as they don't have the training or knowledge to properly serve you.

SELECTING A REPUTABLE TRAVEL AGENT
OR OTHER TRAVEL COMPANY

This brings up another point. If you do use a travel agent to help you design a vacation, try to go to one who is well-traveled and highly experienced as a travel agent. If your agent has only read travel brochures, he or she will probably not be able to offer you a lot of firsthand knowledge. In these cases, you would probably do just as well to make your own travel arrangements and buy a reputable travel guidebook. Finally, buying airline tickets from an unknown individual opens you up to purchasing stolen tickets. If this happens to you, the ticket will be confiscated and you could possibly face criminal charges, and at the very least be questioned by authorities.

Here are some helpful guidelines for selecting reputable travel agents or travel companies:

- Check with the Better Business Bureau to see if there have been any complaints or pending legal action against the travel agent or company.

- Ask the agency or company how long they have been in business and ask the agents what their personal travel experience is.

- Only use travel agents who are certified with the American Society of Travel Agents (ASTA).

How Not to Book Your Vacation

A new year inevitably brings about a list of resolutions, such as losing weight, saving money, living a less stressful life, or taking that dream trip. Well, I can't help with the first three, but I can give you some advice on how to book your travel—or, rather, how *not* to book your travel— which, come to think of it, could indeed save you money and relieve some stress.

Learn some lessons from my friend Maryam, who should have known better. Maryam planned a family trip to Hawai'i over the holidays, from December 21 to January 2. That was her first mistake, as this is one of the busiest tourist seasons in Hawai'i, so there are few deals and room upgrades available. Don't get me wrong, if a white Christmas doesn't get you going, Hawai'i is a wonderful place to be. Just expect to pay top dollar.

Maryam would have been better off waiting a week. She lives in Orange County, California, just ten minutes from the beach, where temperatures topped 75 degrees on Christmas Day. What's more, her kids didn't return to school until the second week in January, giving her ample time for a Hawai'ian adventure during a less-traveled time period.

Maryam's second mistake was a whopper. After doing all the research and planning on her own, Maryam allowed a travel agent to book her hotel and airfare at no savings to her. In fact, it cost her. It turns out that the agent booked Maryam's vacation under an unpublished consolidation rate and fare that gave the agent a bigger commission but put Maryam in the "Do Not Upgrade" category for both her hotel and air travel.

Unpublished rates and fares are the goat's tail when it comes to getting upgraded. Even though Maryam paid for her travel six months in advance, met all eligibility criteria, and had enough points and miles to upgrade her room and her flight, she was barred from all upgrades because of the way the agent booked her ticket. The lesson is one I have articulated many times in the past: Unless your itinerary is very complex or requires special expertise (say, for an African safari), book your travel yourself. Above all, make sure you are upgrade-eligible.

Maryam's last mistake was a failure of initiative. Maryam wanted a room upgrade badly. (Who can blame her? Because of the high rate, her family of four was booked into one room). After her travel agent told her there was nothing she could do, I advised Maryam to call the hotel's manager and see if an upgrade could be arranged directly through him.

This is a somewhat tricky call, I admit, but when well executed, it can reap a number of rewards. It would involve phoning in advance, asking for the manager, getting his or her name, explaining the situation, asking for special consideration, and letting the manager know that if he could help her, Maryam would remember the effort.

Maryam was reluctant to make the call. As a result, her family ended up crammed into their one room without so much as a view. Hotel managers do have discretion to override room bookings, but if you don't ask, you certainly won't receive.

Most New Year's resolutions get lost in the shuffle of everyday life. Don't let this be one of them. Good travel planning requires no dieting or heavy effort, only some foresight and confidence—and the benefits are all yours.

TRAVEL AGENT OF THE FUTURE

Although controversial with some, my take on using travel agents is that it is not entirely necessary for most basic routes. Unless you're traveling to an exotic location, prefer handholding, don't have time, or lack access to the internet, you can mostly likely get the best deals from coordinating your own travels. Remember that many travel agents charge a fee to book basic airline tickets, whereas on an airline's web site you're not usually charged a booking fee. There is, however, one innovative travel agent (craigstravel.com) that I believe provides very good value to his clients. His first difference is that he only works with a limited number of clients whom he charges a flat annual fee for his service. For this fee, which runs slightly over $2,000, he offers a complete travel approach for his clients, many of whom take exotic journeys to new locations. In addition since he has long-term relationships with certain travel providers, he is able to offer significant cost savings if his clients choose to go with one of his preferred vendors. He is also available 24/7 for his clients, so if they're in Bangladesh and have a problem they can call him and he'll solve their problems. To me this is really the only type of travel agent you should be dealing with. If you travel enough then the annual fee will more than pay for itself. In essence, he offers a concierge travel booking service with the added benefit of cost savings.

COUPON BROKERS: A RISKY VENTURE

On occasion, I have spoken with individuals who have purchased airline tickets through coupon brokers. Most often the traveler ended up getting burned. First of all, by purchasing your tickets through coupon brokers, you will not get any frequent flyer miles or continue to build loyalty with an airline. In addition, when buying tickets from coupon brokers you do not get to confirm your seats. Therefore, you might arrive at the airport and find that your reservation is not in the airline's reservation system. And in some cases, you may end up paying for a ticket you never receive.

Selling your miles to a coupon broker is also a bad idea. These brokers sometimes operate under shady circumstances and most definitely without any authority from the airlines. Under present law these coupon brokers do not violate any federal or state statutes; however, they most certainly infringe upon stipulations made in the printed information of the airlines' frequent-flyer programs. If the airlines find out that you sold a free ticket you earned to a coupon broker, they will deny boarding on the ticket and most likely close your frequent-flyer account. These harsh penalties are just not worth it. Instead, use your extra miles to give free tickets and upgrades to family and friends.

Also, as mentioned above, there are some reports that coupon brokers have pulled fast ones on both ticket sellers and buyers. Under this scam they promise to sell your miles to a buyer, then collect those miles from you in the form of a ticket, but disappear before paying you. Or they will offer to sell you a ticket, insist you pay for the ticket in advance, and disappear with your money. Moreover some coupon brokers could use the information they gained from you about your frequent-flyer account (such as account numbers or PIN codes) to pilfer miles from your account. My advice is to stick to the straight and narrow, avoid the gimmicks, and focus on luxury travels.

TIMESHARES

Although I do not mean to imply that the selling of time-share vacations is by nature a fraudulent practice, and while admittedly my knowledge of timeshares is limited, you should be aware of their potential disadvantages. After buying a timeshare, many people have felt that they were misled about what a good investment it was and how it would enable them to travel to many different locations. The usual complaints were an inability to trade for other locations or an inability to sell the timeshare for the same amount of money they paid, let alone make a profit. Other buyers have found that the buildings and grounds of the timeshare property were not always maintained properly over time. If you are looking for a guaranteed place to stay in a particular location for a particular week or weeks during the year, then a timeshare might be what you want. But if you're looking for flexibility of destinations and a return on your investment, make sure you do a lot of research before you buy.

Another very common complaint about timeshares is that the people who sell them can be very aggressive. Usually, you will have to sit through an interminable sales presentation, then be pushed into making a decision on the spot. To entice you to attend the sales presentation you will be offered free boat rides, dinners, electronic equipment, or a free stay at a hotel, whatever the promoters think is an enticing lure. However, you might find that the length and pressure of the sales presentation outweigh any free incentives you might be offered.

You should also be wary of timeshare sales companies that are located offshore, because they would not be subject to many of the U.S. consumer protection laws. On the other hand, there are some very well-established companies who offer timeshare properties, including The Marriott Hotels, The Hilton Hotel Corporation, and The Walt Disney Company. If you find timeshare traveling appealing, you should consider contacting one of these or other reputable companies.

PROMOTION SCAMS

One last "deal" to watch for is the promotion scam. This would involve a company that says if you buy their product (such as a car, television, washer/dryer, or other item), they will give you free airfare to a fabulous resort or a certain number of days at a resort hotel. This is a particularly enticing scam, because often the companies who offer the airfare or hotel stays are very reputable and trusted companies. The problem is that the company from whom you bought the product gives you a certificate or some form of a voucher for your travel and that's it. When you read the fine print on these vouchers, you discover that you need to fly on a designated airline paying a specific fare basis in order to get your free hotel room, or you need to stay at a hotel and pay a mandatory rate in order to get your free airfare. These rates are often higher than you might find on your own. The key here is to look at the real cost involved and read the fine print before you make any commitments.

Maintain Your Own Integrity

You, the traveler, also have a responsibility to act in an ethical manner. For example, I have read numerous articles and books advocating enticing airfare trickery that breaks airline rules and at the very least is questionable and shady. Although you may profit in the short run from some of these tricks—which I will not mention in this book—the possible consequences include: having your tickets confiscated or voided, being denied boarding, or losing your frequent-flyer account. Above all, you are building a long-term relationship with your travel providers, and as with any partners in a relationship, you do not want to deceive them. I have flown more than 1,000 flights in first class paying coach fares and have never cheated the system.

Bona Fide Deals

Just as you should be wary of travel frauds and deals that are too good to be true, you should always be on the lookout for legitimate discounts and travel deals.

Some Advantageous and Legitimate Discounts

◆ Senior Discounts. Senior citizen airline discounts or books of discount airline coupons that can be bought at discounted rates. These rates and discounts are offered by most of the major air carriers.

◆ Student Discounts. Likewise, many airlines offer similar discounts to students.

◆ Airfare Wars. The best deals to profit from are the airfare wars, which have been a common occurrence over the past few years.

◆ Book Early. You can often get the best rates if you can book your travel early and do your homework while maintaining flexibility.

◆ Companion Fares. In many cases, you can buy one ticket and get a companion ticket for free or half price.

◆ The AAA Discount. This very reputable automobile club offers its members a wide range of discounts from airlines to hotels, cruise ships, and rental cars. In addition, they have a resourceful travel staff to assist members with their travel plans.

◆ Last minute fares. Many airlines and hotels have "last minute fares" when they have not been able to book the desired number of passengers or guests for a particular flight or day. These last minute specials, which are distributed via e-mail, are a great way to save if you are flexible and can travel without much notice. To get on these e-mail lists, contact your travel partner.

As often is the case in life, there are no real shortcuts. Take the time to become a prudent consumer of reputable travel companies' services and you'll experience the peace of mind that comes with first-class travel.

Key Points

➤ *Think twice before you spend.*
If you are considering buying a costly piece of art, sleep on it. If you are considering taking an organized tour, be sure it will not lead to a tourist trap.

➤ *Exercise caution whenever you consider hiring a private guide.*
The right guide can be a wonderful alternative to organized group tours. The wrong one can be dangerous. Consider hiring an off-duty hotel employee or someone recommended by your hotel.

➤ *Take only licensed cabs or buses.*
Go to designated taxi stands, or have the hotel or restaurant call you a cab.

➤ *Spot pickpockets before they target you.*
Beware of strangers approaching you, set strong personal boundaries, don't wander from the herd, use the hotel's safe, carry only as much cash as you need, and wear a money belt.

➤ *Look for signs of travel fraud.*
Avoid deals that involve high pressure, 900-numbers, inappropriate requests for credit card numbers, or a sixty-day waiting period to use a purchased travel voucher.

➤ *Be wary.*
Steer clear of companies that have P.O. boxes as an address, toll-free numbers that go unanswered, or that refuse to take credit cards. Search the internet for travel scams.

➤ *Check your travel company's references.*
Stick to well-established travel companies and travel agents who are affiliated with ASTA. Ask the Better Business Bureau about them.

➤ *Avoid coupon brokers.*
You could end up losing miles, money, or even your

frequent-flyer account, without getting anything in
return.

➤ *Watch out for promotion scams.*
The travel vouchers you receive in return for purchasing
merchandise are often laden with restrictions that
involve costly hotel rates and airfares.

➤ *Look carefully at timeshare offers.*
These offers often sound better than they are. Although
there are certainly some reputable timeshare companies,
be sure of what you're getting before you make a commitment.

How to Book Your Vacation

When I write about trips gone bad, like the one I
described in an earlier sidebar in this chapter, the topic
generates a lot of interest. But this time I want to illustrate a memorable trip that my friend Robert took, which
was a result of following the principles of sound travel
planning.

Robert started off on the right foot by following a key
strategy, i.e., he booked his travel with providers with
whom he had a loyal relationship. Knowing that he wanted to take his wife to Rome for their twentieth anniversary,
Robert called his preferred airline and checked for dates
and flights that would allow him to upgrade his seat. After
securing his own upgradeable ticket, Robert then purchased a ticket for his wife. At this point, Robert's goal was
to save some money, so he purchased his wife a lower-
priced coach ticket. Of course, Robert risked having to

give up his first-class seat to his wife if he couldn't get her upgraded, but he had a plan.

Robert watched the bookings of the flight on his airline's web site. As the flight date approached, he saw that half of the first-class cabin remained open, giving him confidence that he wouldn't be sitting in coach. Then he strategically selected the seat for his upgrade. After consulting with me, he chose Seat 1B. I recommended this seat because I have found that the accompanying seat, Seat 1A, remains open on about 90% of the international flights I take. For some reason, people aren't keen on the bulkhead window seat.

On flight day, Seat 1A remained open, so Robert approached the gate agent and asked if he could upgrade his wife to the open seat next to him. No go! Robert was careful not to push the issue. He knew that it is increasingly difficult for gate agents to make a seat change without justification, and he didn't want an unpleasant confrontation to influence his next target: the flight attendants.

Robert boarded the flight with his wife and made a joke to the flight attendant standing at the front of the plane that his poor wife had to go sit in the back. Robert got comfortable in his seat and when the flight attendant offered him a pre-departure drink, he mentioned that his wife was in the back. Again, the reply was, "Sorry, sir, we can't bring her up." Keeping his cool, Robert patiently waited for the flight to get underway. Once he saw the lead flight attendant with a free moment, he approached her and told his story, mentioning that he held the highest level of the airline's elite frequent-flyer status. Soon husband and wife were reunited.

According to Robert, the flight crew couldn't have been more pleasant. This has also been my experience in similar situations. Most people do want to help others when given the chance. In this case, Robert's politeness and loyalty paid off in a romantic trans-Atlantic flight, side-by-side with his wife in first class. Mind you, this kind of travel benefit is one you can only negotiate on your own.

Robert was equally proactive when he planned his hotel stay. As a loyal guest with a particular hotel group, he had gotten to know the managers of two European hotels within the hotel's group of properties. When it came time to book his stay in Rome, Robert emailed the managers and asked if they would introduce him to the manager of the hotel he was planning to visit with his wife. The introduction was made, and the manager of the hotel in Rome emailed Robert with his direct number, asking him to call. When he did, the manager immediately asked for Robert's phone number and called him back, so Robert needn't pay for the call—a very nice touch, Robert thought. Even though Robert had already booked his room on the hotel's web site, the manager offered him a special rate, took down some information about the anniversary, and told Robert the best way to get to the hotel from the airport. Robert appreciated this personal touch, but was really surprised by what the manager had in store for the couple's anniversary: the hotel's house seats to the theater, and a chauffeur-driven Mercedes-Benz to take them to the event.

The main difference between Robert's trip and those that go awry is that Robert took a proactive approach to his travel planning, knowing what he wanted and how he wanted to get it. He did not rely on idle advice or on the impersonal data-crunching of third-party web sites. By building his own personal and loyal relationships, Robert was able to finesse a memorable trip and a wonderful anniversary.

12

Travel Mishaps

Turning Misfortune into Fortune

While staying at the Hilton Towers in Chicago, an early morning meeting required that I leave the hotel shortly before 6:30 A.M. During this stay I had been upgraded to the concierge level, but the lounge that offered complimentary coffee and breakfast to concierge-level guests did not open until 6:30 A.M. When I approached the lounge at 6:25, I saw a hotel employee preparing to open up the lounge. Speaking through the closed door, I politely asked if I could have a cup of coffee. But the employee refused, brusquely informing me that they would not open until 6:30.

Later that day, I told the hotel's general manager what had transpired that morning. He was so apologetic that he waived all my charges for my current stay. In addition, he offered me a complimentary stay on my next trip to Chicago.

EVEN THE BEST MAKE MISTAKES

When travel service companies make mistakes, the knowledgeable traveler can turn misfortune into fortune. Most upscale travel service companies strive to maintain a credible reputation for providing exceptional service. Even with the best travel providers, however, you will experience isolated incidents in which they do not meet their usual high standards. Consequently, any time a dissatisfied customer has a legitimate complaint, quality-oriented companies will usually go out of their way to make amends to maintain their reputation. The circumstances of your mishap and the courteous manner in which you present your case will usually dictate what compensation the company chooses to offer.

FIRST, DO YOUR PART TO AVOID UNSATISFACTORY TRAVELS

Before I get into the specifics of how to turn travel misfortune into fortune, it is important to stress that the responsibility for the quality of your travels starts with you. Over the years I have become extremely knowledgeable about the advantages and disadvantages of Delta Air Line's various routes and flights. I know what planes fly on what routes, how many seats there are in the first-class cabin, and what flights will generally have a heavy load of passengers. Out of Orange County, where I live, Delta has relatively few flights; therefore, I have made it a point to study what flights best fit my needs and opt for those first. Furthermore, I know which flights offer the best opportunity for upgrades and which flights offer me the best chance to clear a wait list for first class.

Also, while you might assume that all first-class cabins are created equal, they are not. On one of the routes that I regularly fly, the first leg of the journey is on an older plane with only eight first-class seats that are quite roomy and comfortable. On the second leg of the journey, however, the newer aircraft has a first-class cabin with twelve smaller and less comfortable seats. Consequently, I've found that if I take an earlier flight on that route, I am able to fly both legs of the journey on planes offering the roomier and more comfortable first-class seats. In addition, you will find that some flights offer drinks and snacks rather than full meals, even in the first-class cabin. This is why being a student of your chosen airline is very important. Get to know the specific seating configurations and cabin service (meals and movies) offered on the planes that fly particular routes. This information is usually available in the airline's schedule book, frequent-flyer onboard magazines, and on the web sites of some airlines. In fact, there is a web site, www.SeatGuru.com, that provides seating configurations for all modern planes, knowledge that you can apply to all airlines. You can also ask the reservation agent for this information.

By developing a thorough understanding of your travel provider you can leverage your knowledge and take an alternate route or flight that would offer you a more comfortable environment.

As you build your relationship with your air carrier or with any of your other travel providers, you will develop your own personal strategy for optimizing your first-class travels. The more you become familiar with the particular idiosyncrasies of your travel providers, the less chance there will be for disappointments and mishaps. However, even the most carefully planned travels with the highest quality travel providers can occasionally result in a disappointing or unsatisfactory experience. When this happens, use the following specific techniques to receive compensation for your dissatisfaction.

Complaints

Complain only when you have a legitimate concern. It is important to point out that although quality travel companies want to appease dissatisfied customers, you as a customer have a responsibility not to take advantage of these companies' efforts to maintain goodwill. If you regularly make vague, unreasonable, or false complaints, these companies will eventually learn to be skeptical of your motives and will be less likely to try to make amends. With this in mind, choose carefully the people to whom you complain, and complain only when you have a legitimate concern.

Know what to reasonably expect from a legitimate complaint. When voicing your dissatisfaction, you should have a clear idea of what type of compensation you are seeking. However, depending on the circumstances and what your intuition tells you, either bring up your suggestion for appropriate amends or let the company make the first offer. In many cases I like to first give the travel company representative an opportunity to specify the form of amends he would like to make. Then, if I feel the offer is insufficient, I will suggest what I think is fair. In most cases it is a good idea to allow the company to make their offer first, because very often quality companies will offer more than you would even think to ask for. The above story about my stay at the Hilton Towers in Chicago is a case in point. Because I was not able to get a coffee five minutes early, the charges for my current stay were waived, and I was offered a complimentary future stay. Although I was very appreciative of the manager's offer, I was frankly surprised at the extent to which he went to make amends. But again, this is why it pays to spend your travel dollars exclusively on quality companies. They have a reputation to maintain and will go to great lengths to do so.

Another reason to allow the company to make the first offer of compensation is to avoid coming across as a person who is out to take advantage of the situation. However, when you do find it necessary to make a specific request, ask only for what is appropriate for the mistake.

QUICK REVIEW

◆ Quality companies strive to maintain their reputation for quality, which is why they will want to make amends if you are dissatisfied.

◆ Learn the idiosyncrasies of your travel providers to avoid unsatisfactory travel experiences.

◆ Do voice your complaints, but only when you have a legitimate concern. Do not take advantage of a company's goodwill.

◆ Keep in mind what you think would be fair recompense for your dissatisfaction, but in many cases allow the company to make the first offer of amends.

Be Careful What You Say

I have long extolled the benefits of customer databases, which help travelers and travel providers build mutually beneficial relationships. By tracking their best customers' preferences and purchases, providers can reward them with upgrades, special pricing, personalized service, and other perks that make travel more pleasant. But there is a little-known downside to the system: A disgruntled employee can wreak havoc on your record—and your reputation—and you usually won't know a thing about it. It happened to me recently.

I was in Budapest, Hungary, trying to change my return flight when I crossed paths with a very disagreeable airline representative. She called herself Ms. Jones. I assume she made this name up. She certainly made up most of the things she wrote about me in my airline file. These customer files are meant to be kept secret from the customer, but I was inadvertently shown her comments. Ms. Jones called me "rude," "demanding," and several other things that I am not going to repeat, and presented a self-serving version of our unpleasant interaction.

Here's what actually happened: I called the reservations center from my international cell phone, which charges me $1.29 per minute. After waiting five minutes for Ms. Jones to answer my call, I politely informed her (yes, I was polite) that I was in Budapest using my cell phone at a rate of $1.29 per minute, and if she could expedite my call by changing my next flight, I would appreciate it. You'd think I'd demanded her firstborn child.

She told me, tartly, that she didn't know how she could help me because she didn't have my flight information. This, despite that fact that she had addressed me by name when she answered the phone. I've been around this airline long enough to know that when an agent has your name on the screen, they also have all your pending reservations in chronological order right there in front of them.

When I repeated that I needed to change my reservation, she again denied having any information, and declared, angrily this time, "I don't know what you want!"

When I finally made my wishes clear, she told me the flight I wanted was sold out.

"How can that be?" I asked. "The web site shows 26 seats available in coach and 21 seats available in first/business class."

"Sorry, the flight is sold out," she said.

When I asked if she could check again, she put me on hold. She would return periodically, only to say, "Please continue holding," which I did—for 40 minutes. (Let's see, that's $51.60 plus tax.) Finally, I hung up and called my assistant in the States (something I should have done in the first place) and asked her to change the reservation for me. Result? Five minutes later I was booked on the "sold-out" flight. By that time, presumably, Ms. Jones had already entered her invective into my file.

There are a number of lessons to learn here. For one thing, if you are overseas on a by-the-minute phone plan, don't waste your money on an expensive call if other means of communication are available. But the most important lesson is that employees in dicey situations will attempt to cover their backsides. They will annotate your record with a version of events that is favorable to them. It's their way of protecting their jobs should the customer later complain.

If you find yourself in a situation like this, there are a few things you can do to protect your good reputation:

1. If a call or interaction is not going well, bail out as soon as you can. Don't waste your time with someone who

doesn't want to help you. Don't argue with an unrespon-
sive representative.

2. After you disengage from the difficult employee, call
back immediately, ask for a supervisor, and explain the incident. When speaking with the supervisor, never blame the
employee, even if s/he is at fault—it will only make you
look bad. Just state the facts and explain what you need.

3. Stress that you want to build a lasting and mutually
beneficial relationship with the company.

4. Ask whether the difficult employee annotated your
file; if so, request that any inappropriate remarks be delet-
ed or amended with your version of events.

5. If you feel the incident was inexcusable, call the
executive offices of the company (after you have returned
home) and explain your position, again stressing your
desire for a long-term relationship with the company.

Don't get branded as a black sheep by a renegade
employee. Understand the difficulties all travel employees
face, sympathize with stressful circumstances, work hard
to build a mutually beneficial relationship with companies
you like. But never accept less than stellar service from
insolent travel employees. After all, they work in a service
industry.

ASK, AND YOU SHALL RECEIVE

Today's traveler has a lot to complain about. Lines at the
airport are long, and there are increasing security measures
that occasionally include evacuations of airport terminals.

Add to that the usual delays and mix-ups, and travelers are stressed to the max. My friend was traveling with her two young daughters when their plane experienced mechanical difficulties. After sitting on the hot and sweltering runway for two hours, the plane returned to the gate. When she was finally able to locate airline representatives, they said that they could book her on a flight to her destination that left in six hours, offering nothing more than coach seats. She diplomatically told the agent that this offer was unacceptable. What she believed would be fair, she said, was a hotel near the airport, vouchers for dinner and breakfast, phone cards to call home, and a flight on a competitor's airline in the first-class cabin. The agent agreed to fulfill all of her requests. And when my friend returned home, she wrote a letter to that airline and received free vouchers for flights in the future. Remember, although you can profit by complaining, you should only do so when it is legitimate.

On the other hand, my friend Carol wished she had read this book before her mishap at Denver International Airport. Carol was about to fly home from a business meeting when her flight was delayed because United Airlines did not have anyone to fly the plane. When United finally located a flight crew, the pilots refused to fly because they had already worked too many hours. Three hours later, Carol was still stranded. Eventually, all the flights to her destination were canceled and she had to wait until the next day for a flight. When the airline announced that the flights were canceled, they also announced that they did not have any hotels available for the stranded passengers. So they handed out airline blankets and pillows. When Carol finally arrived at her destination the next morning, the nightmare continued. To retrieve her bags, which had been sent ahead the day before, she had to wait in one line to confirm that her bags were there. Then she had to wait in another line to actually get her bags. With all of these mishaps, she was not offered any compensation. However, after speaking with me about it, she sent a letter of complaint to United Airlines, who responded with a letter of apology and a $100 fare voucher.

IF YOU FIND YOURSELF STRANDED AT THE AIRPORT

Your highest priority will be to get on another flight. The quickest way to accomplish this is to head to the nearest pay phone or use your cell phone to call the airline's 800-number reservation service. Do not waste valuable time waiting in long lines of stranded passengers to get re-ticketed.

Here are some tips for getting what you want:

- Do not take "no" for an answer. My friend Susan was stranded in the blackout on the East Coast in August 2003. She stood in line for three hours before getting to a gate agent, who then said, "Sorry, all flights are full." Undeterred, Susan went to the ticket counter and asked to be put on a wait list. The ticket agent said it wouldn't make a difference but she'd do it anyway. And Susan did get on a flight.

- Be polite. Very often the customer-contact people are doing their best, and some things are beyond their control. Try to work with them patiently and politely to resolve the situation.

- Use your leverage. If you are a frequent flyer or elite flyer, use that to your advantage when asking to be re-ticketed.

If you are a member of the airline's private lounge, you can head there for help as well.

♦ Don't waste any time if the airport is closing due to weather or other circumstances. Go right to the rental car lots and get a car, and then go to a hotel that's not right near the airport. (The ones closest to the airport are probably going to be packed, and if they still have rooms available the prices are probably jacked up.) Call the hotel from your cell phone to lock in a reservation. You can get a listing of hotels from the car rental desk.

CONSIDER WHAT A COMPANY CAN AND CANNOT REASONABLY DO

Although the best companies want to provide an exceptional level of customer satisfaction, bear in mind that these companies also need to maintain profitability. Consequently, they cannot give away the store, so do consider what a company or its representatives can and cannot reasonably do. To illustrate, I was checking into a hotel and requested that the hotel provide me with points in my frequent-flyer account. I also requested points in the hotel's frequent-guest program. (At the time, this particular hotel chain was running a promotion that offered additional amenities based on the number of nights you stayed within a given time period. More importantly, I wanted to continue building my loyal customer history with the hotel.) However, the front-desk clerk to whom I had made my request said that she could not give me points in both my frequent-flyer and frequent-guest programs. I explained that this was a perfectly legitimate request that I am granted all the time, but she insisted it was not possible. When I politely asked that she check with her manager, she did, and she found out that what I had requested was allowable. Then, she not only apologized for giving me a hard time, she also upgraded me to a suite. This is why it is crucial to know what you can and cannot legitimately request.

Consider this quite different scenario. Perhaps you've arrived at your hotel late, and due to an error made by the hotel, they overbooked and have absolutely no vacancies. When you express your displeasure, however, the hotel does offer you a free night's stay at a comparable hotel and a free night at one of their own hotels at a later date. In this case, it would be unreasonable and unproductive to argue and demand a room in that hotel for that evening. It would also be unfeasible to expect the hotel to make a guest leave a room.

If an airline has delayed your flight for one hour due to mechanical reasons, you should probably just go with the flow. But if it is delayed for five hours, you might voice your concern and ask for a free ticket, first-class upgrade certificates, or an earlier flight on another airline. Likewise, if your room service meal arrived thirty minutes late, you should not expect the hotel to offer you a free weekend in their presidential suite; however, it is not unreasonable to expect the hotel to adjust your room service charges.

GO UP THE CHAIN OF COMMAND

If you are dissatisfied, try to deal with the problem immediately, and most often your dissatisfaction will be dealt with on the spot. You will also want to be sure that you are dealing with someone who has the willingness, authority, and desire to see to your needs. It is useless and a waste of your efforts to try to resolve a bad situation with someone who has neither the insight nor the authority to resolve the dilemma. You will want to avoid those individuals and seek out the ones who have the attitude and wherewithal to help you. At the airport, speak with the gate supervisor; on a tour, speak to the tour leader; on a cruise, seek out the steward; and at a hotel, speak to the general manager or his or her assistant. (There will be more specific advice about voicing complaints at hotels in the next section.) Don't, however, jump the chain of command unless you find it necessary; whenever possible, start with the source of the problem. If that does not yield the desired results, ask for that person's manager. And if that still does not get results, speak to that person's supervisor. Simply put, if the individual you are working with is unable or unwilling to assist you, seek out someone of higher authority. Do, however, remember to be diplomatic; never act pushy or overbearing.

QUICK REVIEW

- Ask for what you think is fair and appropriate to the circumstances, if what a company offers you to make amends is unacceptable.

- Seek appropriate compensation for your dissatisfaction, but bear in mind what is reasonable and feasible for the company to do. Do not be unreasonable in your requests.

- Deal with the problem immediately, and whenever

possible, begin by voicing your complaint to the person through whom you encountered the problem.

♦ Seek out someone with the willingness, authority, and desire to help you, and ask for a supervisor if you still are not satisfied.

THE BEST HOTELS ARE QUICK TO RESPOND TO CUSTOMER COMPLAINTS

When voicing your complaints to hotel industry companies in particular, you will find that they have great leeway in the amenities they can offer you. A seemingly inconsequential event voiced to the right person will reap surprisingly big rewards. Therefore, when you are at a hotel, if the person immediately assisting you is unwilling or unable to make amends, try to deal with the most senior employee on the premises. If you are unable to speak with the general manager or the property manager, try to speak with at least the assistant manager. The best hotels are very quick to respond to guests making a complaint. The last thing they want is a guest ranting and raving in the lobby, in front of other guests. That's the last thing you want to do as well. Whenever you make a complaint at a hotel—or at any travel company—make sure to do so calmly and courteously. Be understanding enough to realize that mishaps do occur from time to time.

Another thing to keep in mind is that it always gives you an edge when you approach your hotel complaint from the position of a loyal customer who cares about the overall service of the hotel. You could say, for example, "I have stayed here in the past, and on this occasion I am somewhat disappointed." Or you might say, "Is this hotel going through some changes, because..." Or you could also say, "In the past while staying at one of your hotels, I never had this kind of problem; is something wrong here?" If you are unable to meet and express your displeasure to the hotel's manager during your stay, you can also write a letter after checking out. In most instances, the manager will respond and usually offer you a free night's stay.

James was traveling with his wife and children on a return trip from Paris with a one-day stopover in Seattle, Washington. At the last minute, they rearranged their travel plans so they could stay at the airport Hilton Hotel. Unbeknownst to him at the time he made his reservation, that particular Hilton was due for extensive improvements. Their non-smoking room smelled of tobacco and the hallway carpets were badly stained. They were, however, too tired to complain at the time. The next day, my friend's wife approached the hotel manager and told him that their experience was atypical of the Hilton chain. Without another word, the manager zeroed out their charges, apologized for the shabby demeanor of the hotel, told her about the new improvements taking place, and invited her and her family back for a complimentary visit after the renovations were complete.

It is very easy for hotels to offer compensation for your dissatisfaction, because—believe it or not—so few people actually complain. A column in *The New York Times* quoted one Hyatt official who estimated that only one in every hundred people complain, and more times than not, that one person never asks the hotel to make specific amends. However, according to this article, those who do complain can expect appropriate compensation.

Complaints that might merit a free night's stay:

- A closed pool
- The sound of a jackhammer in the early morning
- No beach on the hotel property when the brochure showed pictures of a beach
- False fire alarms throughout the night
- No hot water
- Hotel under construction, causing inconveniences
- King-size bed is replaced with twin beds

Annoyances that might merit a free meal or drinks:

- Hotel employee is rude
- Excessive wait for a room
- Spa is closed
- Being stranded in the lobby without a bellhop
- A nonsmoking room reeks of cigarette smoke

CHOOSE YOUR BATTLES

At this point, it would be wise to make mention of employee attitudes. As you travel, you will come across some employees who have an excellent attitude, while other employees might be having a rough day or perhaps are not suited for a customer service job. On one occasion, I was traveling in the state of Washington and needed to take a carrier with whom I rarely fly. Prior to the flight, I called the airline's marketing department and asked if they would upgrade me, which they did. On my outbound flight, I was upgraded without a hitch. However, when I checked in for my return flight, the counter agent gave me a boarding pass for coach. Without looking at the boarding pass, I approached the gate agent to show my ID and asked her if I had an aisle seat in first class. She looked at me and sneered back, "You are not in first class." I replied that I was and asked her to double check. "No," she replied, "you are not in first class. Go to customer service if you want help." (By the way, I was the only person in line at the gate counter.)

In a somewhat foul mood, I went to customer service and asked for help. The woman there cheerfully informed me that I was issued the wrong boarding pass and took care of the problem. In this situation, I did not even bother to seek any amends from the company, because it is unlikely I will be flying with them again. This brings up another important point: Pick and choose your battles. Sometimes, it's just not worth it to complain. Your best payback is to not do any more business with them.

My advice is this: When you come across someone with a poor attitude, whether it's an airline employee or an employee of another kind of travel company, your best bet is to deal with someone else. The goal here is not to get into a clash with anyone. If you are on the phone with a difficult person, just end the call politely, call back, and get a more civil representative. Before you end your call with an unpleasant employee, however, do try to get that person's name, and when you speak to the new representative, tell her that you were just dealing with an unpleasant person. This will usually encourage the new representative to be extra nice to you. If you are dealing with someone unpleasant face to face, kindly ask to speak to that person's supervisor. And when the supervisor arrives, always be civil, no matter how upset you are. This will make you look blameless, and the supervisor will work harder to assist you.

DO ALL YOU CAN TO RESOLVE AIRLINE COMPLAINTS
BEFORE BOARDING

When voicing a complaint to airline industry companies, keep the following in mind: If you are dealing with an airline representative over the phone and are not satisfied, ask for customer service or the supervisor of the representative who is unwilling to meet your needs. And always try to get that person's name. If you complain while at the airport, you might try first to resolve your dilemma with the counter agent. If that is not successful, or if the counter agent does not have the authority or willingness to resolve the situation, then go higher. This probably will be a gate agent supervisor. You might also try to resolve your dilemma in the private members' lounge; usually those representatives provide a high level of quality service.

If you are on the plane, you will want to refrain from making complaints unless the situation is dire, such as finding yourself sitting next to an abusive or uncontrollably drunk person, or if you feel you're in real danger from a fellow passenger. Nevertheless, you must approach such situations with extreme delicacy. Do remember the caveat from Chapter 6: Flight crews are hypervigilant for anything that can be construed as a possible danger to them. If anyone on the flight crew perceives you as interfering with their duties—even if you are making a legitimate complaint about what you consider to be a serious situation—you could be liable for a fine by the FAA or even find yourself strong-armed by airline security once the plane lands.

Therefore, proceed with extreme caution while on board. If the flight crew is unwilling or too busy to deal with your problem, remain very polite and do not push the matter. Wait until after the flight and call the airline's corporate office, and be sure to document everything, including names.

THE REWARDS OF BEING BUMPED

Here is an interesting perspective on another sort of travel mishap—getting bumped from an airline flight. Being asked to give up your seat on an overbooked flight can be seen as an inconvenience; however, it can also work to your advantage. My friend Blake, who frequently flies in connection with his work for the government, was booked at the last minute on a Continental flight. Unfortunately, he did not have an advance opportunity to secure an upgrade to first class. So when the gate agent came back into the crowded and cramped coach section to ask if anyone would be willing to give up his seat, Blake readily volunteered. In return, Blake was offered a first-class seat on a flight one hour later and two vouchers for free future flights.

Getting bumped can reap valuable rewards, and according to the Department of Transportation, about 40% of passengers are bumped or volunteer their seats each year. If you are bumped, you can typically expect to receive a voucher worth a couple hundred dollars for a delay of a few hours, and a voucher worth $400 or more for a longer delay. However, as in Blake's case, compensation can be negotiated, leading to multiple tickets, cash, upgrade certificates, and more. When a gate agent enters the plane asking for volunteers is the time when the airline is the most desperate and the most lucrative incentives will be offered.

The same family who had the poor night at the Hilton in Seattle voluntarily gave up their five seats on an overbooked Chicago-to-Paris flight. For the minor inconvenience of spending one very pleasant night at the Hilton, they were rewarded with ticket vouchers worth $2,500. In addition, the gate agent called their Paris hotel to inform them of the family's delay.

THE POWER OF BUMPING

My friend Gail told me about a couple she knows that can turn one ticket into multiple international flights. Having a solid bumping strategy, they were able to parlay a flight to Costa Rica to a flight to Belize, and then another flight to Argentina—all for free from being bumped.

How did they do this? During a busy holiday season they were bumped from their original flight and received certificates for a free future flight, as well as $300. Then they ran to the next gate and put themselves on the bump list which led to another $300 and free flight. The gate agents were so friendly to this couple that when it became apparent that they would have to stay overnight they were offered a hotel room and were given insider information on the best restaurants and casinos.

Getting bumped can also be a good strategy for flying first class if you were otherwise unsuccessful in obtaining a first-class upgrade. Just make sure that as part of your compensation, you receive a first-class seat on the next flight. By the way, if you are already booked in first class, you will not usually be asked to give up your seat.

Your chances of being bumped are greater if you book your flight during a peak time (Thursday, Friday, or Sunday between 3 P.M. and 7 P.M.). If you're traveling on a route that has frequent departing flights, ask to be booked on a flight that is already full, but unless you want to risk spending the night in that city, make sure there's a later flight. Some travelers enjoy the fruits of being bumped several times on the same trip by traveling during peak periods, on busy holidays, and by volunteering to be bumped. Incidentally, if you did not get a boarding pass when you received your ticket, you have a better chance of being bumped. However, to be eligible for full compensation, you must be checked in at least twenty minutes before the flight. Finally, if your airline places you on another airline's flight as compensation, make sure to request that you receive "qualifying mileage" credit on your chosen airline for that flight. This will help you continue to build your loyal customer status with your airline.

NOTHING BUT THE BEST

The aforementioned techniques for voicing complaints with the airlines and hotels can be applied to a broad range of situations. These methods will also be effective if you experience trouble with a car rental company or a cruise line. Virtually any time a quality travel company fails to meet your standards, these strategies will work to correct the mishap. In fact, if you effectively voice a legitimate complaint to any type of service-related company, you can receive appropriate compensation. For example, if a retailer fails to deliver your new television set on time, you can usually negotiate a free service contract or voucher for free merchandise. I once received a $50 store certificate when Circuit City failed to properly deliver my television. Or if a restaurant does not properly prepare your meal, speak up in a courteous and respectful manner. In fact, today's diners at all levels of restaurants are more likely to send their plates back if they are not satisfied. One restaurateur, Ron Trimberger, was quoted in *The Wall Street Journal* as saying that more customers today "know what they want and what they don't want." This trend is true of all industries, particularly the travel industry. Today's consumers have a wide array of choices available to them, and companies know that dissatisfied consumers will simply take their business elsewhere.

As a consumer on a quest for first-class travel, you have the right to expect and receive nothing less than the best. If a travel company fails to meet your (and its) high standards, inform the highest-ranking official in a professional and caring manner. This will always ensure that you maintain your own high standards of traveling in an ultra-luxurious mode.

Key Points

➤ *Understand that high quality companies strive to maintain their reputations.*
This allows the savvy traveler the opportunity to benefit when a quality travel company makes an error or otherwise fails to maintain its high standards.

➤ *Do not take advantage of a travel company's goodwill.*
It is unwise and unethical to exploit the good intentions of quality travel companies. Taking advantage will prevent you from building a solid, long-term relationship with those companies, because eventually they will lose interest in serving you.

➤ *Complain in a way that will get results:*

1. If your complaint is escalated to a higher level by a helpful employee, start by praising the employee who was assisting you beforehand.

2. Always voice your complaint in a positive manner. Do not approach the situation as adversarial.

3. Try to work for a mutually beneficial relationship.

4. Let the company know that you are not pleased with their service and that you would return if more appropriate service is offered next time.

5. Use the power of the pen/e-mail and voice your complaint to the CEO's office.

➤ *Restrain your eagerness to initially request a specific form of amends.*

In many cases, you will be better off allowing the company's representative to make the first offer of amends. If you make a preemptive request, you might come across as trying to exploit the situation. Quite often the company's offer will exceed what you might have requested.

➤ *Seek compensation that is appropriate and reasonable for the mistake and the circumstances.*

When you do request specific compensation for your dissatisfaction, ask for something that is reasonable and fair. Do not request a free week at a hotel for late room service.

➤ *Don't waste your time wrangling with someone who has a poor attitude.*

Seek out another representative (or a competing company) who is willing to help you. When voicing pre- or post-flight complaints to an airline, go up the chain of command until you are satisfied. However, be extremely careful to avoid being perceived as troublesome when you are in-flight. There can be serious consequences.

13

Using the Internet for Traveling First Class at Coach Prices

New Resources for Getting What You Want

It is estimated that approximately 80% of U.S. households have access to the worldwide web. With this growth in the number of people connected, the internet has become an indispensable tool for finding bargains of all kinds. However, you need to understand the potential pitfalls to optimize your chances of luxury travel.

Travel booking has become one of the biggest areas of e-commerce on the internet. The internet has virtually turned scores of armchair travelers into travel agents. For my taste, unless it's a first-class upgrade, a hotel suite, or a luxury car, my travel philosophy is to know what to expect—no surprises. I want to feel confident that I've sufficiently pre-planned my trip to ensure the most luxurious experience possible. With the wealth of unbiased and valuable information available online, there is no reason to be surprised.

That said, some of the information on the internet is dubious at best. There are a wide range of people with entirely different travel goals and objectives from your own. Information may also be tainted because it was written and posted by travel suppliers whose only interest is to get your money. (See the sidebar in Chapter 7 about hotel travel reviews.) My goal for using the internet is to find the most valuable information (including the lowest price) in the fewest number of mouse clicks. This includes: flight options (most convenient times, fewest stops, best seats, penalties), hotel options (room types with photos, availability of upgrades, who is the manager), resort information (weather conditions, restaurants, tee times, pool locations, ski conditions), city information (maps, shopping, where to eat, tours, subways, sights to see), car rentals (size, options, charges/fees, cost for upgrading). Or more subjective information, such as: the best tour guide in Milan, the best walking tour in New England, the hottest shopping tips for Hong Kong, the trendiest clubs in Paris, the best way to get from the charming city of Cusco, Peru to majestic Machu Picchu, Peru.

The internet also contains a multitude of time saving travel advice essential to navigating today's multifarious world of travel. Whether you're at your home computer, in the office, accessing wi-fi on the road, or traveling with a mobile device of any kind, the internet can inform you well in advance of other travelers when your flight is canceled. It can assist with finding alternative accommodations when your hotel tells you that they gave your room to someone else. The advantage of using the internet is growing exponentially each day. However, there can be pitfalls with having too much information.

SIMPLICITY IS BEST

Many of my colleagues spend literally hours each day searching for the best travel deals. One such individual told me over our morning breakfast that he got the greatest deal the night before by surfing the internet for the best rate. He told me that he saved $20 on a ticket from San Francisco to New York. My first question was how long it took to find this fare. His response was five hours. I then asked him if he could upgrade his flight. Since he booked the ticket on a third-party site, his ticket was not upgradeable. To make matters worse, while he was in New York, there was a snowstorm and since his ticket was booked on a third-party site, the airline referred him to the web site's 800-number where he encountered busy lines and extended wait times. After he returned from his trip I asked him to calculate the time he missed from his family while booking the ticket and what he considered to be the cost of the stress trying to re-book his flight. Clearly a $20 savings did not outweigh the hassles associated with his ticket.

My first bit of advice is to keep it simple. There are far too many choices and internet sites to explore. Trying to research the entire worldwide web would literally take you eons. It is important to develop and stick to a stated goal or objective. Ask yourself what it is you're trying to achieve when researching your travels. The foremost goal of the penny-pinching luxury traveler is to discover hidden treasures in the vast array of travel choices that are available.

Focus your search by following the foremost principle of this book, which is building mutually beneficial relationships with a select number of travel providers. Ideally, at this stage you have already chosen a preferred airline, one to three groups of hotels, and two car rental companies to work with. Search their sites for special deals, and also sign up for a limited number of travel newsletters. I recommend www.elliott.org, The Frequent Flyer Crier (www.frequent-flyer.com), and www.webflyer.com.

In my opinion, these web sites, along with the dedicated sites of your travel providers, will provide you with all the information you need to know. Incidentally, each of the newsletters I mentioned are free and has links to other travel web sites if you really need them.

A WORD ABOUT THIRD-PARTY SITES

All major travel providers have dedicated sites where you can research and book your travel. There are also third-party sites, such as Expedia, Orbitz, Travelocity, priceline.com, hotels.com, and many more. If you truly want to travel in luxury by building mutually beneficial relationships, then you will book your travel directly through your travel provider, and not through these third-party sites. This not only benefits your travel provider by lowering their cost of distribution, it provides you with the opportunity to earn bonus miles and other discounts. In addition, it allows you to deal directly with your travel provider when something goes wrong, such as if a flight is canceled or delayed or whatever else can happen in the world of travel.

I do not use any of the third-party sites, but some travelers have told me they love them and others have had very bad experiences with them. For example, I recently read about a traveler who booked his ticket through one of the third-party sites, and when he arrived at the airport he was told that he did not have a reservation. In this situation, the traveler had to purchase new tickets at the airport and try to sort out the issue with the third-party provider. Earlier in this book I wrote about the time I arrived at the ticket counter and the agent told me that I did not have a reservation. Well, of course I knew I had one, so fortunately I found a ticket agent whom I knew and the whole matter was sorted out in minutes. If I were in the habit of booking through third parties, however, I would not have had the opportunity to develop the all-important personal relationships that I have developed with my travel providers, relationships that pave the way to the highest level of service in all my transactions.

However, not all third party web sites are dubious. I like the sites of Kayak.com and SideStep.com. Both of these are what they call mega sites, meaning that they search virtually all travel providers' fares and rates, and then direct you to the actual provider's site. These sites are a wonderful means for searching and determining if you're getting the best value in your travel bookings.

WHAT ABOUT PRICE—ISN'T IT CHEAPER BOOKING TRAVEL ON THIRD-PARTY SITES?

From the enormous amount of data that I have reviewed, including sources from the Department of Transportation, Air Transport Association Office of Economics, academic studies, and the work I did for my doctoral dissertation in industrial organizational psychology, I have concluded that over the long run there is not enough of a variance in price to give third-party sites a competitive price advantage. Likewise, using a sophisticated tool to assess the competitiveness of prices found on travel web sites, FareChase, Inc. analyzed 350 of the nation's busiest travel markets and found that no single web site or internet source offers the lower price.

Certainly there are times when you will find the golden goose of a deal. But many times the amount of money you save has a bigger price tag: time, as in the case of my friend and his ticket to New York I mentioned a few pages earlier. Another friend told me he'd saved $57 on a $625 ticket by booking through a third-party site. For his 9% savings he spent four hours on the internet, which is four hours that he could have spent with his wife and kids. Ask yourself what your own time and peace of mind are worth to you.

The main point to keep in mind is my mantra throughout this book: Build mutually beneficial relationships. Booking directly through your travel provider helps accomplish this. This is one of the many important principles to follow if you want to travel in a luxurious fashion while paying discounted prices. It is just as important as following the contrarian travel strategy, using your tips as an investment, making prudent use of credit cards, and using the internet as a tool of convenience rather than a time-consuming anchor.

It is not my intent to disparage third-party travel providers; again, I have spoken with a number of travelers who have had good experiences with them. However, I have spoken to an equal if not greater number whose experiences were not so pleasant.

The internet is a living reference providing the most updated and useful information for travel. The "living" part is the fact that the internet is continuously updated with the most current information. Judicial use of this tool will aid travelers for years to come. Your key is to find your most useful information, giving you the highest level of confidence while spending the least amount of time. After all, you don't want to spend more time researching your trip than taking it.

Key Points

➤ Increasingly the internet is becoming the preferred mode of purchasing travel services. In 2006, 60% of all airline tickets were booked on the internet. It is expected that 77% of all airline tickets will be booked on the internet in 2008.

➤ Keep it simple to preserve your time and sanity. Currently one can surf over 100 million travel sites. Clearly, it would take an immeasurable amount of time to surf all these sites. Therefore, focus on a few sites that will provide you with clear, unbiased, and timely information. The reference section of this book offers a few web sites that should fit the bill.

➤ Use the web sites of your preferred travel providers. Very often their prices will be the same or less than what you will find on third party sites, such as Orbitz and Travelocity. In fact, many travel providers, including the Hilton and Hyatt groups of hotels, offer a low price guarantee, promising that you will not find a lower price on any other travel site. This is a policy that all direct travel providers will eventually implement.

➤ Studies show that there are no competitive advantages by shopping around on a multitude of travel web sites versus purchasing travel on one particular web site. However do check with third party web sites just to confirm that you are getting the best price on your preferred travel provider's web site.

For the Best Value, Book Direct

Third-party sites have revolutionized travel, but their time has passed. For all their usefulness, third-party travel web sites can be as much a burden as a boon. The conventional wisdom is to check three or four web sites before purchasing travel services. I say: Hold on a minute. The guy who spoke to me after a speech in San Francisco would agree. He had spent six hours searching web sites for bargain airfares and found he could save only $25.

"It's not worth it," he said. In the end, he purchased the ticket directly from the airline's web site. In my opinion, that's what he should have done in the first place.

The online sale of airline tickets dates back to December 1995, when Alaska Airlines sold airline tickets to a family of four over the internet. That simple transaction changed consumers' travel planning forever. Before the advent of travel web sites, it was difficult for travelers to access products, pricing, and other travel information There was not a lot of marketplace transparency, i.e., customers couldn't easily compare prices among competing airlines and other travel providers. As a result, customers leaned on travel agents and ticket sellers to guide their travel experiences. Thanks to sites like Expedia, Travelocity, and Orbitz, transparency is now the industry standard and consumers are both savvier and better served. Travelers literally have a world of information available through their computers.

Credit for a revolutionary change in travel booking should be given to the early trailblazers. But I'm afraid their time has come and gone. According to PhoCusWright, an independent consulting firm, online bookings through a third-party agency will comprise 55% of all travel bookings in 2007, a market share that represents $136 billion in business. These are big numbers, and they have gotten the attention of direct service providers, e.g., airlines, hotels, and car-rental agencies. These suppliers have responded with low-price guarantees, bonus miles, and a seamless booking experience for customers who book directly with them, whether online or by phone. PhoCusWright reports that consumer perceptions of direct-supplier web sites have improved in recent years; in fact, a 2004 study found that 55% of consumers believed that direct travel providers offer the best price. I suspect the numbers are much higher today.

It makes sense when you think about it. Whenever you have a middleman, prices are going to be higher. If I sell my used car directly, I avoid paying distribution or commission costs; if I sell it on eBay, I pay to use their services. Sometimes a broker or intermediary can provide added value, but when you're booking a single hotel room, a car rental, or a flight from point A to point B, there really isn't much to it.

Today, third-party web sites cannot compete with direct providers in terms of price and service. Let me give you a few recent examples.

I needed to book a flight from Tel Aviv, Israel, to Amman, Jordan. Using a metasearch engine, I found that Royal Jordanian Air offered a flight (I will explain metasearch engines in a moment). The best fare I could find was about $240. When I called Delta Air Lines to see if they could book this flight for me (I was already flying Delta from the United States to Tel Aviv), the agent offered me a rate of $200. In another case, a third-party web site offered me a $638 round trip fare between Barcelona, Spain and Budapest, Hungary, while Malev Airline's web site offered me the same flight for 195 euros. Even with the exchange rate, I fared far better.

Other airlines offer incentives for travelers booking direct. For example, Frontier Airlines offered free DIRECTV service for travelers who purchased tickets online before a certain date last year, as long as the travel commenced before the end of the year.

Better service and cost savings are not limited to the airlines. Back in March, I booked a room at the Grand Hyatt Kauai for a trip in May. Weeks later, I noticed that the room rate offered on the hotel's web site was $50 a night less. I called Hyatt's reservations line, explained the situation, was placed on hold for 30 seconds and, presto, I had a new rate and confirmation e-mailed to me. This simple phone call direct to the company netted me a savings of $200—enough to pay for the rental car. Would this have happened with a third-party site? From the scores of letters I have received seeking advice about how to deal with similar situations, I doubt it.

In another instance, I booked a room for the San Francisco Hilton. I mistakenly booked the wrong date and did not notice my error for a few weeks. I finally realized what had happened when I saw the room charge on my credit card. When I called the hotel and explained my mistake, the Hilton not only refunded the no-show charge but also honored the lower rate I had booked, even though the room rate had risen by more than $100.

These stories go on and on. The point is that direct providers of services have a greater vested interest in your booking than do third-party providers, so they work harder to assure your customer satisfaction.

Still, there are a few occasions when a third-party web site can offer good value.

1. **Specialized or exotic travel.** If you are planning a trip to Africa or other exotic locale, a resourceful site or travel agent can be of great help. Likewise, a site like Road Trips, which offers "The Ultimate in Sports Roadtrips, Travel and Tours," is indeed a source of added value for those seeking a unique sports outing.

2. **Metasearch engines.** These sites search numerous providers (airlines, car rental companies, and hotels) to find the lowest price and then direct you to the provider for booking. This is particularly useful when you're not sure what is available, as was the case when I was searching for a flight from Tel Aviv to Amman. In that case, I used the site Kayak.com. Metasearch sites usually do not book travel but rather redirect you to the provider's own web site; they earn a nominal fee for each referral. Since the price quoted can be higher than you need to pay (as was the case with my Tel Aviv/Amman ticket), I tend to gather information from the metasearch sites, then go directly to my provider of choice for booking. Mobissimo, Qixo, and Sidestep are other popular metasearch sites for travel services.

3. **Strong performers.** If you're intent on using third-party sites, be aware that some appear to do a better job with price then others. For example, according to PhoCusWright, hotel rates available through the American Automobile Association (AAA) were generally lower in

twenty key metropolitan areas than those on Expedia, Hotels.com, Orbitz, and Travelocity.

The choice is yours: Spend endless hours surfing the web, or go direct to save time and money—and get better service.

AND NOW YOU ARE ON YOUR WAY

**PROVIDE ME WITH GOOD SERVICE—I'M A LOYAL CUS-
TOMER. TREAT ME OTHERWISE—YOU HAVE COMPETITION.**

The philosophy behind this book is to promote an understanding of the finer points of travel, hospitality, and luxury, cultivating an environment in which you can indulge in a lifestyle of unparalleled comfort.

I for one count myself fortunate to have experienced the global universe we are all a part of. Most telling during my travels is how similar we all are. Whether I'm sitting along a road in a far-off village in Ethiopia buying beers for the locals or enjoying the cache of a Paris café, I find we all have a common thread, and for me travel has been a road to experience the wonders of our world. However and wherever you choose to travel, maintaining a principle of seeking travel experiences of exceptional quality through superior personal service can bestow a sense of pride and satisfaction, and memories of a lifetime.

As I've explained, we do this through the creation of alliances with the finest luxury travel companies, and our success depends on the united efforts of many—we are most effective when we work together cooperatively, respecting each others' contributions and importance.

Accordingly, in our careful interactions with travel providers, we seek to deal with others as we would have them deal with us. The cornerstone of the Penny Pincher's philosophy is this mutual respect, and the understanding that you represent value to travel companies—and that they in turn deserve to earn a fair and reasonable profit so they can continue to meet your needs.

Whenever you travel, embark with the trust that your travel partners will deliver comprehensive, highly personalized service that feels complete and consistent, clearly reflecting an ambiance of the best that the world has to offer. And for those you come into contact with, whether it's a bell person or housekeeper, get to know them and spread the warmth of the world. You'll be amazed how this feel-good action pays dividends, just as much as sitting in first class or staying at the best hotels. Remember when it is all said and done the true beauty of travel is the interaction we have with the natural beauty of the world and those who surround us.

Throughout this book it has not been my intention to be a spokesman for any particular travel provider. All I know is that by following the principles outlined here, I have traveled the world first class at coach prices.

My best to you, and may your journeys fulfill your innermost desires.

RESOURCES
— *and* —
REFERENCES

Traveling First Class at Coach Prices

As I've said throughout this book, researching your journeys in order to travel in a luxurious fashion while paying discounted prices is extrememly important. Focus your research and follow the contrarian travel strategy so you can travel to the destinations where and when your business will be the most needed and appreciated. Remember that when a travel company has low demand and high supply, you will get a lower price and a higher level of preferential treatment.

Today's information age has made it relatively simple to become a travel agent. You can research every aspect of your trips before departing, giving you more control of your travel experience. Travel providers have developed easy-to-use web sites that allow you to book your own flights and hotel rooms and also check on the number of points listed in your frequent-user accounts.

The benefit of researching your travels is that you will be contacting your travel partners directly. This is an essential step in securing the best possible travel experiences at the lowest possible prices. Researching your travels also provides an opportunity to spend a few minutes talking with a travel company representative who will give you a good sense of what is available. This also helps you to negotiate the lowest price. Another reason to call directly is so that you can ascertain the ideal travel times for your needs. You can ask an airline representative which flights are not as heavily booked and which ones will allow you the best chance of an upgrade. You will be able to ask the hotel representative when a hotel has a high or low occupancy rate, thus allowing you to determine the best opportunities for an upgrade. This also holds true for getting the best rental cars and the most luxurious cabin on the cruise ship. Calling directly also provides you with the flexibility to alter your travel decisions on the spot. If you are working through a travel agent, on the other hand, often the agent will have to get back to you with a few options that might not be available by the time he calls you back. Researching your travel might take a little more time and effort on your part, but when the result is a luxurious travel experience, I am sure you will agree that it is well worth it.

Insiders' Tips

Here's a refresher list of tips from *The Penny Pincher's Passport to Luxury Travel*:

- *Feel secure when you buy*—as a general rule, airfares that range from $199 to $373 (domestically), and less than $599 (internationally) represent a fair price. Luxury hotels rooms ranging from $125 to $225 both domestically and internationally suggest an excellent value. Car rentals ranging from $19 per day to a weekly rate of $99 will also provide you with good value.

- *Get a lower fare after you paid*—most travel providers will lower your existing rate or fare if their prices drop after you purchased their travel services. In most instances, hotels and car rental companies will simply adjust your rate. On occasion, airlines will try to charge you a change fee of as much as $100. If this is the case, ask for a voucher good for up to a year on a future flight.

- *Stay informed*—get on the list for e-mail notifications of special opportunities with your travel providers. This will open the door to exclusive fares, rates, upgrades, and special mileage earning possibilities.

- *Be flexible*—fly a day earlier or later. This might provide you better pricing and upgrading opportunities.

- *Get the best seat on the plane*—when making your flight reservation, ask the agent what type of aircraft is used on this route. Then go onto the airline's web site or click on www.seatguru.com to see the cabin configuration of the plane. This will help you avoid getting a seat that does not recline because of an emergency row.

- *Be nice to gate agents*—the gate agent is your most powerful ally. She can make your trip more enjoyable (i.e. better seating, an upgrade, a meal voucher, frequent-flyer miles, endorsing your ticket to another airline, etc.).

- *Stand-by for the flight you want*—sometimes an upgrade or a better fare is only available on a later flight. If you encounter this but prefer a different flight, try to fly stand-by on the early flight or the flight of your preference. It is best to call your airline and check on the flight's load factor so that you do not needlessly wait at the airport. The lower the load factor the better.

- *Get to your seat early*—this will help you find overhead bin space before it all fills up. Most airlines allow any elite frequent-flyer member to board early.

- *Facing a delay or cancellation*—try flying out of a nearby alternative airport. For example, if your flight at LAX is cancelled, you might try flying out of John Wayne or Long Beach airports.

♦ *Getting bumped*—when you are bumped from your airline seat, whether voluntarily or involuntarily, the amount of compensation is negotiable. Hold out for a worthwhile prize such as upgrade coupons or free flights, and on your reconnected flight make sure that your seat is in first class.

♦ *Keep your schedule simple*—usually this means taking a non-stop flight (if available) to avoid potential problems such as a mechanical delay, a wait at security, or just bad weather.

♦ *Take your luggage with you*—when possible, try to carry on your luggage. This will save you time and prevent your belongings from getting lost. (Make sure to check tsa.gov or your airline's web site for the latest carry-on restrictions.) If traveling on a long trip with a lot of luggage or bringing items prohibited onboard, check your bags at the ticket counter or with a sky cap. But be warned—recently some airlines are starting to charge for checking in more than one bag. Alternatively you can ship your items, relatively inexpensively, using UPS or FedEx ground services.

♦ *Handing over your luggage*—the surcharges for oversized and heavy bags can run as high as $180 on some airlines. Instead of checking your big bags in at the ticket counter, have the sky cap process your bag—but remember to tip accordingly. If the sky cap takes your baggage without charge, a tip from $5 to $20 is appropriate, depending on the size and number of bags.

- *Ask about surcharges*—often travel rates can be laden with extra charges that are not disclosed until you buy your ticket, check out of a hotel, or return your car. These can be in the form of taxes, city fees, phone connection charges, drop-off fees, or a special assessment—know before you go.

- *Check-out those special rates*—many travelers innocently accept group rates or conference rates as the lowest price. This is not always true, so call the travel provider directly to see what rates would be offered if you were not part of a group or conference.

- *Be a contrarian*—maintain an open mind for your leisure trips by being flexible enough to travel on several possible dates and times. Also consider destinations off the beaten path or an off-season destination, this will help you avoid high prices and big crowds.

- *Keep the faith*—even if you are told by a gate agent that only three upgrades are available and you are number five on the wait-list, all is not lost. Often, passengers will have already boarded the plane or there can be no-shows, thus leaving the upgrade for you.

- *Use your partners*—travel alliances have expanded your ability to travel where and when you want, and to use your award miles. Don't forget to ask about partner affiliates; this includes both airlines and hotel companies.

- *Make the fast track to elite status*—many travel providers offer end-of-year specials making it easier to earn elite status. For example, airlines will credit your account with bonus elite-qualifying miles for flying certain routes or flying a specific number of flights before the end of the year. Typically these programs are announced in October. Some programs require that you sign up for their promotions, so check with your travel provider for specific details.

- *Seek out other elite promotions*—many travel providers quietly offer promotional incentives to tie consumers into their loyalty programs by allowing them to earn elite status in special ways. Currently, American Airlines and America West offer a chance to earn elite status with only two trips. Check with your travel providers for any such programs.

- *Switching your elite status*—once you have earned elite status with a travel provider you can usually switch that status to a competing provider by calling your preferred vendor and requesting it.

- *Be persistent*—if you have tried everything to get an upgrade for a flight, hotel room, or luxury rental car without luck, ask to be added to the waiting list. As flights fill up, yield management determines whether revenue seats are being purchased as scheduled. If it looks as if too many seats will go empty on a flight, or too many hotel rooms or rental cars will go unsold, the providers will loosen capacity controls for lower fares and award travel.

- *Checking the stars*—hotel ratings are increasingly becoming an important decision barometer for would-be travelers. However, all stars are not equal. Due to the prestigious recognition of ratings from the American Automobile Association (AAA) and Mobil Travel Guides, many web sites and hotels have begun to arbitrarily assign their own ratings. A five-star rating from travel web sites trying to sell rooms very often can be a three-star rating under more rigorous independent assessment. Before confirming your five-star room, check the hotel's quality with impartial raters such as: AAA and the *Mobil Travel Guide* (www.aaa.com, www.mobiltravelguide.com). The *Mobil Travel Guide* tends to be more meticulous and does not rely on advertising from hotels. If you cannot find your hotel's listing among these guides, check out the other hotels within the brand name. For example, if it is a Kempinski Hotel, check out the Kempinski web site to get an idea of what their other hotels are like.

What Do I Read?

A FIRST-CLASS LIST OF TRAVEL EXPERTS

- FlyerTalk (www.flyertalk.com)—when you want to know what travelers are saying about various airlines, hotels, etc., check out Randy Peterson's web site. An excellent source for the real inside story for the Sky Warrior community.

- Christopher Elliott's site (www.elliott.org)—this site offers an excellent weekly newsletter, filled with insightful commentaries, articles, and the latest travel information. Chris also includes links to articles from other writers, which I find very helpful.

- FrequentFlier.com (www.frequentflier.com)—this site is an excellent resource for researching travel programs and the latest opportunities for earning bonus miles.

- Johnny Jet (www.johnnyjet.com)—the ultimate travel portal with links to every imaginable travel-related site, including links to all of the weekly newspaper and TV stories about travel.

- SmarterLiving (www.smarterliving.com)—this site is an excellent collection of newsletters, and articles from informative travel writers.

- Airliners.net (www.airliners.net)—this is a comprehensive site for aviation enthusiasts.

- MSNBC.com—offers a variety of travel destination stories, as well as travel tips.

How to Compare and Research Fares and Rates from Your Travel Provider

Use the following sites to cross-reference the fares and rates from your travel providers.

- Kayak.com

- SideStep.com

General Information Travel Web Sites

- Air Traffic Control System Command Center (www.fly.faa.gov)—a handy site for checking real-time flight status at airports across the country.

- Aviation Consumer Protection Division (http://airconsumer.ost.dot.gov)—in the event your service is not what it should be, this is the site to write an airline's consumer representative, or to register a formal complaint with the government.

- CDC Travelers' Health (www.cdc.gov/travel)—this site provides health information on specific destinations. What to know before you go.

- SeatGuru (www.seatguru.com)—a useful site for determining the best seats on a number of airline flights. Includes cabin configurations and advice about what seats to get and what ones to avoid.

- Transportation Security Administration (www.tsa.gov)—for the most up-to-date information on security issues at the nation's airports.

- U.S. Department of State Bureau of Consular Affairs (travel.state.gov)—official travel warnings and advisories for all countries of the world.

- World Travel Watch (www.worldtravelwatch.com)— updates on changing travel conditions, from security issues to transit strikes to border closings.

My Select List of Hotel Chains

A list of hotel chains that offer considerable global coverage and great loyalty rewards.

Four Seasons Hotels & Resorts
(www.fourseasons.com)
800-332-3442

The Four Seasons group of hotels specializes in offering a travel experience of exceptional quality. They strive to be recognized as the world's finest collection of hotels and resorts. Their properties offer an experience of enduring value using superior service, supported with a deeply instilled ethic of personal service. The Four Seasons meets the needs and tastes of the most discriminating travelers, making them the world's premier luxury hospitality company. The Four Seasons currently manages 59 properties in 28 countries.

Hyatt
(www.hyatt.com)
800-233-1234

Hyatt has long been regarded as a leader in the hospitality industry serving business, group, and leisure customers and has been on the forefront in developing faster, more efficient check-in options, including 1-800-CHECKIN, which allows guests to check in to their hotel rooms in the U.S. and Canada by telephone. The company also is known for introducing other concepts to the hotel industry, including Regency Club floors that offer premium VIP services with a

concierge and club lounge on every floor. There are 207
Hyatt hotels and resorts around the world. The Park Hyatt
brand is a favorite of mine.

Preferred Hotels & Resorts
(www.preferredhotels.com)
800-323-7500

Worldwide hotelier with such high-end properties as the
Montage Laguna Beach, the Broadmoor, and the Landmark
London. The majority of properties are in the U.S., but
Europe, Asia, the Middle East, and the Caribbean also have
a good variety of resorts to choose from.

Shangri-La Hotels & Resorts
(www.shangri-la.com)
800-942-5050

Asia's leading luxury hotel group, with 44 properties in Asia
Pacific and the Middle East, Shangri-La provides the very
finest elements of Asian hospitality and service. Their guests
enjoy exceptional consistency in delivery of service.

St. Regis Hotels & Resorts
(www.starwood.com/stregis)
800-325-3589

A division of Starwood Hotels & Resorts Worldwide, Inc.,
the flagship hotel of this chain is the St. Regis New York,
built in 1904 by John Jacob Astor IV. Fourteen properties are
located around the world, with ten more slated to open in
the near future.

The Leading Hotels of the World
(www.lhw.com)
800-745-8883

Leading Hotels of the World understands the finer points of hospitality and luxury. Their philosophy embraces a lifestyle of 5-star luxury and unparalleled comfort, catering to the discriminating few, where first-class service is a norm rather than an exception. Leading Hotels of the World features small luxury hotels, resort hotels, as well as world-renowned stately hotels offering all the possibilities for family getaways, romantic escapades, and business meetings. Each year, The Leading Hotels of the World, Ltd. publishes a directory of its member hotels which includes many Four Seasons, Ritz-Carlton, and St. Regis properties.

Car Rental Companies

My top list of car rental companies that operate on a worldwide basis:

Avis Rent A Car
www.avis.com/AvisWeb/home/AvisHome
800-831-2847

Hertz Rent A Car
www.hertz.com
800-654-3131

Europcar
www.europcar.com

Credit Card Frequently Asked Questions

Q. What kind of a rewards card gives you the "best bang for your buck"?

A. It depends on your personal travel preference. For example:

- If you fly frequently then airline cards are your best bet.
- If you want a card that provides various travel options, then American Express or Diners Club Card is the way to go.
- If you desire cash, then Discover Card or American Express Blue would be the best.

Q. How do you accumulate airline miles?

A. You can earn miles when you use an award-based credit card to pay for traveling expenses, everyday purchases, and paying your bills. It is generally best to use a card that is associated with your preferred airline. These cards typically offer bonus miles for travel-related purchases. However, calculate the fees associated with the card (annual fees, APR, overseas transaction fees) and determine your projected spending to decide if using the card provides good value.

Q. Which mileage-earning credit cards allow you to transfer miles to any airline?

A. American Express and Diners Club.

Q. Is there a credit card where I can earn 1 airline mile for each $1 spent?

A. Yes, most credit cards affiliated with a specific airline (i.e., United Mileage Plus Visa) offer one mile for each dollar charged. Moreover, when purchasing tickets with the affiliated airline you usually earn bonus miles. Also, many airline cards offer sign-up and annual renewal bonuses that can be as much as 15,000 miles.

Q. Which credit cards earn miles but have no annual fee?

A. American Express Delta SkyMiles Options Card

Q. Are airline credit card reward programs a good deal?

A. It depends on your spending habits. Consumers who charge a lot and pay off the balance each month benefit the most from these programs. For example, if you expect to spend more than $9,000 per year and do not consistently carry over a balance of more than $1,000, then it can be a good deal. In general, the annual fees are fairly high and the interest rates are normally not attractive.

Q. Are there debit cards that are tied with loyalty reward programs?

A. Yes. Alaska Airlines Visa Check Card, Citibank AAdvantage Debit Card, America West Flight Fund Visa Check Card, Continental OnePass Banking Card, Northwest WorldPerks Check Card, and U.S. Airways Dividend Miles Visa Check Card.

Q. When I transfer my balance to a new card do I earn points?

A. It depends on the card issuer's program policy. Some will offer points for balance transfers as a special incentive to sign up, but afterwards do not award points for these purchases.

Q. How are sky-miles redeemed?

A. If you belong to an air-mileage program that is affiliated with a major airline, then you simply contact the airline and tell them you intend to use your miles for a trip. If the air-mileage program is not directly affiliated with an airline and is operated by the credit card issuer or a third party, then you need to contact the issuer for details on how to redeem the miles for free or discounted travel.

Q. Which credit cards give you airline miles?

A. Unbranded mileage cards are offered through a number of banks under the Visa and MasterCard brand. Likewise, American Express and Diners Club cards have mileage-earning programs. The benefit of these programs is having redemption options with many different airlines. However, the best mileage-earning opportunities are usually connected to cards affiliated with a specific airline.

Q. Where can I find the exchange rate a credit card issuer charges for foreign currency?

A. This information can usually be found on the card issuer's web site. You can also call the card issuer's customer service center to verify the current policy on foreign transactions. In any event, it is a good idea to call your card issuer when traveling overseas, so your card is not flagged or suspended for a security alert.

Q. Which credit card gives the best exchange rates for foreign purchases?

A. Cards issued by smaller institutions such as community banks and credit unions charge a 1% fee. Most of the top issuers now charge a 3% foreign transaction fee. Call your issuer and check on the fee before heading overseas.

Q. My credit card issuer has raised its fee on international transactions to 4%. When I complained to my card issuer, they told me that all credit card companies have raised their fees, and that theirs are competitive. Is this correct?

A. No, most credit card issuers continue to charge a 1% foreign exchange fee. Most issuers of the major co-branded airline cards charge a 3% fee. American Express and Diners Club generally charge a 2% fee.

Q. What is the best card to use in European countries?

A. Generally, there is wide acceptance of any Visa, Master-Card, Diners Club, or American Express cards.

Q. Are there any credit cards that don't charge fees for international transactions?

A. No. All credit card issuers charge a minimum fee of 1%. Usually the fee is not noticed because it is masked in the currency conversion transaction. Keep in mind that this fee is 1% over the wholesale exchange rate, which is a good deal compared to using cash or other forms of payment. However, recently some card issuers have raised their fees. If you plan to use your card overseas, call the issuer and check on their most current conversion rates and fees.

Q. Are cash withdrawals overseas possible?

A. Yes, if you have a PIN to access an ATM machine.

APPENDIX

Frequent Flyer, Elite Status, and Upgrade Information

Many frequent-flyer programs announced major changes to their programs on January 1, 2004. Many airlines are now rewarding qualifying miles for elite status based on the type and cost of the fare. The following illustrates the most common method of accruing base miles for elite status.

Purchased Fare	Elite Qualifying Miles Earned
First Class	1.5–2.0% of Actual Flight Miles
Business Class	1.25% of Actual Flight Miles
Full-fare Economy Class	1.00% of Actual Flight Miles
Discount Economy Class	0.50% of Actual Flight Miles

Here are the most common U.S. Airlines and web sites for you to check your earning ability and new rules in your preferred program:

AirTran Airways	800-247-8726	www.airtran.com
American Airlines	800-433-7300	www.aa.com
American Trans Air	800-435-9282	www.ata.com
Continental Airlines	800-523-3273	www.continental.com
Delta Air Lines	800-221-1212	www.delta.com
JetBlue Airways	800-538-2583	www.jetblue.com
Northwest Airlines	800-225-2525	www.nwa.com
Southwest Airlines	800-435-9792	www.iflyswa.com

Spirit Airlines	800-772-7117	www.spiritair.com
United Airlines	800-241-6522	www.ual.com
US Airways	800-428-4322	www.usairways.com

Insider Jargon to Make You Sound Like a Pro

actual flying time: The actual time that an aircraft is in the air. Does not include time on the ground (waiting in line for take-off, for example).

ADCOL: The abbreviated form for additional collection. Used by computer reservations systems, airports, and travel agencies. ADCOL is used to collect additional fees. For example, paying to upgrade a ticket from economy to business class would require an ADCOL.

ADT: The abbreviated form for Approved Departure Time.

airline designator: The code designated by the International Air Transport Association/(IATA) to represent the name of an airline (UA is United Airlines, QF is Qantas, etc.).

airport codes: Three letter codes used to identify airports (YVR is Vancouver, Canada, EWR is Newark, New Jersey, etc.).

air rage: When passengers become violent towards crew members or passengers.

AOG: Act of God—also known as a *"force majeure."* This encompasses the situations where airlines are not legally responsible to provide lodging, transport, or other expenses that travelers may incur as a result of an AOG. Inclement weather, civil disruptions, and other unanticipated events may be classified as an AOG. Sometimes it is also used to state the Aircraft is On the Ground—when an aircraft urgently needs some sort of maintenance on the ground when it is supposed to be in the air.

APEX: Abbreviated form for Advance Purchase Excursion Fare. Usually refers to international fares that have been discounted.

ARNK: Pronounced Arunk—the abbreviated form of Arrival Not Known. Used in computer reservations systems to indicate a portion of an air travel itinerary that does not involve a flight. A passenger travels from Boston to Madrid. He makes his way to Barcelona by train. He flies back to Boston from Barcelona. The portion from Madrid to Barcelona would be an ARNK.

ATA: The abbreviated form for Actual Time of Arrival of a flight.

ATC: The abbreviated form for Air Traffic Control.

AVIH: Indicates that an animal is in the cargo hold and not in the passenger cabin of an aircraft. Used in computer reservations systems.

back-to-back ticketing: Considered an illegal practice by the airlines. When a passenger does not meet the requirements of a discounted ticket (usually the Saturday night stay requirement), and is traveling more than once to a destination on business, a passenger may purchase two tickets.

base fare: The price of a ticket before any taxes have been added.

bereavement fare: Also known as compassionate fare. A discounted fare offered to family members traveling because of an imminent death or death in the family. Most airlines that offer bereavement fares will require information about the situation.

black box: Also known as the cockpit recorder or the flight data recorder. Records all of the data transmissions such as altitude, air speed, etc., and the voice and sound transmissions. Black boxes are not black, they are brightly colored in order to find them more easily amongst the wreckage after an accident.

blackout dates: The dates on which certain fares or certain types of tickets are not permitted.

bucket shop: The British term for a consolidator. A bucket shop deals in discounted fares.

bulkhead: The physical walls on an aircraft that separate the plane into different sections (such as business class and economy class).

bulkhead seating: The seats on an airplane that are immediately behind the bulkhead (see definition of bulkhead). These seats usually have limited storage, and may have either more leg room or less leg room.

bumping: Passengers who are denied a seat on the flight they originally booked due to a flight being oversold. They will then be bumped to another flight.

call sign: The title used to identify an aircraft for communication purposes. An example would be Air Canada 856 (a flight from Toronto to London).

carry-on: Luggage that is permitted to be brought on the aircraft by the passenger.

circle trip: A trip that involves more than one destination.

cockpit: The compartment at the front of the plane containing all of the devices required to fly an aircraft.

code share: An agreement between airlines to sell space on each others' flights.

commercial airline: An airline that transports passengers.

comp: The abbreviated form of complimentary—any freebies or complimentary extras.

connection: The additional flight(s) required to get from the airport of origin to the final arrival airport.

consolidator: A company that negotiates the purchase of blocks of tickets from an airline and sells that space (at some sort of discount) to the traveling public.

contract of carriage: The legal contract between the passenger and the airline, issued with the ticket.

DALPO: The abbreviated form of Do All Possible, used in computer reservations systems.

destination: The place a person is traveling to.

direct flight: A flight that stops at another airport, but passengers do not change planes.

discount fare: A lower-priced fare, usually offered for a limited time.

double booking: Booking two or more reservations when only one will be used. Doing this can lead to all reservations involved being canceled.

ETA: The abbreviated form of Estimated Time of Arrival, used in computer reservations systems, airports, and by the travel industry.

e-tickets: Also known as electronic tickets or ticketless travel.

excess baggage: Luggage that exceeds the airline's allowable limit for weight or number of pieces. Passengers are usually charged extra for excess baggage, if excess baggage is permitted at all.

excursion fare: A lower-priced fare with restrictions, like advance purchase, non-refundable, etc.

extra section: A second flight added to a flight schedule in order to accommodate additional passengers.

fare basis: Representing a specific fare and class of service with letters, numbers, or a combination of both. For example, the letter Y on its own represents full-fare economy.

FIM: Abbreviated form of Flight Interruption Manifest.

final approach: A common term for landing an aircraft at the end of a flight.

FIRAV: The abbreviated form for First Available Flight, used in computer reservations systems.

FLIFO: The abbreviated form for Flight Information, used in computer reservations systems.

FQTV: The abbreviated form for Frequent Traveler, used in computer reservations systems.

fuel surcharge: A fee added to a ticket by an airline to cover the increased cost of fuel. Usually lumped onto the cost of a ticket as if it were a tax.

fuselage: The central body of the aircraft.

gates: The physical areas of the airport where flights depart and arrive.

hidden cities: When a passenger books an itinerary that is farther than his/her destination in order to get a lower fare.

HK: Also KK and GK—the most frequently used codes to indicate confirmed space on a flight, used in computer reservations systems.

HL: The abbreviated form of Have Waitlisted (HL is a code representing wait-listing), used in computer reservations systems.

holding pattern: When air traffic control has a flight turn away from the airport and remain at an assigned altitude instead of landing. The pilots then await further instructions.

hub: An airport where an airline bases many of its major flight operations, and uses many of the gates for its aircraft.

IATA: The abbreviated form of the International Air Transport Association.

illegal connection: Connections that do not adhere to the minimum connection time, and are thus not legal connections because it is deemed that there is not enough time to connect.

inbound: The return flight portion of a ticket.

inflight: Services provided during a flight.

in transit: A passenger is currently traveling to his/her destination.

INVOL: The abbreviated form of Involuntary Denied Boarding.

itinerary: A list of flights that a passenger is scheduled to take.

jet lag: The tired, often disorienting way a passenger feels after traveling through many time zones in a short amount of time.

joint fare: An agreement between certain airlines to charge specific fares when a passenger uses more than one airline.

landing fee: A fee that the airlines pay for the right to land at an airport.

layover: Usually an overnight stop during the flight portion of a trip, involving a change of airplanes or another form of transportation.

leg: One single flight portion of an itinerary.

low season: The time of year when prices of tickets decline because it is a less popular time to travel to a destination.

MAAS: The abbreviated form for Meet and Assist, used in computer reservations systems. Indicates that the passenger needs to be assisted in some way by an airline agent.

MCO: The abbreviated form of Miscellaneous Charge Order, used by airlines and travel agencies.

minimum connection time: The legal minimum time necessary to change planes at a given airport. If this is ignored, the connection is called an illegal connection.

Min/Max: The abbreviated form for Minimum/Maximum stay—refers to the minimum and maximum times allowed for travel on a ticket.

NN: The abbreviated form of needed or required space on a flight or another air travel related service, used in computer reservations systems.

non-refundable: If a passenger does not use a ticket, none of the money paid for the ticket will be returned.

non-refundable airline ticket: The less expensive airline tickets are almost always called "non-refundable." Although you can't get a full cash refund, you can exchange these tickets for a fee—usually $100—plus the difference in the new fare.

non-stop flight: A flight that does not stop at another airport before reaching its point of arrival.

no-show hotel charge: Most hotels require a credit card number to hold your reservation. If you do not show up to check-in for your reservation, the hotel will charge you a no-show fee. This is often one night's stay.

non-transferable: The only person who can use the ticket is the one who has his/her name on the ticket.

NOOP: The abbreviated form for Not Operating, used in computer reservations systems. In other words, the flight is not operating because it has been removed from the airline's schedule, or has been canceled.

NOREC: The abbreviated form for No Record, used in computer reservations systems. Indicates no record of a passenger's booking can be found.

NOSHO: Also known as No Show. A passenger who doesn't show up to take the flight that he/she is booked on.

off-line connection: A connection that not only involves a change of planes, but a change of airlines as well.

on-line connection: A connection that involves a change of airplanes but not a change of airlines.

open jaw: A flight itinerary where the departure city is different on the way out than the return.

open ticket: A ticket with no date specified and the passenger books a flight when ready to travel. These are usually full-fare tickets, as opposed to a discounted, restricted fares.

outbound: The portion of the trip where a passenger is leaving the first city of a flight itinerary and is traveling to a desti-nation, or destinations.

overbook: When an airline takes more reservations for a flight than it has seats on an aircraft.

oversell: As with overbooking, it is when an airline takes more reservations than it has seats on an aircraft.

PAX: Also PSGR—The abbreviated form of Passenger, used in computer reservations systems.

PIL: The abbreviated form for Passenger Information List.

PNR: The abbreviated form for Passenger Name Record or Personal Name Record, used in computer reservations systems.

published fare: A fare that is available for purchase to anyone.

record locator: A combination of letters, numbers, or both forming a unique code which identifies a passenger's booking.

red eye: An overnight flight that arrives early the following morning.

refundable airline ticket: Refundable tickets are the most expen-sive coach tickets as well as business and first-class tickets. They are completely refundable. In the past, airlines would refund if you didn't show up for a flight. Now, most airlines require you to contact them before the flight in order to get a full refund.

revalidation sticker: Also known as a Validation Sticker. A sticker placed on a flight coupon to indicate a change in flight number, time, class of service, etc.

RMKS: The abbreviated form for Remarks, used in computer reservations systems.

round trip: A flight itinerary that involves flying to a single destination and back.

routing: The sequence of airports used (whether it be
connections or destinations) in order to build an airfare.

SC: The abbreviated form for Schedule Change, used in
computer reservations systems. Indicates some sort of
change in the arrival or departure times of a flight.

segment: As with Leg, it is a single portion of a flight itinerary.

short haul: Shorter flights, both in terms of distance and
duration.

shoulder season: The travel season that falls between low
and high seasons, offering fares that also fall somewhere
between low and high seasons.

standby: The procedure of waiting for a seat to open up on a
flight on which a passenger is not booked/confirmed.

stopover: A planned stop of at least one night (or more than
four hours domestically), and then continuing the next
part of a flight itinerary.

through fare: The fare to a destination reached by traveling
through a gateway city.

ticket: A contractual travel document between a traveler
and an airline.

ticket stock: Blank airline tickets.

UM: The abbreviated form for Unaccompanied Minor, used in
computer reservations systems. An unaccompanied minor
is a child traveling without a parent or guardian.

unrestricted fare: A more expensive fare that offers greater
flexibility (allowing changes, refunds, etc.).

UTR: The abbreviated form for Unable to Reach, used in
computer reservations systems.

VOL: The abbreviated form of Voluntary Denied Boarding.
Refers to passengers who volunteer to take a later flight
due to an oversold flight situation (and are compensated for
doing so).

WK: Code used to indicate space was confirmed on a flight but no longer is, used in computer reservations systems.

XCL: Also XXL—The abbreviated form of canceled, used in computer reservations systems.

Zulu time: Also known as UTC (Universal Time Co-ordinated), was GMT (Greenwich Mean Time)—Zulu time is the standard time used for flight operations globally.

Acknowledgments

The first two editions of *The Penny Pincher's Passport to Luxury Travel* grew from a simple idea that there was a better way to travel while maintaining a budget. To my surprise and delight, Travelers' Tales believed in my inspiration and provided me the opportunity to express myself. With their wonderful support and nurturing, the first edition of this book was a success. Once again I find myself indebted to Travelers' Tales, especially James O'Reilly, Sean O'Reilly, and Larry Habegger,who believed in my passion and devotion for updating this edition to provide readers with a new path to luxury travel. The earliest draft of my manuscript was brilliantly critiqued by Larry and James, whose experience and willingness to share their time is an extraordinary contribution. Susan Brady for once again graciously dealing with my time-challenged edits and magically pulling everything together. I also wish to express how much I appreciate my agent, Pat Snell, without whose guidance, friendship and dedication these pages would not exist. Lastly, I owe so much to the readers who have written me offering their advice and tips, encouragement and criticism—thank you all!

About the Author

Joel L. Widzer's travels have taken him to more than a hundred countries, logging over 250,000 air miles a year, and accumulating more than 3 million frequent-flyer miles. Joel has developed the unique ability to approach travel from the point of view of a consumer as well as from a business perspective. He regularly speaks to travelers and business people, sharing the secrets of crisscrossing the world in luxury while paying coach prices.

A sought-after speaker and media presence, Joel's innovative approach to travel has received extensive media coverage. He has appeared on CBS, NBC, and ABC networks, MSNBC News Network, The FOX News Channel, The Travel Channel, *The Today Show*, CNN, *Inside Edition*, and in print media including *USA Today*, *The Wall Street Journal*, and *The Washington Post*. He writes regular travel columns for MSNBC and *Forbes*. Joel holds a doctoral degree in the field of industrial organizational psychology.

When Joel is not off on one of his many global journeys, he takes to the skies as an instrument-rated pilot. More information on Joel and *The Penny Pincher's Passport to Luxury Travel* can be found at www.JetReady.com and travelerstales.com.

Joel is based in southern California.

Notes

Notes

Notes

Notes

Notes